Governance of Private Enterprises in Modern China

Governance of Private Enterprises in Modern China

Zhong Qin

NorthAmerican
Business Press

Atlanta – Seattle – South Florida - Toronto

North American Business Press, Inc

Atlanta, Georgia

Seattle, Washington

South Florida

Toronto, Canada

Governance of Private Enterprises in Modern China

(Modern China Series)

ISBN: 9780985394998

© 2013 All Rights Reserved.

Supported by the Publication Fund of Shantou University

Along with trade books for various business disciplines, the North American Business Press also publishes a variety of academic-peer reviewed journals.

Library of Congress Control Number: 2013931702

Library of Congress

Cataloging in Publication Division

101 Independence Ave., SE

Washington, DC 20540-4320

Printed in theUnited States of America

First Edition:

ABSTRACT

Domestic private enterprises have dramatically re-emerged in China's unique transition from a planned to a market-oriented economy, where the private sector plays an increasingly important role. The development of Chinese private enterprises differs from what standard property rights theory describes, particularly in the early stages of development. This gives rise to a concern that standard property rights theory may not be sufficient to explain the success of Chinese private enterprises.

Based on the experience of private enterprises in Zhejiang province, this book incorporates standard property rights theory, including agency theory and endogenous ownership theory, with a cultural perspective to discuss the development of Chinese private enterprises. Over the last decade, there has been a decline of "red-hat" enterprises and an increased dominance of family businesses among private enterprises. This book employs the concept of trust (*Guanxi* in Chinese), which stems from traditional culture and comprises two important components (government and family), to investigate the changing patterns of corporate governance.

The core argument of this book is that family businesses, which are now the major form of corporate governance among Chinese private enterprises, have become dominant not only due to an improvement in the economic environment, but also because of the tendency for family trust (*Guanxi*) to replace government trust (*Guanxi*). The property rights theory developed in this book extends orthodox ownership theory to include a developing market such as China, representing a combination of endogenous ownership theory and agency theory. This extension provides a better understanding of the development of Chinese private enterprises. Policy implications are also presented with respect to the future development of private enterprises in the market-oriented reforms in China.

BRIEF BIOGRAPHY OF THE AUTHOR

Dr. Zhong Qin is a Professor of Economics at Business School of Shantou University, China. Dr. Qin's research interests and peer-reviewed publications are mainly in the study of ownership and corporate governance, as well as industrial organizations, with the integration of macroeconomics and microeconomics. Dr. Qin is a member of the Economic Academy of Guangdong Province, China. He obtained his Ph. D. degree in Economics from Monash University, Australia, in 2007. He had been an officer at Department of Planning and Development, Hainan Provincial Government, engaging in the macroeconomic policymaking and development studies from 1991 to 2003.

ACKNOWLEDGEMENTS

This book is based on my PhD thesis in the Department of Economics, Monash University, Australia. I am very grateful to my supervisors, Professor Russell Smyth and Doctor Wenli Cheng, for their guidance, understanding and support. This book would not have been possible without their valuable insights and comments. I am especially indebted to Professor Russell Smyth, who has been a mentor throughout my PhD candidature, for his tireless revising of almost every chapter of my PhD thesis, and for his preface to this book.

I am also thankful to my previous associate supervisor, Doctor Zhongmin Wang, and research fellow, Doctor Dingsheng Zhang, in the Department of Economics for their help with the analysis in the mathematical models in Chapter 4. Thanks also to participants in the fieldwork research in Ningbo City, Zhejiang province, China.

This book has benefited from issues raised by the participants at various seminars and the PhD conference in the Department of Economics during the period from 2003 to 2006. Financial support in the form of research scholarships from the Monash Graduate Research School and the Faculty of Business and Economics, Monash University are graciously acknowledged.

The book is sponsored benevolently by the publishing fund from Shantou University, China. I am very grateful to Doctor Guang Tian, and Marius Lazau, the Director of Publications, North American Business Press, who gave lots of help for the publication.

Finally, I am deeply indebted to my family for their constant support. The most heartfelt gratitude is owed to my dear wife Qiao Wang, who has always supported my academic endeavours, encouraged me and shared the ups and downs of this journey.

TABLE OF CONTENTS

LIST OF TABLES

LIST OF FIGURES

PREFACE TO THE BOOK

China has undergone a massive economic transformation over the course of the last three decades. The Chinese economy of today would be barely recognizable to the architects of China's market reforms in the late 1970s. An important component of China's economic transition has been the emergence of non-state enterprises. For a long period in the reform era collective township and village enterprises (CTVEs) were the engine room driving China's high growth rate while state-owned enterprises, at least small and medium-sized state-owned enterprises, represented a considerable drag on resources. For most of this period there were two distinct models – the Wenzhou model dominant in Zhejiang and the Sunan model, which originated in southern Jiangsu. The development of both models of CTVEs has challenged the view in standard western property rights theory that well-defined property rights are a prerequisite for economic success. In this volume Dr. Qin examines the Wenzhou model from a range of perspectives including agency theory, standard property rights and endogenous ownership theory with particular emphasis on the role of culture.

Dr. Qin focuses on two aspects of the changing structure of private enterprises since the 1980s. The first is the decline in the phenomenon of 'red hat' firms. Red hat firms were commonplace in the 1980s and early 1990s and shared many similarities with the Sunan model of CTVEs. The second feature of the Wenzhou model has been the involvement of family members, resulting in the prevalence of family businesses among private enterprises. Since the mid-1990s there has been a decline of red-hat enterprises and an increased proportion of private enterprises that are family businesses. Dr. Qin employs the concept of trust, which stems from traditional culture to examine the changing patterns of corporate governance in private enterprises. An innovative feature of Dr. Qin's approach is differentiating between what he terms 'family' and 'government' trust. The core argument Dr. Qin makes is that family businesses - the major form of corporate governance among Chinese private enterprises – has become dominant not only due to economic reforms, but also because of the tendency for family trust to replace government trust.

Dr. Qin makes several contributions to the literature on China's private enterprises. First, he provides a theoretical treatment of the interaction between family and government trust in Chinese private enterprises. The mathematical model Dr. Qin presents highlights the important role played by institutional foundations of trust in Chinese private enterprises. Specifically, the model predicts that the interaction between government and family trust will result in government trust being replaced by family trust in private enterprises. Second, Dr. Qin tests the predictions of the theoretical model through an empirical study of the relative importance of family and government trust in private enterprises in Zhejiang. To be precise, Dr. Qin examines the relative importance of family and government trust in terms of firm characteristics such as age, size, and business instability. An important finding from the study is that there is strong evidence that family trust has come to dominate government trust in facilitating cooperation in Chinese private enterprises in Zhejiang province. Third, Dr. Qin presents an empirical study of the effect of corporate governance on firm performance in private enterprises in Zhejiang. This study shows that ownership arrangements are important to firm performance in an economic environment which combines both orthodox endogenous ownership theory and agency theory. Both empirical studies are based on a large-scale survey conducted by Dr. Qin in Zhejiang, through which he was able to compile a unique dataset to examine these issues.

It is often said that the twenty-first century will be the Chinese century. The growing economic might of China has increased the world's interest in its economic performance and the institutions that have generated that performance. Compared with the much studied state-owned sector, there is relatively little serious research on the role of China's private enterprises. Through combining a sound theoretical framework with empirical research based on fieldwork in Zhejiang, Dr. Qin has made an important contribution to understanding the rapidly changing nature of China's private enterprises and, in so doing, has started to fill this largely missing gap on China's enterprise performance. As such, this is a volume of interest not only to academics, but all those interested in China's economy. I warmly commend it to all.

RUSSELL SMYTH
Monash University
July, 2012.

Notes: Russell Smyth is a Professor, and the Head of Department of Economics, Monash University. His research interests encompass Asian economies, Chinese economic reform, empirical legal studies, law and economics, migration and applied time series econometrics. From 1998 to 2008 he was Editor of Economic Papers, the policy journal of the Economic

Society of Australia and was a member of the Central Council of the Economic Society of Australia. In 2008 he received the Honorary Fellow Award of the Economic Society of Australia. He is currently an Associate Editor of the B.E. Press journal, *Asia Pacific Law and Economics Review and Pacific Economic Review* and sits on the Editorial Board of a further four journals.

CHAPTER 1

Introduction

This book is a research endeavour based on the changing patterns in corporate governance in Chinese private enterprises. At the beginning of this book, it is necessary to introduce the background and structure of the book.

1.1 Background and Objectives

China has achieved remarkable economic growth since the introduction of market-oriented reforms and an open door policy in the late 1970s. These reforms have transformed China's economy from a planned to a market-socialist economy. The re-emergence of a substantial private sector has been one of the most important outcomes of these changes.[1] Initially permitted only on the fringes of the economy, the domestic private sector was estimated to account for about one-quarter of gross domestic product (GDP) in 2005 (Yearbook of State's Industrial and Commercial Administration, 2005), and it has been officially recognized as an important component of the economy in the Chinese Constitution since 1999.[2] The private sector is the most dynamic sector of China's economy and is playing an increasingly important role in the national economy.

The overriding objective of this book is to analyse the development of Chinese private enterprises from the perspective of property rights theory. China's experience with the development of domestic private enterprises appears to represent a challenge to standard property rights critiques. The conventional wisdom in this area is that clearly defined property rights are a prerequisite for economic prosperity so that rapid privatization is seen as desirable for a transitional economy. However, it is commonly acknowledged that China has pursued a gradual approach to privatization. In particular, a clearly demarcated property rights system and a corresponding legal system, which are the central elements of a sound free-market system, are not well established in China. The contrast between the gradual privatization and rapid economic growth in China and the rapid privatization and recession in

---

[1] China's private enterprises were almost eliminated in 1957, several years after the establishment of the People's Republic of China, due to socialist reforms. Private enterprises emerged again after 1978 and it is this period on which this book focuses.

[2] Throughout this study, the "domestic private sector" refers to business enterprises under the effective private control of resident Chinese private persons, whatever the legal status of the enterprises or formal ownership rights. That is, this book focuses on domestic private enterprises but not foreign-invested enterprises.

1

Central and Eastern Europe, as well as the former Soviet Union, has puzzled many economists. This puzzle provides a backdrop for the study of property rights and the development of Chinese private enterprises in this book.

Since their re-emergence in the late 1970s, the development of Chinese private enterprises has been characterized by two main institutional features. One is the significant involvement of local governments in the firm's economic activities. From the firm's perspective, local government involvement serves to avoid government predation and ideological harassment, and facilitates material needs and information for successful production. The important role that the government has played in private enterprise development is represented by the phenomenon of "red-hat" firms, which were commonplace in the 1980s and early 1990s and which shared similarities to the well-known township-village enterprises (TVEs).[3] The second feature of Chinese private enterprises has been the involvement of family members, resulting in the prevalence of family businesses among private enterprises.[4]

These two features—family and government involvement—seemingly represent serious shortcomings from the conventional perspective of good corporate governance (Singh, 2003). This is because property rights of private enterprises with government involvement are vaguely defined (see, for example, Weitzman and Xu, 1994; Smyth, 1997; Tian, 2000) while private enterprises with pervasive involvement of family members find it difficult to take advantages of economies of specialization and scale, which has been shown to be conducive to good performance (Fama and Jensen, 1983; Demsetz, 1997). These corporate governance patterns indicate that standard property rights theory may not adequately explain the success of Chinese private enterprises. Given the existence of institutional impediments, both in terms of the overall market environment and in ownership arrangements within the firm, what are the characteristics of private enterprises that have facilitated their contribution to China's remarkable economic growth, particularly over the last three decades?

---

[3] "Red-hat" firms referred to private firms that put on a "hat" of collective ownership to evade the government's prohibition on private firms and associated ideological harassment. According to a spot-check of 178,000 collective enterprises in 16 provinces and 35 cities (counties) by the State Bureau of Industrial and Commercial Administration in 1995, 20.8% of firms were "fake collectives" because more than 51% of these firms' assets were privately-owned (Report of China's Citizen-Run Enterprises, No.1, 2004, p.180). In the 1980s and first half of the 1990s, most TVEs in the Zhejiang (Wenzhou) model were "red-hat" enterprises (see Chapters 2 and 3).

[4] It is estimated that family businesses account for about 90% of total Chinese private enterprises (Blue Book of Private Enterprises, 2001, 2002; Gan, 2002).

To address this issue, this book will seek to incorporate traditional Chinese culture into standard property rights theory. Building upon the work of North (1990) and others, this study links the immature institutional environment in China with the institutional arrangements within private enterprises, with emphasis placed on the role of the informal constraints, or implicit contracts, that stem from traditional culture in influencing the development of Chinese private enterprises. Building on the study by Weitzman and Xu (1994), this book considers two institutional arrangements for a private enterprise: a *non-cooperative arrangement* corresponding to what standard property rights theory describes, and a *cooperative arrangement* that incorporates traditional Chinese cultural and sociological perspectives. In this book, the concept of *trust* is treated as synonymous with *Guanxi*. Generally speaking, trust (*Guanxi*) is a culturally-determined manifestation of implicit contracts, and is employed in this book to represent the role played by traditional culture. In terms of the roles of the government and family members in the development of Chinese private enterprises, trust (*Guanxi*) comprises two components: government and family trust (*Guanxi*). The notions of family and government trust (*Guanxi*) provide the conceptual framework for the book.

1.2 Contributions of This Book

This book has contributed to the extant literature as follows:

First, this book provides a theoretical exposition of the interaction between family and government trust (*Guanxi*) in Chinese private enterprises. Building on Tian's (2000) framework, the mathematical models in this book highlight the important role played by institutional foundations of trust (*Guanxi*) in Chinese private enterprises. Furthermore, they illustrate the incentive-based reasons for ownership arrangements of private enterprises by taking the economic institutional environment as exogenous. The main difference from Tian's study is that the roles of both the government and family members are examined in the book while Tian discusses only the role played by the government. In this respect, Tian's model is a special case of the model developed in this book. This model further predicts that the interaction between government and family trust (*Guanxi*) will result in government trust (*Guanxi*) being replaced by family trust (*Guanxi*) in private enterprises.

Second, this book provides an empirical study of the effect of corporate governance on firm performance in private enterprises in Zhejiang province, China. The empirical study is based on this researcher's survey in this area, with the Zhejiang model being representative of the development of Chinese

3

private enterprises. While the relationship between ownership structure and firm performance is far from conclusive (Demsetz and Villalonga, 2001), this study shows that ownership arrangements are important to firm performance in a given economic environment, which combines both orthodox endogenous ownership theory and agency theory.

Third, the book provides an empirical study of the relative importance of family and government *Guanxi* in private enterprises in Zhejiang province, China. This study fills a gap in the extant literature where previously family and government *Guanxi* have been examined separately. Specifically, the study examines the relative importance of family and government *Guanxi* in terms of firm characteristics such as age, size, and business instability, and provides strong evidence of the preference for family *Guanxi* over government *Guanxi* in facilitating cooperation in Chinese private enterprises.

To sum up, this book extends standard property rights theory to include a developing market such as China, and provides an explanation for why family businesses constitute the majority of Chinese private enterprises.

1.3 Structure of the Book

The remainder of the book is organized as follows. Chapter 2 reviews the literature on conventional property rights theory, with particular emphasis on agency theory and endogenous ownership theory. The main theme of this chapter is that conventional property rights theory may not provide an adequate explanation of the relationship between corporate governance and firm performance in a developing market such as China. Consequently, standard property rights theory needs to take account of the traditional cultural context in which economies such as China have evolved, particularly the role of trust (*Guanxi*). The distinction between government and family trust (*Guanxi*) in private enterprises in China, which forms the backdrop for the theoretical exposition later in the book, is also introduced and discussed in this chapter.

Chapter 3 describes the general evolution of private enterprises in China, with particular emphasis on the development of private enterprises in Zhejiang province. The rise of Zhejiang private enterprises confirms not only that well-defined property rights are a precondition of economic prosperity, but also that there is no commonly accepted approach to achieving private ownership. This chapter concludes with a discussion of the roles played by the government in the Zhejiang model and the characteristics of family businesses among private enterprises.

Building on Tian (2000), Chapter 4 presents two related mathematical models to explain the important features of private enterprises in Zhejiang by specifying management ability and *Guanxi* ability as important non-marketed resources for a firm's production. These models represent a combination of endogenous ownership theory and agency theory. While the first model proposes that the optimal ownership arrangement of private enterprises is related to the degree of imperfection of the market environment as well as the ability of management in those firms, the second model proposes that family trust (*Guanxi*) is replacing government trust (*Guanxi*) in private enterprises.

The mathematical models develop two hypotheses: that firm performance has a close link with its ownership arrangement in a given market environment, and that there is a tendency for family trust (*Guanxi*) to replace government trust (*Guanxi*) in private enterprises. Chapters 5 and 6 contain empirical studies which test the two hypotheses. The first empirical study in Chapter 5 examines the effect of corporate governance on firm performance in Chinese private enterprise. The main finding from this study is that the combination of ownership and control, particularly ownership concentration, in the hands of the single largest owner and top management, is beneficial for private enterprises. However, family shareholding does not have a statistically significant effect on firm performance, suggesting that there may be other factors at play. One such factor could be trust (*Guanxi*), which is not well explained by orthodox ownership theory.

The second empirical study in Chapter 6 examines the relative importance of government and family trust (*Guanxi*) in Chinese private enterprises. The main findings from this study are twofold. First, both government and family *Guanxi* are perceived as important for the development of private enterprises, particularly in the current imperfect market environment. Second, government trust (*Guanxi*) is being replaced by family trust (*Guanxi*) in private enterprises, which is consistent with the second hypothesis developed in the mathematical models.

Based on the above analysis, policy implications are presented in Chapter 7. Emphasis is placed on the future development of Chinese private enterprises with discussion of the different roles played by the government and family. One key policy implication is that the government should shift from being an active participant in a firm's economic activities to focus on improving the overall market environment where private enterprises operate. Another key implication is that private enterprises must adopt an appropriate governance form corresponding to the changing economic environment and the evolving cultural context in which family trust (*Guanxi*) still plays an important role. Chapter 8 concludes the study of this book, reiterating the contributions of the book to the literature and pointing out directions for further research.

1.4 The Link between the Theoretical Modelling and Empirical Testing

The theoretical model in this book extends the theoretical work of Tian (2000) in which private ownership prevents a firm from obtaining help in procurement (of some key production factors) from government officials. Correspondingly, the non-cooperative arrangement in the theoretical model prevents a private firm from obtaining assistance in procuring *Guanxi* from government officials. The concept of *Guanxi* employed in this book is treated, the same as procurement ability, as a non-market resource that can not be readily acquired from the market. However, more space in the theoretical model is devoted to discussing the interaction of family and government *Guanxi* within private firms under the cooperative arrangement.

In the empirical part, all sample firms were already private-owned at the end of this researcher's survey. This does not mean that government *Guanxi* is currently not important at all. Instead, it indicates that the theoretical model and empirical test cannot be tightly linked in the sense that variables in the theoretical model correspond on a one-to-one basis with the empirics. In other words, the lack of tight linkage is dictated by the availability of data. To address this point, the empirical model is designed to test the broad tenants of the theoretical model.

The empirical studies presented in this book are also grounded in an alternative theoretical foundation in the management literature. The first model in Chapter 5 is based on studies on the relationship between ownership structure and firm performance (see, for example, Demsetz, 1983; Demsetz and Lehn, 1985; and Demsetz and Villalonga, 2001), while the second model in Chapter 6 is based on the studies of *Guanxi* (see, for example, Yang, 1994; Xin and Pearce, 1996; and Lovett et al., 1999).

CHAPTER 2

Conventional Property Rights Theory
Implicit Contracts and Private Enterprises

Chinese private enterprises have re-emerged and mushroomed since the introduction of market reforms and the open door policy in 1978. Despite the progress of private enterprises in China, research on Chinese private enterprises is a relatively recent phenomenon. Some initial research has been carried out to analyse the development of private enterprises, focusing on their definition, ownership characteristics, and contribution to economic growth (Chen and Feng, 2000; Gregory et al., 2000; Lin, 2000; Roberts and Zhou, 2000; Sun, 2000; Flynn and Xu, 2001; Schlevogt, 2001; Tian, 2001; Gan, 2002; Sun and Wong, 2002; Zhao, 2002; Blue Book of Private Enterprises, 2001, 2002). This book attempts to integrate standard property rights theory with a cultural perspective to explain the development of Chinese private enterprises, with a focus on the definition and development pattern of Chinese private enterprises, ownership arrangements, and traditional cultural factors.

This chapter proceeds as follows. Section 2.1 discusses the definition of private enterprises in a specifically Chinese context, and shows that the "red-hat" phenomenon as a specific development pattern of Chinese private enterprises differs from private firms in Western countries. Section 2.2 reviews standard property rights theory in general, and emphasizes agency theory and endogenous ownership theory. The discussion in this section proposes that standard property rights theory may not be adequate to explain ownership characteristics in an imperfect market such as China, and consequently standard property rights theory needs to incorporate a traditional cultural perspective. Following this argument, trust (*Guanxi*), which is a manifestation of implicit contracts and stems from traditional culture, is discussed in Section 2.3. This section further discusses two important aspects of trust (*Guanxi*), government and family, which provides the conceptual framework for this book. Section 2.4 concludes the literature review and shows how the concepts discussed in this chapter are linked to the remainder of the book.

2.1 Definition of Private Enterprises

China's unique approach to market-oriented reforms has influenced the way in which the private sector has developed since its re-emergence in the late 1970s. The definition of private enterprises in China has changed greatly and will continue to evolve. Therefore, it is important from the beginning to define Chinese private enterprises.

2.1.1 From "other ownership" (*Qitasuoyouzhi*) to domestic private enterprises (DPEs)

One view in the literature is that the private sector is simply categorized as "enterprises outside the state and collective sectors" (Schlevogt, 2001, p.3), and it is consequently subsumed into "other ownership (*Qitasuoyouzhi*)" including foreign-invested, shareholding, and private domestic firms (Jefferson et al., 2000, p.787). Although this view corresponds to the official statistics, especially during the early reform period in the 1980s, it takes a general definition of private enterprises and thus lacks a clear benchmark to distinguish between different types of private enterprises.

The private sector in China is separated into two types of business structures: domestic private enterprises (DPEs), and foreign-invested enterprises (FIEs). This approach has been adopted by many scholars, although there are some subtle distinctions in categorization. For example, Lin (2000, p.517) states "[domestic] individual enterprises are owned by individuals or a group of individuals and are not affiliated with any government organizations. They can determine what and how to produce, and they sell their products in the market. These enterprises are clearly private enterprises ... other enterprises include foreign enterprises and joint ventures between domestic firms and foreign firms, and joint ventures between state enterprises and private enterprises. Since these enterprises are market oriented and pursue profits, we put them in the same category as private enterprises." Similarly, Zhu (1995, p.38) argues that "traditionally, there [were] three main types of firms before reform started: SOEs (state-owned enterprise), COEs (collective-owned enterprise) and DPEs." But "since the early 1980s, foreign investment from different sources has poured into the country." He then concludes that the private sector includes "both domestic and foreign firms." Zhao (2002) also argues that private-owned firms consist of domestic private enterprises (DPE) and foreign invested enterprises (FIE), while Chow and Fung (1998) use the terms local private enterprises and DPE interchangeably.

To sum up, a broad definition of private enterprises in China includes both domestic private and foreign enterprises, as many scholars have recently argued. More specifically, domestic private businesses include individual businesses, single industrial and commercial proprietors, specialized households and privately-run enterprises, while foreign-invested enterprises include equity joint ventures, cooperative joint ventures, and wholly foreign owned enterprises. In contrast, a narrow definition of private enterprises refers only to domestic private enterprises (DPEs). This book adopts the narrow definition of private enterprises because the main aim of the book is to analyse private enterprises in China's specific transitional context, which differs notably from conventional Western firms.[5] In short, "private enterprises" in this book refers to domestic private enterprises (DPEs) unless otherwise indicated.

2.1.2 Formal definitions of Chinese private enterprises

2.1.2.1 Policy definitions

The evolution of the definition of Chinese private enterprises pieced together from government documents is presented in Table 2.1. The government documents here include a set of regulations issued by the State Council such as "Stipulations on Urban Non-Agricultural Individual Economy" in 1981, "Several Issues on the Temporary Rural Economy" in 1983, and "Tentative Stipulations on Private Enterprises" (TSPE) in 1988.

Table 2.1 Summary of Policy Definitions of Private Enterprises

Policy Definitions	Year	Areas	Industrial Distribution	Employee Require-ment
Individual Business (*Getihu*)	1978-83	Rural and urban	Consumer goods and services	Not available
Specialized Households (*Zhuanyehu*)	Early 1980s	Rural	Non-agricultural activities	Not available
Single Industrial/Commercial Proprietor (*Getigongshanghu*)	1981	Urban	(Certain limits)	No more than eight
Privately-Run Enterprises (*Siyingqiye*)	1988	Urban	Various	More than eight

The first row of Table 2.1 refers to the Individual Business/Entrepreneur (*Getihu*). The 1978-83 phase is marked by the official revival of private business. During that period, the private sector was limited to individual

---

[5] Foreign-invested enterprises (FIE) in China have been studied in the literature (see, for example, Gregory et al., 2000; Schlevogt, 2001). In general, FIEs are almost the same as private firms in Western countries although they are also influenced by Chinese policies and regulations (Blue Book of Private Enterprises, 2001).

9

businesses. The private sector was intended to play a marginal, stop-gap role and to act as a "supplement" to the state and collective sectors, "filling the gaps" the collective and state sectors left in the economy, particularly in the distribution of consumer goods and services and in employment.

The second row of Table 2.1 describes the Specialized Households (*Zhuanyehu*). In the early 1980s the private enterprise boom began in rural areas. The contract responsibility system evolved into a fundamental reform in agriculture because economic management devolved to households. Some households then specialized in non-agricultural activities and became "specialized households." Many of these were in fact private non-agricultural businesses.

The third row of Table 2.1 refers to the Single Industrial and Commercial Proprietor (*Getigongshanghu*). This business category was introduced in July 1981 by the State Council regulations on the urban non-agricultural individual economy. The government moved with caution when developing the *Getihu*. The July 1981 document capped the number of employees a *Getihu* could hire at eight. In addition, it specified that individual businesses were only supplements to state and collective economic units, and could develop only within certain limits. Because they originated within the collective agricultural economy, their private nature could be ignored, which overcame the need for guidelines or regulations dealing with them.

The last row of Table 2.1 describes the Privately-Run Enterprises (*Siyingqiye*). Such enterprises, defined as privately owned enterprises employing more than eight people, began to develop as early as 1981 as a separate category from the smaller individual enterprises (*Getihu*). However, the *Siyingqiye* were not covered by regulations until 1988. At that time, the private sector continued to be regarded as a supplement to the public sector and until as recently as 1999, they were not recognized as an important component of the economy.

2.1.2.2 Legal definitions

In June 1988, the State Council issued the Tentative Stipulations on Private Enterprises (TSPE) to govern the registration and management of private firms. This document defines a private firm as "an enterprise running for profit, whose capital belongs to individuals and hires more than eight workers," and it also defines three kinds of private company: a solely-owned company, partnership, and a limited liability company. The Company Law of the People's Republic of China, promulgated in 1993, unified the legislation on companies as formal organizations, including the title of a firm, legal person, registered capital, major business scope and sideline activities. The Company Law goes further than the TSPE in the definition of "company" by defining two different types of company: a limited liability company and a company limited by shares. This book focuses on analysis of private enterprises employing more than eight people.

There are four types of private enterprises in terms of legal definition. A *solely-owned company* is owned by one proprietor who has unlimited responsibility for his or her company's liability, while a *partnership* is a company in which the acts of each partner are binding upon the others and each is liable for all debts. There are at least two owners bound by a contract.

A *limited liability company* is one of the two forms of corporate entities allowed under the Company Law. The registered capital of a limited liability company is not divided into shares, but instead is accounted for by the distribution of capital contribution certificates. These acknowledge the registered capital investment of the investor and are issued in proportion to the amount contributed by each investor. Capital contribution certificates thus serve the role of shares, although they cannot be traded on the stock exchange. A limited liability company must have between two and 50 shareholders.

A *company limited by shares (joint-stock company)* is the second type of corporate entity allowed under the Company Law. In order to commence operations, a company limited by shares must have between two and 200 founding shareholders. The registered capital of these initial investors is divided into shares of equal value and then issued to shareholders in proportion to their investment. Every share carries one vote at the shareholders' meetings, and shareholders generally enjoy rights and obligations in accordance with their shareholding. Shares can be transferred or traded according to law.

2.1.3 Private enterprises and township-village enterprises (TVEs)

2.1.3.1 Confusion with TVEs

To a certain extent, many private enterprises and township-village enterprises (TVEs) originated within rural individual households (Gregory et al., 2000; Report of China's Citizen-run Enterprises, No.1, 2004). Thus, confusion between private enterprises and TVEs is evident in the literature. Some scholars regard TVEs as predominantly private enterprises in disguise (Kornai, 1992; Wong, 1996). This is because given government policy discriminated against private firms and favoured collective firms, many private firms claimed to be collective firms in order to avoid discrimination against private enterprises in the early reform years, and to take advantage of special tax allowances even after private enterprises were formally approved in 1988. As a consequence, some studies speak in terms of rural township, village, and private enterprises (TVP) (Gregory and Meng, 1995) including TVEs and private enterprises.

Despite the presence of ill-defined institutional arrangements in China, TVEs cannot be simply considered private enterprises, which is the view embodied in much of the literature. While Singh et al. (1993, p.5) argue that TVEs are either actually private enterprises or operate with sufficient autonomy so as to "mimic" private ownership, Naughton (1994) and Rawski (1995) suggest that property rights, even if legally ill-defined, are in practice clearly exercised by Township and Village Governments (TVGs). More recently, Che and Qian (1998) regard a TVE as an industrial business unit belonging to all residents in the relevant rural community. In other words, TVEs are best characterized as government-structured community enterprises controlled by the community government. Furthermore, Bowles and Dong (1999, p.4) argue that "for some, TVEs are simply private enterprises in disguise and behaviourally equivalent; for others, TVEs represent a unique form of enterprise organization based on collective ownership." This view has been supported by Smyth (1997), who argues that the actual TVE's ownership structure varies between regions, with the township and village government being important in the Sunan pattern in southern Jiangsu, while most TVEs are privately owned in the Wenzhou model in southern Zhejiang.[6] He therefore concludes that the TVE is not a private enterprise with well-defined property rights. If these arguments are accepted, it is inaccurate to regard TVEs as organizationally and behaviourally equivalent to private enterprises.

2.1.3.2 The phenomenon of "red-hat" enterprises

In TVEs, the situation is complicated in some enterprises which claim to be collective-owned but are operated by individual entrepreneurs (Smyth, 1997; Sun, 2000). In agriculture, although the collective ownership of land was formally maintained, "the land was re-privatized de facto" under the household contract responsibility system (Kornai, 1990, p. 451), because "such a long duration brought lease contracts close to full ownership" (Krug, 1997, p.279).[7] In industry and commerce, many TVEs were found to be fake

---

[6] The Wenzhou model will be discussed in Chapter 3 in the context of the "Zhejiang model."

[7] From the mid-1980s onwards in rural areas in China the length of the land contracts was

collectives in the sense that they were private enterprises in nature although they used the collective label for political protection and economic benefit (Oi and Walder, 1999; Tian, 2001). Because some TVEs are in fact private enterprises, but with ill-defined property rights, it is impossible to estimate the number of private enterprises hidden among TVEs (Wong, 1996; Oi and Walder, 1999; Tian, 2001). These firms are called "red-hat" enterprises, which mean that the private owners put on a "hat" of collective ownership to evade the government's prohibition on private firms and associated ideological harassment. The "red-hat" phenomenon remained important until the end of the 1990s because government policies favoured collective-owned enterprises (mainly TVEs) in terms of approval, taxation, and bank loans. In the late 1980s and the early 1990s, a considerable number of registered private enterprises were transferred into collective firms (Gregory et al., 2000).[8] In certain cases, distributing shares or profits as bonuses to employees was enough to qualify these private enterprises as collectives (Gregory et al., 2000).

Ownership reform in SOEs and TVEs from 1995 (with a lag of one or two years before the enforcement of ownership reform policy in many provinces), together with the change of legal status of private enterprises in 1999, resulted in many "red-hat" firms resuming the nature of private enterprises. There have been almost no private enterprises registered as "red-hat" firms since 2000 (see Chapter 3). This book deals with private enterprise with well-defined property rights excluding collective TVEs, particularly when citing official statistics. However, "red-hat" firms are viewed as private enterprises when discussing the role played by the government in a firm's economic activities. That is, the "red-hat" phenomenon is one of the two main features characterizing the development pattern of Chinese private enterprises, which differs notably from private firms in Western countries. The other is the nature of family business, which will be discussed later in the book.

2.2 General Property Rights Theory

In general, there is no single universally accepted statement of property rights theory, because most presentations of the theory are essentially verbal expositions which represent a combination of philosophical thinking, empirical generalizations, and reasoned theoretical assertions (Weitzman and

---

extended, first to a minimum duration of 15 years, and then 30 years. In the meantime, the land could be subcontracted, the rights to use land could be traded, and a secondary market emerged (Tian, 2001).

[8] This period was influenced by the Tiananmen Square Incident in 1989, see Chapter 3.

Xu, 1994). However, there are consistent themes within a significant body of property rights literature.

2.2.1 Property rights, ownership, and the modern theory of the firm

According to the property rights literature, the scope and content of property rights assignments over resources affect the way that people behave in a world of scarcity. Although there are many categories of property rights, the right of ownership, which is actually a subcategory of the general concept of property rights, consists of three elements: the right to use the asset, to appropriate returns from the asset, and to change the asset's form and/or substance (Furubotn and Pejovich, 1974). Among them, the last right is fundamental, which implies the owner has the legal freedom to transfer rights in the asset to others at a mutually agreed-upon price by law. This also implies that the mobility of property rights is important to understand the firm's behaviour. Because it is difficult to define general property rights such as ethics and/or customs in an effective manner, many economists treat ownership as the control of property rights;[9] that is, ownership of a firm represents property rights in the firm. This book follows the literature in this respect.

According to the modern theory of the firm, the firm is a nexus of (incomplete) contracts, which represents a means of exchanging property rights between individuals (Coase, 1937; Jensen and Meckling, 1976). In other words, property rights are the pre-condition of exchange while ownership of the firm is the pattern and consequence of exchange (Zhang, 1999). Property rights theory and the modern theory of the firm are in essence consistent with each other. Generally speaking, the modern theory of the firm consists of two streams: transaction cost theory and agency theory.[10] A brief summary of the theory of the firm in the literature is presented below, with a more detailed treatment to follow in the remaining sections.

In transaction cost theory, which emphasizes the substitution of firm and market, the firm exists simply because of positive transaction costs. If transaction costs are zero, the firm ceases to exist and all activities are accomplished by the market. As transaction costs increase, the market is weak in favour of within-firm allocation of resources due to the substitution

---

[9] For example, Demsetz (1967, p.357) refers to "effective ownership, i.e., effective control of property" while Grossman and Hart (1986, p.693) refer to "control (i.e., ownership)."
[10] In essence, transaction cost theory and agency theory are the same, because they both discuss the nature of the firm as a nexus of (incomplete) contracts.

14

of the firm for the market (Coase, 1937). Williamson (1975, 1979, 1985) regards firms as vertical integration entities induced by incomplete contracts in continuously productive processes, and argues that firms exist because vertical integration (of market and firm) can reduce or eliminate the problem of opportunism by asset-specificity. Asset specificity, which Williamson claims is the most important "transaction dimension," refers to the extent to which the investment is idiosyncratic or transaction specific. In his opinion, there are three different degrees of asset specificity, i.e., non-specific, semi-specific, and highly specific. Classical market contracting will be efficacious when assets are non-specific to the trading parties, but bilateral market contracting will take over if assets are semi-specific and internal organization will replace bilateral contracting if assets are highly specific. Grossman and Hart (1986) and Hart and Moore (1990) further develop the ownership structure model, and distinguish between the residual rights to claim and the residual rights to control. It is commonly accepted that the most important aspect of ownership and property rights within firms is the residual right to control (Weitzman and Xu, 1994; Chang and Wang, 1994).

2.2.2 Clearly defined property rights are a prerequisite for economic prosperity

The conventional wisdom in the property rights literature is that clearly defined property rights are a prerequisite for economic prosperity. According to property rights theory, clearly defined property rights typically include three basic elements (Demsetz, 1967; Furubotn and Pejovich, 1974). First, every piece of property is assigned to a well-defined owner, or owners, with exclusive rights of ownership. Second, the owner of the property receives the residual income accruing from the asset. Third, the owner has the right to control or determine the use of the existing assets, to restructure the property, and to sell or lease it.

Property rights assignment is strongly reflected in the competition between private and public ownership, which has existed throughout history. However, private ownership has generally grown in importance relative to public ownership (Demsetz, 2003). Alchain (1974), the founding father of the new property rights theory, stresses that private property rights are a precondition of a well-functioning market economy, although he admits that the argument is "not yet derivable from economic theory nor fully validated by sufficient evidence"; however, the logic of competition indicates that a more complete and definite specification of individual property rights diminishes uncertainty and tends to promote efficient allocation and use of resources although the costs will be incurred by individuals in defining, policing, negotiating, and enforcing property rights (Furubotn and Pejovich, 1974). The transformation from socialism to post-socialist and capitalist economies that has occurred in Central and Eastern Europe, the former Soviet Union, and China over the last three decades supports this argument.

In the context of China, research on resource allocation and efficiency of private enterprises, compared with SOEs and TVEs, has been undertaken by some scholars, who have found that the provinces in China with the fastest rates of privatization show the largest gains in the marginal productivity of capital and economic growth (Lin, 2000; Tian, 2001). This is evident in the rapid development of private enterprises that has been strongly contributing to economic growth in Zhejiang province (see Chapter 3). In short, the analysis of property rights assignment has been applied to the ownership reform of Chinese SOEs and the transfer of TVEs by some scholars, who emphasize the importance of private ownership. For instance, Zhang (1999) emphasizes entrepreneurship in the process of ownership reform. In other words, the essence of ownership reform policy in China confirms that clearly defined property rights have been recognized as a prerequisite for economic prosperity.

2.2.3 Agency theory and ownership structure

The assignment of property rights (ownership structure), which is the basic factor of corporate governance within private firms (Zhang, 1999), is very important to firm performance. While there is a large literature discussing ownership structure within a firm, agency theory is emphasized here because it is most closely related to the analysis in the following chapters of this book.

Generally speaking, agency theory formalizes a trade-off between efficient risk sharing and effective incentive mechanisms, showing that only the second best partial equilibrium contract can be obtained (Hart and Holmstrom, 1987). The principal-agent problem comes from hidden action ("moral hazard") due to asymmetric information. According to Alchian and Demsetz (1972), the essence of a firm is that it permits people to work as a team. Team production occurs when an output is produced by the simultaneous co-operation of several team members. Thus, the agency problem inevitably arises in corporate governance, which describes the conflict of interests between owners/shareholders as the principals and managers as the agents. Consequently, residual control rights fall into the hands of management instead of the residual cash flow claimants. Jensen and Meckling (1976) further describe the cost of agency as the sum of monitoring expenditures incurred by the principal, bonding expenditures incurred by the agent (to guarantee that the agent will not take actions to harm the principal), and the value of the lost residual borne by the principal. In general, when ownership of a firm becomes more diffuse, the agency problem will be exacerbated due to the inability of relatively small shareholders to police the behaviour of management. The monitoring of managers by shareholders is also weakened by the well-known free-rider problem. In short, agency costs increase when the ownership of a firm becomes more diffuse.

2.2.3.1 What do managers really maximize?

The principal-agent problem emphasises the role played by the agent (manager), which can be dated back to Adam Smith's statement (1776 [1937], p.700):

> "The directors of such (joint-stock) companies, however, being the managers rather of other people's money than of their own, it cannot well be expected, that they should watch over it with the same anxious vigilance with which the partners in a private copartnery frequently watch over their own. Like the stewards of a rich man, they are apt to consider attention to small matters as not for their master's honour, and very easily give themselves a dispensation from having it. Negligence and profusion, therefore, must always prevail, more or less, in the management of the affairs of such a company."

As Jensen and Meckling (1976) stress, managers will act in their own economic self-interest. Empirically, Murphy (1985), Ang et al. (1999), and Denis and Sarin (1999) find an inverse relationship between the manager's ownership share and agency costs. To mitigate the problem of agency, an obvious remedy is to increase management shareholding, making the manager a significant residual claimant. This is an important issue when analysing corporate governance in family businesses, as in the theoretical model presented in Chapter 4.

However, although it seems that a firm performs better when ownership is in the hands of management, the relationship between the ownership structure and firm performance is inconclusive. This debate dates back to Berle and Means (1932), who suggest that an inverse correlation exists between the diffusion of shareholding and firm performance. This is because managers' interests do not coincide with the interest of shareholders so that corporate resources are not used for the maximization of shareholders' wealth. This view has been supported by many scholars. Shleifer and Vishny (1986), McConnell and Servaes (1990) and Zingales (1995) find a strong positive relationship between ownership concentration and corporate performance in the United States and other market economies and attribute this result to the impact of better monitoring. In transitional economies, Xu and Wang (1997), and Chen (2001) find a positive relationship between actual firm performance and ownership concentration for a sample of listed Chinese companies. Other studies also reach a similar result for Russia (Barberis et al., 1996) and for the Czech Republic (Claessens and Djankov, 1999). However, this poses a question: why do diffuse ownership structures survive over time, as has occurred in many Western enterprises?

2.2.3.2 Endogenous ownership structure

There is another stream of literature discussing the relationship between ownership structure and firm performance; that is, endogenous ownership theory, which emphasizes the role of market discipline. Firms owned and managed by a single person cannot be the optimal organization for most firms because specialization and scale can be productive, which usually requires the use of agents. In Demsetz's (1997, p.29) words, "by choosing a more diffuse ownership structure, owners are choosing to increase the agency cost they bear. However, this reduces the risk-weighted cost of capital to the firm, so that the total cost of operating the firm is not necessarily raised by greater agency cost." Demsetz (1983, 1985) further argues that ownership structure is endogenously determined in equilibrium. The ownership structure of a corporation should be thought of as an endogenous outcome of decisions that reflect the influence of shareholders and of trading on the market for shares. Thus, there is not a monotonic relationship between firm performance and ownership structure. This view has been supported by some other scholars (Morck et al., 1988; Hermalin and Weisbach, 1988; Loderer and Martin, 1997; Cho, 1998; Himmelberg et al., 1999; Holderness et al., 1999). However, these studies use samples of large companies in market economies and hence restrict the endogenous ownership structure to be the outcome of a perfect market. In Demsetz and Villalonga's (2001, p.228) words,

> "[T]he market succeeds in bringing forth ownerships structures, whether these be diffuse or concentrated, that are of approximate appropriateness for the firms they serve. These structures differ across firms because of difference in the circumstance facing firms, particularly in regard to scale economies, regulation, and the stability of the environment in which they operate. If these structures were the outcomes of perfect markets for control, they would eliminate any systematic relation

between firm performance and ownership structure."

One important implication of endogenous ownership theory is that it does not matter whether ownership is in the hands of management for firm performance. The reason underlining this implication is that the division of property rights allows individuals the option of combining "ownership" and control in any mixture that they wish, subject to the budget that they face (Demsetz, 1983). If the interests of the firm's managers and its shareholders are (perfectly) aligned, and firm decisions are in the shareholders' interests, firm performance is not affected by the managers' shareholdings. But perfect alignment is implausible in theory and impossible in practice. The above studies of endogenous ownership theory focus on market economies with low transaction costs in changing ownership. Even though the ownership structure is dispersed, effective monitoring is in place since such firms are frequently in the public eye due to analysts' reports. In such cases, an investor would need a relatively small share to promote changes in management or alter its behavior.

At first sight, endogenous ownership structure does not seem to be an accurate representation of firm structure in China (Xu and Wang, 1999; Chen, 2001). The reasons include the following. First, the decision to transform the ownership arrangement of SOEs and TVEs was taken by the state, while the rules prevent participating agents from obtaining an optimal ownership structure. Second, shares cannot be freely traded, except for publicly listed companies and there are only a relatively few publicly listed private enterprises.

However, endogenous ownership as a theoretical construction cannot easily be rejected. The key is not only the role of the manager, but also the discipline of the market. The high concentration of ownership in Chinese private enterprises, particularly family businesses, is an appropriate governance form for private enterprises, subject to the constraints imposed by the current immature market system in which family members provide cheap and flexible resources to fill the void created by imperfect capital and labour markets (see Chapter 3). That is, the ownership structure of private firms corresponds to the market environment. This notion is developed in the theoretical models presented later in the book, which extend endogenous ownership theory to take account of developing markets while emphasising the role of management (see Chapter 4). In short, given the legal and regulatory environment in China, the ownership arrangements of Chinese private enterprises should not be treated exogenously.

This conclusion suggests that there is a close link between property rights assignment and the market environment, which is more generally known as the "institutional environment." However, the institutional environment is difficult to measure clearly. Davis and North (1971, pp.6-7) state:

> "The institutional environment is the set of fundamental political, social, and legal ground rules that establish the basis for production, exchange, and distribution. Rules governing elections, property rights, and the right of contract are examples of the ground rules that make up the economic environment ... An institutional arrangement is an arrangement between economic units that governs the ways in which these units can cooperate and/or compete. It ... [can] provide a structure within its members can cooperate ... or [it can] provide a mechanism that can effect a change in laws or property rights."

An ownership arrangement is an institutional arrangement that allocates property rights to an individual, a group of individuals, or even a government. The distinction between the institutional environment and an institutional arrangement is important to an understanding of the analysis in the theoretical models (see Chapter 4), in which the institutional environment is treated as exogenous to avoid measurement problems.[11] However, changes in the institutional environment certainly occur in transitional economies such as China.

2.2.4 The paradox of Chinese township-village enterprises (TVEs)

Because government involvement in "red-hat" firms in Chinese private enterprises resemble the nature of government involvement in TVEs, as discussed in Section 2.1.3, the analysis of TVEs sheds light on the analysis of this segment of private enterprises prominent in the 1980s and 1990s.

A typical TVE is characterized by two main features: vaguely defined property rights and a significant role for the government (Weitzman and Xu, 1994; Chang and Wang, 1994; Smyth, 1997, 1998, 2002; Hsiao et al., 1998; Tian, 2000). The success of TVEs from the beginning of the reform period in the late 1970s until the end of the 1990s is commonly acknowledged in most of the literature which discusses TVEs.[12] There are many explanations for the success of TVEs. Among them, one is sociological and uses traditional Chinese culture as an explanation (Weitzman and Xu, 1994). Weitzman and Xu (1994) argue that because of relatively strong cooperative culture in

---

[11] This approach is the same as that adopted by Davis and North (1971) in analysing economic growth in the United States.

[12] There is a huge body of literature discussing TVEs; see also Section 2.1.3.

China, a TVE is best described as a vaguely defined cooperative, meaning an essentially communal organization quite far removed from having a well-defined ownership structure.[13] Building on this explanation, Smyth (1997, 1998) further argues that reputation is the strategic core asset of a TVE, and the TVE's incentive to cultivate a reputation for meeting its informal obligation is that if it does not it will impose extra costs, manifest in a risk premium, on forming informal contracts. A second explanation is politically focused and is based on the interaction of the central and local governments. Chang and Wang (1994) argues that TVEs can be viewed as the solution to the central government's problem of improving citizens' welfare subject to the constraints that the current political system be preserved and that local agents (governments) be provided with incentives. The third is a risk-sharing explanation suggested by Li (1996), which proffers that collective ownership arrangement are optimal in a grey market environment with ambiguous property rights. A fourth explanation, given by Che and Qian (1998) interprets the firm boundaries of TVEs at the community level rather than at the enterprise level. A fifth explanation is the principal-agent approach of Hsiao et al. (1998), which assumes double-sided moral hazard between the local government and the TVE. A final explanation is provided by Tian (2000), who focuses on special resources in which administrative bureaucrats may have a comparative advantage of procurement ability in irregular economics.

There is a common aspect emphasized in the literature regarding Chinese TVEs, the involvement of government, particularly the local governments, which constitutes the ill-defined property rights of TVEs. Within a typical TVE, control rights are given to the government, meaning that the government is in fact the executive owner of the firm who decides the revenue shares and the appointment of managers (Weitzman and Xu, 1994; Chang and Wang, 1994). The involvement of government is also manifest in procurement ability, which is essential for success in production (Tian, 2000). On the other hand, despite the lack of political liberalization, it has been recognized that the government generally functions as a "helping hand" rather than a "grabbing hand" for the TVEs' development (Li, 1998). More concretely, an extensive administrative and fiscal decentralization within the government has been conducted, which is so-called federalism as a commitment to preserving market incentives by local governments. Consequently, inter-jurisdictional competition across different regions (local governments) has played an important role in promoting markets (Sun, 2000). In short, due to the success of TVEs, the significant involvement of

---

[13] See further Section 2.3.1 below.

government within the firm seems a serious challenge to standard property rights theory (Weitzman and Xu, 1994; Chang and Wang, 1994; Smyth, 1997, 1998; Bowles and Dong, 1999; Jefferson et al., 2000).

However, in this researcher's opinion, the experience of Chinese TVEs is not a major challenge to standard property rights theory, but rather a transitional phase as part of a strategy of gradual privatization. As noted by Oi and Walder (1999), there has been fierce debate over the approach to privatization in transitional economies. While some argue for a comprehensive and rapid privatization such as in Central and Eastern Europe and the former Soviet Union, others oppose this approach and argue that it could not succeed in the absence of appropriate institutional and legal frameworks, which cannot be established overnight. Hence, privatization should proceed on a gradual and experimental basis with a range of hybrid or intermediate forms of ownership (Murrell, 1992; Stark, 1996). In general, the process of privatization in China is accepted as a gradual one. This is especially so given support in the literature for viewing TVEs as a form of hidden privatization, informal privatization, partial privatization or covert privatization (Krug, 1997; Francis, 1999).

There has been a reduction in the importance of TVEs since the late 1990s as most traditional Sunan-type TVEs have been converted to shareholding cooperatives (Smyth, 2002). This development supports the view that TVEs are an intermediate form of private enterprise during the process of gradual privatization in China. Furthermore, the policy of transferring TVEs to private enterprises after 1995, together with the ownership reform of SOEs and the development of "pure" private enterprises, actually represents a victory of private ownership over public ownership. In other words, standard property rights theory does work when TVEs are viewed as an intermediate form of private enterprise.

2.3 Implicit Contracts, Cooperative Culture, and Trust (*Guanxi*)

It has been argued that the Chinese experience shows that the growth of private enterprises and market institutions over time create demand for a clear definition and enforcement of private property rights (Gregory et al., 2000). Implicitly, the argument suggests that the development of Chinese private enterprises, at least on the surface, differs from what standard property rights theory describes, especially in the early stages of development. On the relationship between corporate governance and long-term economic growth, Singh (2003, p.457) argues that in China there are acknowledged to be "serious shortcomings from the conventional perspectives of good corporate governance in terms of the legal system, in contract enforcement and in the definition of property rights." But he also suggests that "there are other factors, which may more than compensate for poor corporate governance," where "poor corporate governance" in China also indicates differences from standard economic theory. However, he does not clearly specify the "other factors," although he suggests the system of corporate governance depends on a country's history and its other institutions. In this researcher's opinion, the experience of Chinese private enterprises can be explained more fully by the notion of trust (*Guanxi* in Chinese). However, it is not claimed that trust (*Guanxi*) represents the only way to explain the experience of Chinese private enterprises. Rather, among many possible explanations, trust (*Guanxi*) is regarded here as the most important factor influencing the development of Chinese private enterprises.

2.3.1 Implicit contracts and cooperative culture

The notion of implicit contracts stems from the nature of a firm as a nexus of contracts, whether explicit or implicit. In general, an implicit contract refers to any contract which cannot be enforced by a third party, owing to it being non-verifiable (Lorenz, 1999). Standard economic theory has attached little importance to the role of implicit contracts in market exchange because of the assumption of perfect rationality which allows agents to loosely negotiate comprehensive contracts accounting for all future contingencies relevant to the terms of their exchange (Lorenz, 1999). In such a world, trading partners need not fear that unanticipated developments in an unforeseeable future will trigger opportunistic responses because third-party contract enforcement would be efficient. Therefore, it seems that standard economic theory has placed more importance on the role of comprehensive or explicit contracts, in which entering into and enforcing contracts are basic to market economies. However, the version of a world governed by comprehensive agreements had always been difficult to reconcile with the pervasiveness of incomplete contracts in the real world, especially in the case of long-term trading relations. One of the most notable recent developments in economics has been the effort to bring incomplete contracts within the purview of orthodox theory (see Lorenz, 1999). Contracts are costly to write and enforce, and in many cases they are incomplete because of large transaction costs. If a contract is not enforceable or is prohibitively costly to enforce, the explicit contract will be replaced by a self-enforced implicit contract (Bull, 1987; Hart and Holmstrom, 1987).

The idea of a self-enforcing implicit contract can be illustrated by the frequently cited study of Kreps's (1990) game-theoretic model of reputation, which shows that reputation (or corporate culture) endogenizes the determination of efficient authority. Starting from the folk theorem of non-cooperative game theory,[14] Kreps emphasizes unforeseen contingences and focal principles on the infinitely repeated prisoner's dilemma with complete information, and argues that the reputation of the trusted party can be a powerful tool for avoiding the transaction costs of specifying and enforcing the terms of the transaction. At the same time, a firm is viewed as a "reputation bearer" (p. 111). Thus reputation works as follows: "the trusted party will honor that trust because to abuse it would prelude or substantially limit opportunities to engage in future valuable transactions" (p.116). In short, a good reputation allows for future beneficial transactions. In the final step, Kreps comes to corporate culture, in which ensures a reputation to have an effect. "If individuals within an organization who exercises hierarchical authority are supposed to exercise that authority according to some clear principle, then it becomes easier ex post to monitor their performance", and hence "in the usual fashion, efficiency can be increased by monitoring adherence to the principle (culture)" (p.126).

Therefore, Kreps's (1990) model can be applied to any situation where the possibility of ex post breach of an implicit contract discourages the vulnerable party from entering into a contractual relationship. The logic of Kreps's argument is that agent participation can nonetheless be ensured by the interest the firm has in maintaining its good reputation among the community of potential trading partners. If an ex post breach of promise leads to loss of reputation, the firm will find it difficult to persuade trading partners in the future to participate or will have to pay a premium for this participation. A basic conclusion is that as the expected value of the future gains from participation is greater than the one-time gain from reneging on one's commitments, the firm will have an incentive to behave honestly (Lorenz, 1999). Corporate culture, according to Kreps, not only acts as a "reputation bearer," but also communicates to corporate citizens the rules that they must follow in their interactions with potential partners so that the corporation's reputation can be perpetuated. Corporate culture provides a rationale for introducing an explicit role for reputation in facilitating exchange in order to overcome the (short-run) incentives for agents to deal opportunistically with others (James, 2002). In short, the main purpose of reputation and/or corporate culture is to serve as a check on opportunism (Williamson, 1993).

---

[14] It is called the folk theorem because it has been well-known for so long, and no one has the presumption to claim to have originated it (Kreps, 1990).

Weitzman and Xu (1994) extend the concept of corporate culture to the notion of cooperative culture in the context of explaining the success of Chinese TVEs. Cooperative culture, according to them, refers to the ability of a group to solve potential conflicts internally without explicit rules, laws, rights, procedures and so forth. The main thrust of their argument, however, can also be applied to explain the development of private enterprises, particularly the role played by the government. Commencing with the folk theorem of infinitely repeated games, Weitzman and Xu emphasize a continuum of outcomes (solutions),[15] and use the parameter λ, which is a value between 0 and 1, to stand for the ability of a group of people to resolve prisoner's dilemma-type free-riding problems internally. In their opinion, the parameter λ is a more or less given function of culture, and societies differ in their degree of cooperative culture. In their words, "the existence of varying degrees of cooperating capabilities among people in disparate societies makes the importance of well-defined property rights itself vary across societies." (p.140) Where cooperative culture is weak (low- λ), such as in Western countries, standard property rights theory is applicable. But implicit contracts might be preferable in Eastern countries where cooperative culture is strong (high- λ). In this manner, Weitzman and Xu (1994) argue that standard property rights theory aspires to be a universal or culture-free theory. However, this may be inadequate because it misses the key element of cooperative culture.

The main argument of Weitzman and Xu (1994) provides a useful understanding of cultural influence on a firm's economic activities. As noted by North (1990, p.37), implicit contracts, as informal constraints, come from "socially transmitted information and are a part of the heritage that we call culture," while the traditional Chinese cultural system is strongly influential in all aspects of Chinese social life, including business management (Xing, 1995). In this respect, Weitzman and Xu (1994) link implicit contracts and cooperative culture. However, they just provide the cooperative culture (group cooperative ability) in general and do not discuss it in detail, although they limit group cooperative ability to the (local) government and the firm. It may be arguable that there are different types of group cooperative ability, such as the government-type and family-type cooperative ability that is manifest in the economic activities of Chinese private enterprises, which

---

[15] The folk theorem of infinitely repeated games can be summarized in the following terms (Fudenberg and Tirole, 1992, pp.150-160): if the players discount the future at a sufficiently low rate then individually rational payoffs can be supported by an equilibrium. Thus, in the limit of extreme patience, repeated play allows virtually any payoff to be an equilibrium outcome. Because multiple equilibria are generic in the repeated game, economists typically focus on cooperative results or efficient outcomes.

leads to a more general notion of trust (*Guanxi*) in the literature in the followings.

2.3.2 From cooperative culture to trust (*Guanxi*)

There is no clear definition of trust in the economic literature. Gambetta (1988) speaks in terms of "the elusive notion of trust." Generally, "when we say we trust someone or that someone is trustworthy, we implicitly mean that the probability that he will perform an action that is beneficial or at least not detrimental to us is high enough for us to consider engaging in some form of cooperation with him." (Gambetta, 1988, p.217) Trust can be viewed as an expectation, and it pertains to circumstances in which agents take risky actions in environments characterized by uncertainty or informational incompleteness (James, 2002).[16] While there is no unified definition of trust in the literature, it has been recognized that there are different types of trust (Williamson, 1993; Lorenz, 1999; James, 2002). Williamson (1993) accepts that the notion of reputation (or corporate culture) in Kreps's (1990) study is similar to the notion of trust, although Kreps's use of the word "trust" is merely incidental, and he argues that corporate culture is one kind of institutional (or "hyphenated") trust and "works mainly within particular organizations." (p.478) In this manner, cooperative culture, especially the group cooperative ability developed by Weitzman and Xu (1994), is narrower than the notion of trust. However, it is not claimed here that cooperative culture substantially differs from trust, because culture is also an elusive notion that comprises many elements (Schlevogt, 2001). Rather, "trust" is employed in this book as the most important aspect of cooperative culture, and this is the term often used in the literature, as discussed below.

2.3.2.1 Trust as institutional foundation(s)

Corresponding to institutional economics,[17] there are two levels of trust: the macro variant as the institutional environment, and the micro variant as the institutions of governance (Williamson, 1993). More specifically, Williamson (1993) categorizes trust as the following: institutional trust, including societal culture, politics, regulation, professionalization, networks and corporate culture; calculative trust, which should be "described in calculative terms, to which the language of risk is exactly suited" (p.485-6); and personal trust. The last two categories are subsumed into the institutions of governance. Williamson joins these two levels of trust by treating "the institutional environment in which a transaction (or a related set of

---

[16] Williamson (1993, p.463) even treats "trust" as "risk."
[17] See Davis and North (1971).

26

transaction) is embedded as a set of shift parameters, changes in which elicit shifts in the comparative costs of governance", and he mainly examines "the rudiments of governance" (p.457). In his opinion, transactions are "always organized (governed) with reference to the institutional context (environment) of which they are a part" (p.486).

Trust is an important element in economic exchange. Without trust, "no market could function." (Arrow, 1973, p.24) For example, Fukuyama (1995) concludes that trust (or social capital) is just as important as physical capital in facilitating the creation of large-scale business organizations necessary for economic growth and development. However, economists generally have little understanding of trust and its role in economic exchange (Williamson, 1993), particularly in the absence of incentives for trustworthiness in others (James, 2002). Lorenz (1999) even argues that trust is not relevant to the orthodox economic analysis of incomplete contracts.

As noted by North (1990), there is good reason to believe that "in the modern Western world, we think of life and the economy as being ordered by formal laws and property rights," (p.36) and hence what is missing in orthodox economic theory is "an understanding of the nature of human coordination and cooperation." (p.11) At the same time, trust provides a solid foundation of cooperation; that is, people with a high degree of trust are more willing to cooperate than individuals with low trust levels (Gambetta, 1988; James, 2002). Trust, which has deep embeddedness of particular cultures and hence is culturally determined (Granovetter, 1985; Fukuyama, 1995), overreaches the formal organizational structure in many cases in China. Business contracts are often specified in legal terms, but are implemented on the basis of trust and relationships between the parties involved. In line with Weitzman and Xu's (1994) work, it can be seen that standard property rights theory is generally applicable in Western countries, while trust might be preferable in Eastern countries. As a consequence, there are two institutional (ownership) arrangements for a private enterprise. One is the non-cooperative arrangement, which corresponds to what standard property rights theory describes, and the other is the cooperative arrangement incorporating traditional Chinese culture, i.e., the role of trust (see Chapter 4).

2.3.2.2 Trust and *Guanxi* in China

There is also no clear definition of *Guanxi* in the literature. In general, *Guanxi* may be viewed as networks of informal relationships and exchanges of favours that dominate business activity throughout China and East Asia (Lovett et al., 1999; Li, 2002). In particular, *Guanxi* involves cultivating personal relationships through the exchange of favours and gifts for the purpose of obtaining goods and services, developing networks of mutual dependence, and creating a sense of obligation and indebtedness (Yang, 1994). In this manner, *Guanxi*-based business practices emphasize the importance of interpersonal relationships (Xin and Pearce, 1996; Lovett et al., 1999; Schlevogt, 2001; Sun and Wong, 2002).

In China, one important aspect of *Guanxi* centres on cultivating personal relationships with government officials (Yang, 1994, 2002; Wank, 1996; Guthrie, 1998). Wank (1996) argues that *Guanxi* refers to entrepreneurial ties with officialdom. Sometimes *Guanxi* is honourable, but it also has a dark side, which means that *Guanxi* is often mistaken for bribery and corruption (Sun and Wong, 2002). However, *Guanxi* is more than the exchange of gifts in order to procure favourable business treatment (Standifird and Marshall, 2000). Therefore, it is important to make a distinction between *Guanxi* and bribery, the central difference being that *Guanxi* refers to relationship building while bribery is simply an illicit transaction (Yang, 1994; Lovett et al., 1999). In other words, *Guanxi* places much more emphasis on human feelings, long-term obligations and bonding than the material interest exchanged, whereas with bribery and corruption, the social relationship is a means, not an end, of the exchange. Given this distinction, in this book *Guanxi* is viewed in a positive fashion. We accept the distinction between *Guanxi* and bribery or corruption, and also the argument that *Guanxi* is productive (Wank, 1996). In particular, we see *Guanxi* as productive in providing transaction cost advantages in the transitional economy of China. For instance, Lovett et al. (1999) argue that *Guanxi*-type system reduces contracting costs; Standifird and Marshall (2000) argue that *Guanxi*-based business practices reduce environmental and behavioural uncertainties and opportunistic behaviour; Li (2002) argues that the average transaction cost in relationship (*Guanxi*)-based governance is smaller than that in rule-based governance.

Some studies have attempted to depict practices such as *Guanxi* as a trust-based exchange (see, for example, Hill, 1995). Sun and Wong (2002) argue that trust and expectations behind *Guanxi* are the mechanisms to make *Guanxi* operational in Chinese private enterprises. While Lovett et al. (1999) suggest that trust seems a more complete concept than *Guanxi*, they point out that trust and *Guanxi* cannot be separated from each other in relationship-based business practices. In this researcher's opinion, although *Guanxi* is manifest in personal relationships, it refers to informal institutions, as discussed by North (1990). When discussing the business practices of Chinese private firms, *Guanxi* and trust are interchangeable in much of the literature (Wank, 1996; Xin and Pearce, 1996; Li, 1998; Lovett et al., 1999; Schlevogt, 2001; Sun and Wong, 2002).[18] This book follows the literature in this respect; that is, trust and *Guanxi* are treated as interchangeable terms. *Guanxi* is the most suitable word to capture the various informal business relationships in China (Yang, 1994; Guthrie, 1998).

2.3.3 Government trust (*Guanxi*) and family trust (*Guanxi*)

In explaining the development of private enterprise in China, trust (*Guanxi*) has a multifaceted role. There are at least two important aspects of trust (*Guanxi*) present: trust (*Guanxi*) resulting from family relationships and government trust (*Guanxi*).

2.3.3.1 The dual roles of government trust (*Guanxi*)

Generally speaking, the role of government trust (*Guanxi*) in a private firm has direct and indirect components. The direct role of government trust (*Guanxi*) within Chinese private enterprises is represented by the phenomenon of "red-hat" enterprises. In this case, the government is an active participant in the firm's economic activities, which provides the advantage of avoiding government predation and ideological harassment, especially in the early development stages. In addition, in an imperfect institutional environment such as China, where many exchange relationships are personalized and access to market information and scarce inputs is a matter of privilege, government trust can be represented by procurement ability, which is essential for successful production (Tian, 2000). In this researcher's opinion, a "red-hat" firm is viewed as a cooperative or trust-sharing (*Guanxi*-sharing) arrangement, i.e., an example of cooperation between a private enterprise and the government.

The indirect role of government trust (*Guanxi*) in a firm's economic activities is reflected in its power to provide institutional trust. According to Williamson's (1993) categorizations of trust, institutional trust corresponds to the institutional environment. It has been recognized that in the current transitional period in China, the available institutional backup has to be the government, and private enterprises have flourished by tapping into the institutional capital of the government (Sun and Wong, 2002). In China's case, apart from "red-hat" firms, other private enterprises also reveal a strong degree of dependence on the government (Xin and Pearce, 1996; Flynn and Xu, 2001). Therefore, the first indirect role of government trust (*Guanxi*) is to provide protection within the overall institutional environment in which

---

[18] For example, Li (1998, p.295) writes "trust (*Guanxi*, in general)."

private enterprises operate (Williamson, 1993; Rao et al., 2005). The second indirect role of government trust (*Guanxi*) is to provide useful information, including market entry, access to financial resource, and technological support and services. For example, to access capital in China, the government can provide information about reliability of a private enterprise, which can be illustrated by the importance of obtaining "*Lixiangpiwen*" (official permission for a proposed project) from the government (Sun and Wong, 2002).[19] In short, the indirect role of government trust (*Guanxi*) is to facilitate the development of private enterprises through the provision of institutional trust, which means that the government acts as regulator, arbitrator and service provider.

2.3.3.2 The role of family trust (*Guanxi*)

The importance of family trust (*Guanxi*) has its origins in Adam Smith's conception of self-interest as a means of explaining the way people behave: "every man ... is first and principally recommended to his own care ... after himself, the members of his own family ... are naturally the objectives of his warmest affections. They are naturally and usually the persons upon whose happiness or misery his conduct must have the greatest influence." (Smith, 1759[2002], p.257) In short, there is good reason to believe that feelings of family members are stronger than that of others outside the family.

In essence, family-ism and group-orientation philosophy have made the Chinese cultural system distinctive and powerful. On the one hand, Chinese families, as a basic unit of the society, act to provide not only shelter and food, but also an environment within which people socialize and play the roles defined by traditional Confucianism. In modern times, the Chinese traditional family concept has transformed into "family-ism" and pervades almost all social organizations. In private enterprises, there is much emphasis on family-based relations and respect for collective orientation (Schlevogt, 2001). On the other hand, Chinese group orientation emphasizes ties of kinship and close personal relationships. In business, the importance of groups is reflected in the form of family-ism's claim for solidarity (Xing, 1995). This is also reflected by the argument that trusting relationships between family members underpin the development of private enterprises (Sun and Wong, 2002). Thus, we would rather limit the scope of group

---

[19] This official permission represents governmental confirmation of the legitimacy and necessity of a proposed project. Only with this official permission is an enterprise able to approach banks for loans, and approach higher level government departments for support (Sun and Wong, 2002). However, government support is a necessary, though not sufficient, condition for private enterprises to secure bank loans.

cooperation to the family circle, i.e. the prevailing family business of private enterprises. Furthermore, trust (*Guanxi*) in China, although family centred, has an extraordinary capacity to extend and be network-based; that is, this family-based trust (*Guanxi*) is often extended beyond family members to friends and acquaintances (Sun and Wong, 2002). In this manner, family trust (*Guanxi*) also presents an ability to obtain necessary inputs for successful production. In general, the development pattern of Chinese private enterprises is characterized by the pervading role of family businesses, no matter whether they take the form of "pure" private enterprises or "red-hat" enterprises. This type of family business, in the author's opinion, is also a trust-sharing (*Guanxi*-sharing) arrangement, i.e. cooperation between a private enterprise and the family.

2.3.3.3 Distinction between government and family trust (*Guanxi*)

While both government and family trust (*Guanxi*) have played an important role in the development of Chinese private enterprises, differences between them can be located in terms of three important factors of trustworthiness: ability, benevolence, and integrity (Mayer et al., 1995; Lovett et al., 1999). The meaning of these three factors is somewhat elusive in the literature (Lovett et al., 1999). However, in simple terms, ability refers to competence and expertise, while benevolence refers to loyalty and altruism, and integrity refers to consistency and congruity (Mayer et al., 1995).

In terms of ability, although family members have been a major source of cheap and flexible resources for private enterprises (Roberts and Zhou, 2000), their financial competence is limited compared with that of the government in accessing capital, in particular bank loans, which is critical to enterprise development (Sun and Wong, 2002). In this manner, government trust (*Guanxi*) can be interpreted as being at a higher level of ability than family trust (*Guanxi*). In terms of benevolence, although the government generally acts as a "helping hand" in market-oriented reforms (Li, 1998), this does not mean that government policy always gives priority to the long-term development of private enterprises (Sun and Wong, 2002). Rather, new regulations have often been accompanied by "rectification" campaigns, which have impeded private enterprise development (Gregory et al., 2000). Moreover, there is a tendency for the government to increase rent-seeking in successful enterprises (Sun, 2002; Yang, 2002). In contrast, it is generally accepted that family relationships represent loyalty and altruism simply because family members care more about each other than outsiders (Whyte, 1995; Schlevogt, 2001). In this manner, family trust (*Guanxi*) is at a higher level of benevolence than government trust (*Guanxi*). In terms of integrity, it has been argued that private business was experimental during the reform periods (Gelb et al., 1993) and there was no effective mechanism to ensure that the government could not suddenly reverse the reform process or impose exactions on private enterprises (Li, 2004), while the success of family firms lies in the stability of the family system (James, 1999; Yeung, 2000). In this respect, family trust (*Guanxi*) represents a higher level of integrity than government trust (*Guanxi*). To sum up, among the three aspects of trustworthiness, government trust (*Guanxi*) generally represents a higher level of ability, while family trust (*Guanxi*) generally represents a higher level of benevolence and integrity within private enterprises. These differences between government and family trust (*Guanxi*) affect a firm's decision to cooperate with the government or with the family (see Chapter 6). More importantly, as noted by North (1990, p.37), since governmental institutional arrangements rest on the "coercive" power of government, they stand "on a somewhat different footing than individual and voluntary organization." Therefore, government and family trust (*Guanxi*) have different effects on ownership arrangements of private enterprises. Table 2.2 summaries the nominal ownership, control rights, and the distribution of benefits in the two development patterns of Chinese private enterprises, i.e., "red-hat" enterprises and family businesses, compared with Japanese and American firms. This table is based on the study of TVEs by Chang and Wang (Table 1 in p.442, 1994), where "red-hat" enterprises resemble the nature of government involvement in TVEs, as discussed above.

Table 2.2 Ownership Structure in Different Types of Firms

	Family Business	"Red-hat" Firm (or TVE)	Japanese Firm	American Firm
1.Nominal Owner	Investors	Investors	Shareholders	Share-holders
2.Control Rights	Owner as manager	Manager and/or local government	Workers and managers	Managers
3.Main Beneficiaries	Investors	Investors and government	Workers and shareholders	Share-holders

Within a typical family business, control rights are in the hands of the owner, who is also the manager of the firm (Schlevogt, 2001). In other words, this kind of firm can be viewed as an owner-cum-manager firm (Fama and Jensen, 1983; James, 1999). Moreover, often the investor is also the owner of the firm. In this sense, the management of a family business is called "three roles in one" management (the investor, the owner, and the manager) or "four roles in one" (adding the producer) in some of the literature (Blue Book of Private Enterprises, 2001, 2002; Gan, 2002). In terms of corporate governance, non-separation of ownership and control in family businesses is the main difference compared to the other types of firms.

In contrast, the control rights within a "red-hat" enterprise rest with both the manager and the government (Smyth, 1997; Hsiao et al., 1998),[20] or the government only (Weitzman and Xu, 1994; Chang and Wang, 1994; Che and Qian, 1998). Consequently, the government shares the profits with investors (Pearce, 2001; Rao et al., 2005). However, the conflicts of objectives and interests between the firm and the government are obvious because local governments are not purely economic actors but pursue multiple social, political and economic objectives such as employment maximization (Bowles and Dong, 1999; Sun, 2002). As a consequence, private enterprises often go along with government interference, which often contradicts their interests (Sun and Wong, 2002). In fact, there is a tendency for local governments to misuse their ownership rights over TVEs and "red-hat" enterprises (Sun, 2002). In this manner, corporate governance in a "red-hat" enterprise can be interpreted as separation of ownership and control.

Previous research on the development of Chinese private enterprises has focused exclusively on either government trust (*Guanxi*) (see, for example, Yang, 1994, 2002; Wank, 1996; Xin and Pearce, 1996; Guthrie, 1998) or family trust (*Guanxi*) (see, for example, Xing, 1995; Yeung, 2000; Schlevogt, 2001; Gan, 2002), so that one important element of trust (*Guanxi*) has always been missing. While Sun and Wong (2002) analyse both government and family trust (*Guanxi*) and attempt to make a comparison between the two,[21] their study is limited in that they restrict government trust (*Guanxi*) to

---

[20] For example, Smyth (1997) argues that the control rights of a TVE shift from the township-village government to the managers and skilled workers. This indicates that the government has the rights to control the firm.

[21] For instance, Sun and Wong (2002) divide the concept of trust into three types, namely, trust in one's own person, trust in interpersonal relations, and trust in systems, which correspond to three forms of capital, i.e., human capital, relational capital and institutional capital. They argue that trust in China is family centred, the same conclusion as in the Xing (1995) and Schlevogt's (2001) studies.

providing institutional capital for private enterprises within society and with banks, and they do not adequately explain the role of individual firm characteristics in distinguishing between government and family trust (*Guanxi*). This gap in the literature will be filled by the empirical study in Chapter 6.

2.3.4 Approaches towards dealing with trust (*Guanxi*) within a firm

As Kreps (1990, pp.94-95) has observed in his analysis of reputation and implicit contracts, a firm is "an intangible asset carrying a reputation." The same is true for trust (*Guanxi*). Since trust (*Guanxi*) is an elusive notion, and it stems mainly from social and cultural background, it is difficult to clearly measure it. Williamson (1993) suggests that trust is irrelevant to commercial exchange, indicating that trust can be treated as a special non-market resource within a firm.

A similar approach can be found in the literature, showing that different classes of agents characterized by comparative advantages in different non-marketed resources can be used to explain different organizational arrangements. Reid (1977) was the first to use this idea to study the contractual structure in agricultural tenancy. He considers landlords, as a class, to have a comparative advantage in management, while tenants afford an advantage in labour supervision. Eswaran and Kotwal (1985) model Reid's idea formally and study how each contractual form, i.e., fixed wage contract, fixed rental contract, and share contract, entails a different type of agent, i.e., landlord or tenant, providing non-marketed factor inputs. These scholars discuss the optimal contractual structures in terms of the landlords' profit within specific parameters.

In the Chinese context, Tian (2000) further develops Eswaran and Kotwal's (1985) model to discuss the optimal ownership arrangement between private and collective ownership, by introducing the government's procurement ability into the firm's profit function (this is explained in more detail in Chapter 4). The theoretical models developed later in this book are extensions of Tian's framework, but use the more general notion of trust (*Guanxi*), which comprises both the roles of government and family. Furthermore, emphasis is placed on the interplay of government and family trust (*Guanxi*) to explain the dominant structure of family businesses in Chinese private enterprises.

2.4 Conclusion

The development of Chinese private enterprises is a reflection of China's unique transition from a planned economy to market-oriented economy. However, research on Chinese private enterprises is a relatively recent phenomenon due to their status as a new force. Because of the confusion over the definition of private enterprises, some previous research does not deal with private enterprises independently. For the purposes of this book private enterprises refer only to domestic private enterprises and this book focuses on privately-run enterprises that employ more than eight people.

Recent contributions in the literature on Chinese private enterprises are "broad brushed" in discussing general facts (Gregory et al., 2000; Blue Book of Private Enterprises, 2001, 2002) or are focused on individual, fragmented aspects of private enterprise development (Flynn and Xu, 2001; Schlevogt, 2001; Zhao, 2002), but do not provide a clear theoretical analysis. This book will attempt to integrate standard property rights theory with the traditional cultural context to analyse the development of Chinese private enterprises.

It is commonly acknowledged that clearly defined property rights are a prerequisite for economic prosperity, including the sound development of private enterprises. However, debate still occurs in the discussion of property rights assignments within the firm. While agency theory attaches great attention to the role of management, endogenous ownership theory emphasizes the importance of the market environment. Although this book attempts to discuss the development of private enterprises based on endogenous ownership theory, it also takes into account the importance of management, particularly in discussing the prevailing dominance of family businesses among Chinese private enterprises (see Chapter 4).

In general, the development of private enterprises in China in recent decades not only proves that privatization is an inevitable process for economic prosperity, but also confirms that there is no commonly accepted approach for achieving private ownership (see Chapter 3). More precisely, the Chinese experience demonstrates that implicit contracts, which come from traditional culture, seem not to be sufficiently explored by standard property rights theory. The notion of trust (*Guanxi*), which is culturally determined, is employed in this study. While this book is consistent with the basic arguments raised by Weitzman and Xu (1994) that standard property rights theory needs to incorporate social and cultural backgrounds, it further develops the verbal exposition of "cooperative culture." It does this by mathematically introducing trust (*Guanxi*) as a non-marketed resource into the firm's production function, following Tian's (2000) study. However, this book departs from Tian's work by considering two types of trust (*Guanxi*), government and family, in influencing the development of Chinese private enterprises (see Chapter 4).

In summary, the main purpose of this book is to integrate general property rights theory with a cultural perspective to discuss the development of Chinese private enterprises, using trust (*Guanxi*) as the cultural factor in a firm's economic activities, particularly in the process of production. While filling gaps in the literature, this book also attempts to provide a theoretical explanation for the reduction in government ownership within firms and the prevalence of family businesses in China, thus providing policy implications for the future development of private enterprises.

CHAPTER 3

The Development of Private Enterprises in Zhejiang Province

Since the late 1970s a new type of ownership form has appeared and mushroomed in China's market-socialist economy. An amendment to the Chinese Constitution, passed in 1999, explicitly specifies this emerging phenomenon as the "private economy," which indicates that private enterprises have been legally recognized. [22] This chapter describes the development, history and the present situation of Chinese private enterprises with emphasis on private enterprises in Zhejiang province, because private enterprises in that province have developed more rapidly relative to many other provinces. More importantly, the chapter emphasizes the ownership structure of private enterprises, focusing on the role of government and family. It then provides stylized facts on the characteristics of family businesses.

3.1 General Backgrounds of Private Enterprises in China

3.1.1 The development, history and present situation of Chinese private enterprises

In the early stages of the People's Republic, private enterprises underwent "socialist transformation." At the end of 1957, there were about one million people in cities and towns engaged in the individual, industrial and commercial sectors (the predecessor of private enterprises). Following the Great Leap Forward (1959-1961) which ignored and even denied the commodity economy in theory and government policy, and also three years of natural catastrophe (1959-1961) which resulted in shrinkage of the national economy, this number declined. During the Cultural Revolution (1966-1976), when chaos occurred nationwide and government policies had a strong bias against private ownership (a strategy designed to "cut off the tails of capitalism,"[23]) the individual industrial and commercial sector came under continuous political attack. Consequently, by 1978, there were only 140,000 individuals engaged in the private sector. In short, before the reform and the open door policy began in 1978, the individual industrial and commercial sector was on the brink of extinction, and the private economy had lost its legal status.

---

[22] As discussed in Chapter 2, this book focuses on domestic private enterprises. However, due to the availability of official data, the data cited in this chapter covers only those enterprises registered as private enterprises; that is, the data exclude "red-hat" firms.

[23] "Cutting off the tails of capitalism" means the elimination of private ownership.

The situation has changed since 1978. China's market-oriented reforms have produced impressive results, and perhaps the most important result is the emergence of a significant private sector. The important role of private enterprises has recently been formally recognized by the Chinese government. This can be seen in the changes in the legal status of private enterprises, and the enforcement of reform policies.

3.1.1.1 Legal status of private enterprises: from "a supplement to the socialist publicly-owned economy" to "an important component of the economy"

The Third Plenum of the Chinese Communist Party's (CCP) Eleventh Conference in December 1978 marked the beginning of market-oriented reforms in China. Although the plenum itself made no specific announcements concerning private business, it emphasized economic development and individual incentives that gave impetus to the revival of private business. The private sector was officially recognized as a supplement to the public sector. Following the recovery of private business, in 1981 the number of people engaged in the individual industrial and commercial sector increased to 2,279,000, or about 1,829,000 households in all.

The private economy then grew steadily. In 1988, the Tentative Stipulations on Private Enterprises (TSPE) was issued by the State Council to govern the registration and management of private firms. In this document a privately-run enterprise was defined as "a for-profit organization that is owned by individuals and employs more than eight people." From that time, large private enterprises started to emerge. During 1986-1988, the private economy grew rapidly, but some serious problems, such as products with poor quality and/or fake brand names, also surfaced. Following the Tiananmen Square Incident in 1989, the state became more involved in the administration of the private economy. That is, directed by state policies and influenced by the market mechanism, the private economy became stagnant. As a consequence, the growth of private enterprises slowed and the private economy entered a stage of adjustment and consolidation from 1989 to 1991.

Deng Xiaoping, in his famous southern tour in 1992, called for a broadening of reforms. This was a critical moment in China's transition to the market. It was followed by a major ideological breakthrough at the Fourteenth Conference of the CCP. For the first time, the market-socialist economy was endorsed as China's goal of reform, which was the turning point on the road to a fully fledged private sector. Recognition of the private economy commenced an era of rapid development, and attitudes towards private enterprises changed. The greatest change in official attitudes towards private ownership came in 1999, when private enterprises were recognized in the Chinese Constitution as an important component of the economy. Private enterprises have been legally recognized since that time. In 2001 private entrepreneurs were allowed to join the Communist Party, while legitimate private property was protected by the 22nd amendment to the Chinese Constitution on March 14, 2004, indicating that private property is now officially recognized in "socialist" China.[24]

3.1.1.2 Enforcement of reform policy

The dual-track approach (partial reforms within sectors) has been an important feature of Chinese reforms since 1979 (Gregory et al., 2000). Two-tier pricing was first introduced in rural areas along with the household responsibility system, and later applied to other sectors, including industry (through the contract responsibility system), the national budget (through the fiscal contract responsibility system), and labour markets (through the contract system for new employees in the state sector). The approach was adopted with respect to the development of private enterprises because transfer of ownership was not a part of political debate until well into the second decade of market reforms. In fact, private enterprises were tolerated and even encouraged in areas where large-scale state-owned enterprises (SOEs) did not exist, such as services, light industry, and agriculture.

A policy of ownership reform has been implemented since 1995, when the central government formulated a policy of "grasping the large ones and letting the smaller ones go" (*Zhuadafangxiao*) for SOEs. The central government decided to keep under its ownership 500 to 1,000 large state firms and to reform the smaller SOEs through a package of policy measures including reorganizations, mergers, acquisitions, leasing, and sales. At the same time, collective enterprises (mainly township-village enterprises (TVEs)) were also allowed to change ownership, predominantly through shareholding cooperative reform. When the ownership reform began, the essence of the policy was privatization. This favoured the development of private enterprises.

In conclusion, China's unique approach to market-oriented reforms has

---

[24] However, the protection of legitimate private property differs from the protection of public property because public property is still specified as "sacrosanct and inviolable" in the Chinese Constitution (2004), while at the same time, it is difficult to define whether private property is legitimate or not. Further discussion on this difference is in Section 7.3.1.

influenced the manner in which the private sector has developed since its re-emergence in the late 1970s. Private enterprises first took hold in the rural sector as an outgrowth of the restructuring of the rural economy and in sectors such as trade and services, where there were a limited number of large state enterprises, and distortions from central planning created market opportunities for private enterprises. The scope of private sector activities then gradually expanded to various sectors. During the 1980s, larger private enterprises grew out of these rural and individual enterprises, and out of collectives and state-owned enterprises, although they were not officially recognized until 1988. In the 1990s, government policy placed increasing emphasis on building a market economy and shifted towards a rule-based framework, which paved the way for rapid growth of private enterprises. This was given further impetus by policy changes that encouraged ownership reform of smaller, non-strategic state-owned enterprises, and which allowed collectives to transform into private enterprises.

3.1.1.3 Private enterprises as an unintended result of China's economic reform

The changes in the legal status of private enterprises and the enforcement of reform policies, together with the evolution of the definition of private enterprises (see Chapter 2), reflect the fact that the development of private enterprises was not a clear, careful design on the part of the central and local governments. At the beginning of the reform period, the government did not have a well-defined strategy or a clear blueprint, and did not envision private enterprises as the driving force of economic growth. Rather, private business was revived in the period after the Cultural Revolution as a quick way to respond to the mounting pressures of unemployment and economic stagnation. As some scholars have argued, private business was an experiment, and for most of the reform period it evolved through cycles of unpublicized experimentation, followed by general "in principle" approval,[25] then by ratification and specific regulations (Gelb et al., 1993). Often, new regulations have been accompanied by "rectification" campaigns, which have impeded private enterprise development. In this manner, reforms are implemented over time, but several years may elapse from the beginning of a reform experiment in one region until it is endorsed by the centre or is imitated by other regions. In this sense, the development of private enterprises is not the result of careful design on the part of the government. However, during the reform periods, the Chinese government has generally

---

[25] The "in principle" approval is one feature of Chinese bureaucratic style of work, which means that a way of doing things (or a project) is approved but under some restrictions, usually without extant policies or regulations.

been accepted as a "helping hand" in promoting the development of private enterprises (Li, 1998).

Corresponding to the above changes, continuously changing ownership is a notable feature of the development of private enterprises (Blue Book of Private Enterprises, 2001), in which the government plays an important role and this results in the phenomenon of "red-hat" firms (see Chapter 2).

3.1.2 Contributions of private enterprises to the Chinese economy

3.1.2.1 General development of Chinese private enterprises

In general, private enterprises in China have developed rapidly since 1978. This is reflected in increasing numbers, registered capital, and employees in registered private enterprises, as shown in Table 3.1. At the same time, the number and employees in SOEs and TVEs has experienced a downward trend since the early 1990s (Blue Book of Private Enterprises, 2001, 2002).

In recent years, privately-run enterprises (*Siyingqiye*, employing more than eight people) have developed more rapidly than individual businesses (*Getigongshanghu*, employing no more than eight people). Although the absolute number of privately-run enterprises is smaller than that of individual businesses, registered capital of privately-run enterprises had surpassed that of individual businesses by 1994, and their employees also exceeded employees in individual businesses by 2004. This indicates the rapid development of privately-run enterprises in recent years.

Table 3.1 The General Development of Private Enterprises

Year	Privately-run Enterprises			Individual Businesses			Total
	Heads (millions)	Registered Capital (billions RMB)	Employees (million persons)	Heads (millions)	Registered Capital (billions RMB)	Employees (million persons)	Employees in Private Enterprises (million persons)
1978						0.14	
1981				1.83	0.50	2.27	
1989	0.091	8.40	1.64	12.47	34.70	19.41	21.42
1990	0.098	9.50	1.70	13.29	39.76	21.04	22.74
1991	0.11	12.32	1.84	14.17	48.82	22.58	24.92
1992	0.14	22.12	2.32	15.34	60.10	24.67	26.99
1993	0.23	68.03	3.72	17.67	85.49	29.39	33.12
1994	0.43	144.80	6.48	21.87	131.90	37.76	44.24
1995	0.66	262.20	9.56	25.29	168.90	46.14	55.70
1996	0.82	375.20	11.71	27.04	216.50	50.17	61.88
1997	0.96	514.01	13.49	28.51	257.40	54.42	67.91
1998	1.20	1,020.10	17.09	31.20	312.03	61.14	78.24
1999	1.51	1,028.70	20.22	31.60	343.90	62.41	82.63
2000	1.76	1,330.80	24.07	25.71	331.50	50.70	74.77
2001	2.03	1,821.20	27.14	24.33	343.60	47.60	74.74
2002	2.44	2,475.60	34.09	23.78	378.20	47.43	81.52
2003	3.01	3,630.50	42.99	23.53	418.70	46.37	89.36
2004	3.65	4,793.60	50.17	23.51	505.80	45.87	96.04

(Source: Statistical Yearbook of China,1990-2005; Yearbook of State's Industrial and Commercial Administration,1992-2005)

Notes: 1. Registered capital in this table is calculated at current prices.

3.1.2.2 Contributions of private enterprises to the Chinese economy

As shown in Table 3.2, from 1990 to 2004 (deflated by the Consumer Price Index, 1990=100), the output of private enterprises increased in real terms from 76.4 billion RMB to 1478.5 billion RMB (about USD$178 billion in 2004),[26] with an average annual growth rate of 23.57%. At the same time, retail sales increased from 131.3 billion RMB to 1204.3 billion RMB, with an average annual growth rate of 17.15%, and tax revenue increased from 13.4 billion RMB to 152.7 billion RMB, with an average annual growth rate of 18.98%.

Table 3.2 Contributions of Private Enterprises

Unit: Billions RMB

Year	Output		Retail Sales		Tax Revenue	
	Privately-run Enterprises	Individual Businesses	Privately-run Enterprises	Individual Businesses	Privately-run Enterprises	Individual Businesses
1978						0.33
1989	9.70	56.00	3.40	1147.00	0.01	11.97
1990	12.20	64.20	4.30	127.00	0.20	13.20
1991	14.70	78.20	5.70	152.60	0.34	15.08
1992	20.50	92.70	9.10	186.10	0.46	17.66
1993	42.20	138.70	19.60	271.00	1.05	31.47
1994	114.00	163.80	51.30	421.10	1.75	36.04
1995	229.50	279.10	100.60	535.60	3.56	40.13
1996	322.70	353.90	145.90	670.60	6.02	39.78
1997	392.30	455.30	185.50	807.40	9.05	46.05
1998	585.30	596.00	305.90	978.00	16.38	53.69
1999	768.60	706.30	419.10	1,200.00	25.50	57.58
2000	1,074.00	716.20	581.30	1,135.00	41.44	76.27
2001	1,232.00	731.70	624.50	1,149.00	66.09	91.76
2002	1,534.00	796.80	792.90	1,222.00	94.56	100.50
2003	2,008.30	874.10	1,060.30	1,342.30	138.83	104.75
2004	2,295.04	809.80	1,303.90	1,225.20	199.50	121.20

(Source: Yearbook of State's Industrial and Commercial Administration,1991-2005;
Taxation Yearbook of China, 1991-2005)

Notes: 1. The data in this table are calculated at current prices.

---

[26] USD$1=RMB8.28yuan in 2004, and henceforward.

From official data, it appears that private enterprises have achieved impressive growth with relatively few resources; that is, private enterprises have in general made more efficient use of capital (Gregory et al., 2000). Regarding the share of tax revenue of private enterprises in the national total, it was as low at 8% in 1995 while SOEs and TVEs accounted for 56% and 15% respectively. However, there are several considerations which should be noted. First, there has been an upward trend in the taxation share of private enterprises since 1990 when it was at 6.8%, indicating their potential contribution to tax revenue. Second, because the data exclude "red-hat" firms (fake collectives), the actual share of private enterprises should be higher than the official data indicates. Third, considering the input-output ratio, although the state generally does not invest in private enterprises since the re-emergence of private enterprises, private enterprises still pay tax to the government. Therefore, the contribution to tax revenue by private enterprises is fairly impressive. Private enterprise share of total tax revenue increased 5.7 percentage points from 1990 to 2004 and was 12.5% in 2004.

In summary, private enterprises are the most dynamic component of the domestic economy, and the development of private enterprises constitutes an important component which has contributed to the rapid economic growth in China for more than two decades.

3.1.3 The involvement of the government

As discussed in the previous chapter, the experience of Chinese private enterprises, particularly the phenomenon of "red-hat" firms in which there is a significant role for the government, seems to suggest that a system of well-defined and secure property rights is not necessarily a precondition for the re-emergence and initial development of private business. In this respect, the growth of private enterprises and market institutions over time create demand for a clear definition and enforcement of private property rights (Gregory et al, 2000). Small businesses, which constitute the majority of private enterprises in the initial stage of development, need little in the way of legal protection. They are typically owned by a single individual or a small group of people who know each other very well, and do not raise capital from the public. What they need most is to have the state eliminate the obstacles that have been put in their path, and then to stand on an equal footing with SOEs and TVEs (Blue Book of Private Enterprises, 2001, and 2002). Although the central government's policy toward private enterprises has been getting better, there is still a problem of how to execute the central policy by the local government(s). Indeed, local governments in China often interpreted new regulations as a signal allowing them to interfere in the activities of private enterprises. For instance, land use fees in some areas have increased to some extent, and have resulted in that some private enterprises moved to other areas [Report of the Asian Development Bank (ADB) and the China General Chamber of Commerce (CGCC), 2001]. On taxation, private enterprises do not enjoy policy preference as foreign enterprises although they generally do not use state investment. However, various fees, such as for annual examination of both lightning arrester by the meteorological bureau and fire prevention by the fire-controlling bureau, are exceedingly high. Restricted market access for some industries, such as production and sale of gold and silver products, primary real estate market, and important raw materials, is also a result of a policy decision which prevents from operating as private enterprises. Besides, there are restrictions on direct access to foreign trade in which private firms were not allowed to export directly prior to 1998. This leads to the collusion between local governments and enterprises, with the local governments acting as patrons rather than regulators in many cases. That is, since private enterprises have made increasing contributions to the financial revenue, local governments also have an incentive to cooperate with private firms, resulting in rent-seeking activities. However, private firms with the collusion of local governments generally suffer less from government rent-seeking activities than other private firms without it, particularly in the early development stage (Sun, 2002).

On the other hand, the collusion makes private entrepreneurs more susceptible to interference from the local governments. The former reliance on personal connections in the relationship with the government has been transplanted to the marketplace and dominates market exchange. Therefore, private enterprises have to rely heavily on personal relationships for vital information and necessary inputs. In addition, faced with a plethora of restrictions and biases, private enterprises have to establish a close link with the local bureaucracy, which indicates the important role played by the government in the firm's economic activities.

3.2 The Development of Private Enterprises in Zhejiang Province

The development of private enterprises in Zhejiang province generally corresponds to the evolutionary trend of private enterprises in China, as discussed above. According to a Report of Zhejiang Statistical Bureau (2003), at the beginning of the foundation of the People's Republic, there were 600,000 individual businesses with 990,000 employees, and 7,650 privately-run enterprises with 107,000 employees. After the socialist transformation and the Cultural Revolution, there were only 2,086 individual

45

businesses on the eve of market reform in 1978. Since the commencement of the reform period, Zhejiang private enterprises have developed more rapidly compared with many other provinces. The characteristics of the development of Zhejiang private enterprises constitute the so-called "Zhejiang model," which is now used as a reference by other provinces to achieve high and sustainable economic growth. This section discusses the historical development, current state, and some stylized facts of Zhejiang private enterprises since 1978.

3.2.1 Historical development of Zhejiang private enterprises

Chronologically the development of Zhejiang private enterprises spans three periods since 1978. The first period was from the commencement of reforms in the late 1970s to the early 1990s, when private enterprises re-emerged and experienced an initial spurt of market-oriented development. In 1978, the share of GDP produced by private enterprises was only 5.7%. Since then, private enterprises in Zhejiang have developed rapidly. However, initially many private enterprises claimed they were collectives to avoid government predation and ideological harassment. Therefore, this period was characterized by the development of collective enterprises, many of which were "red-hat" firms, while registered private enterprises represented a small proportion of the provincial economy. In 1990, the share of GDP produced by private enterprises was still low at 15.7% (while the share of GDP by collective enterprises was high at 53.1%) (Zhejiang Statistical Yearbook, 2005).

Table 3.3 The General Development of Zhejiang Private Enterprises

Year	Privately-run Enterprises			Individual Businesses			Total
	Heads (thousands)	Registered Capital (billions RMB)	Employees (million persons)	Heads (millions)	Registered Capital (billions RMB)	Employees (million persons)	Employees in Private Enterprises (million persons)
1990	11.00			1.00		1.53	
1991	11.00	0.73	0.15	1.00	4.00	1.55	1.70
1992	11.50	1.10	0.18	1.12	5.22	1.74	1.92
1993	19.40	4.29	0.26	1.24	8.07	1.97	2.23
1994	46.00	13.67	0.68	1.43	12.20	2.32	3.00
1995	72.00	25.12	1.05	1.54	17.30	2.54	3.59
1996	87.70	34.70	1.17	1.68	22.70	2.65	3.82
1997	91.80	47.01	1.36	1.53	21.99	2.56	3.92
1998	100.20	78.80	1.53	1.58	22.67	2.68	4.21
1999	146.40	97.60	1.92	1.64	25.03	2.81	4.73
2000	178.80	136.90	3.00	1.59	29.96	2.72	5.72
2001	208.80	179.50	3.47	1.58	31.11	2.77	6.24
2002	247.30	205.70	4.04	1.53	33.23	2.76	6.80
2003	302.20	286.00	4.84	1.59	40.75	2.98	7.82
2004	333.20	390.60	5.09	1.68	49.83	3.21	8.30

(Source: Zhejiang Statistical Yearbook,1990-2005; Yearbook of State's Industrial and Commercial Administration,1992-2005)

The second period was from the early 1990s to the late 1990s, when registered private enterprises obtained prominence. Following Deng Xiaoping's 1992 speech, private enterprises began to enter the period of the first "leap," while many "red-hat" firms took off their "red-hats" and registered as private enterprises. As shown in Table 3.3, from 1991 to 1997, registered individual businesses (*Getigongshanghu*) and privately-run enterprises (*Siyingqiye*) increased from 1 million to 1.53 million firms, and from 11,000 to 92,000 firms, respectively. At the same time, their workforce increased from 1.56 million to 2.56 million and from 0.17 million to 1.36 million employees, respectively. In 1997, the share of GDP produced by private enterprises accounted for 33.7%; that is, one third of provincial GDP (while the share of GDP by collective enterprises declined to 36.7%) (Zhejiang Statistical Yearbook, 2005).

The third period is the latest period of development for private enterprises dating from the late 1990s. As shown in Table 3.3, the number of privately-run enterprises reached 333,200 firms in 2004, which placed Zhejiang third among China's provinces in terms of number of enterprises,[27] while the number of Zhejiang's individual businesses reached 1.68 million, which ranked second among China's provinces.[28] The registered capital of privately-run enterprises accounted for 390.6 billion RMB, while that of individual businesses was 49.83 billion RMB in 2004, with average real annual growth rates since 1991 of 53% and 15% respectively. In addition, the workforce in private enterprises increased to 8.3 million employees in 2004. The share of GDP produced by domestic private enterprises continued to increase, and reached 55.1% of the provincial total in 2004 (while foreign-invested enterprises accounted for only 7.4%) (Zhejiang Statistical Yearbook, 2005). In short, private enterprises now underpin more than half of the provincial economy, becoming the main force to economic growth in Zhejiang.

3.2.2 Current state of Zhejiang private enterprises

3.2.2.1 Standing at the forefront of private enterprise development in China

Zhejiang stands at the forefront of private enterprise development in China's provinces. This is reflected not only in the figures presented above, but also the increase in industrial output, retail sales of social consumer goods, tax revenue, and export value, as shown in Table 3.4. Calculated in real terms from 1990 to 2004 (deflated by the Consumer Price Index, 1990=100), the output of private enterprises increased from 14.1 billion RMB to 471.9 billion RMB, with an average annual growth rate of 28.5%. At the same time, retail sales increased from 7.1 billion RMB to 159.8 billion RMB, with an average annual growth rate of 24.9%, and tax revenue increased from 0.8 billion RMB to 15.4 billion RMB, with an average annual growth rate of 23.5%. The average annual growth rates in Zhejiang for these three indicators are higher than the corresponding national average annual growth rates during the same period at 4.9%, 7.7%, and 4.5%, respectively. The private sector has also been an important contributor to exports. In 2004, the direct export value of private enterprises reached 14.9 billion US dollars, accounting for 25.7% of total provincial export values and surpassing the

---

[27] The first was Jiangsu province with 401,000 privately-run enterprises, and the second was Guangdong province with 389,800 privately-run enterprises (Report of China's Citizen-run Enterprises, No.1, 2004).

[28] The first was Guangdong province with 1.7 million (Report of China's Citizen-run Enterprises, No.1, 2004).

export shares by state and collective firms (25.1%) for the first time (Report of China's Citizen-run Enterprises, No.1, 2004, p.184).[29] The development of private enterprises in Zhejiang has become an important component of the provincial economy (Report of China's Citizen-run Enterprises, No.2, 2004).

Table 3.4 Contributions of Zhejiang Private Enterprises

Year	Industrial Output (billions RMB)	Retail Sales (billions RMB)	Tax Revenue (billions RMB)	Export (billions US Dollars)
1990	14.10	7.10	0.80	0.05
1991	17.30	7.80	1.00	0.07
1992	20.90	8.70	1.60	0.10
1993	28.70	12.60	2.32	0.06
1994	79.00	32.90	2.89	0.22
1995	173.30	89.20	2.85	0.45
1996	238.80	121.60	3.95	0.58
1997	257.90	125.00	3.90	0.71
1998	317.30	128.80	4.88	1.30
1999	399.30	154.40	6.04	2.82
2000	573.70	200.60	9.00	6.50
2001	645.30	222.50	12.69	8.24
2002	742.70	267.70	16.98	8.91
2003	827.10	290.80	22.05	9.94
2004	990.98	335.60	32.36	14.90

(Source: Zhejiang Statistical Yearbook, 1990-2005; Yearbook of State's Industrial and Commercial Administration, 1992-2005; Taxation Yearbook of China, 1990-2005)

Private enterprises also became a main channel for increasing employment. From 1979 to 2004, 17.13 million new employees had been absorbed by the private sector, while the number of employees within the public sector declined by 4.56 million. In 2004, employees within the private sector accounted for nearly 60% of total employees in Zhejiang province. Besides, investment by the private sector has become an important source of social investment. In 2004, the private sector invested 221 billion RMB, accounting for 52.9% of total social investment. Moreover, the private sector also played an important role in increasing rural and urban residents' income.

---

[29] Together with foreign invested companies, the export values of private sector accounted for 60% of the provincial total in 2004.

Table 3.5 Zhejiang's Economic Indices and Position among China's 31 Provinces, Autonomous Regions, and Direct-Jurisdiction Cities in 2004

Economic Indices	Zhejiang's Level	National Average level	Zhejiang's Ranks in China
Population (million persons)	47.20	1,299.88	--
GDP (billion RMB)	1,124.30	13,687.59	4
Per Capita GDP (RMB)	23,942.00	10,561.00	4
Disposable income of Urban Residents (RMB/per person)	14,546.38	9,421.61	3
Net income of Rural Residents (RMB/per person)	5,944.06	2,936.40	3
Consumption Expenditures of Urban Residents (RMB/per person)	10,636.14	7,182.10	4
Living Consumption Expenditures of Rural Residents (RMB/per person)	4,659.11	2,184.65	2

(Source: Statistical Yearbook of China, 2005)

In summary, following more than two decades of private enterprise development in Zhejiang, the industrial output, sales revenue, retail sales of social consumer goods, and exports of private enterprises have shown a continual upward trend, strongly contributing to the provincial economy. Zhejiang was ranked first nationwide in terms of absolute numbers in each of these categories over seven years from 1998 to 2004 (Report of China's Citizen-run Enterprises, No.2, 2004, p.182). In terms of current prices,[30] from 1978 to 2004, 53% of GDP was contributed by private enterprises (Report of China's Citizen-run Enterprises, No.1, 2004, p.183). In 1978 Zhejiang's GDP was only 12.4 billion RMB, which ranked twenty-fourth nationwide, while in 2004 its GDP reached 1,124.3 billion RMB, which placed it fourth in China. At the same time, it was estimated that Zhejiang's per capita GDP also ranked fourth in China in 2004, only less than that of Shanghai, Beijing, and Tianjin, as shown in Table 3.5. This shows that Zhejiang province, the former economically small province with poor resources, has become one of those provinces that perform well in the economy. In other words, Zhejiang province, as a leader in economic growth,

---

[30] The price is not discounted here.

sets a good example for the development of the private economy in other provinces in China.

3.2.2.2 The industrial distribution of Zhejiang private enterprises

The scope of private sector activities has expanded from sales, services, and small transportation, to almost every industrial sector, except for a few industries prohibited by state policy such as basic energy and military industries. At present, Zhejiang individual businesses (*Getigongshanghu*, employing no more than eight people) are concentrated in tertiary industry while privately-run enterprises (*Siyingqiye*, employing more than eight people) are mainly concentrated in secondary industry, which has become a new area of provincial economic growth. In 2004, among the total incremental industrial output produced by private enterprises, secondary industry accounted for 65.2%, while tertiary industry accounted for 30.6% and primary industry accounted for only 4.2% (Report of China's Citizen-run Enterprises, No.2, 2004, p.182). In general, the industrial distribution of Zhejiang privately-run enterprises has shifted from "primary, then secondary, and then tertiary industries" at the beginning of the reform period to "secondary, then tertiary, and then primary industries" at present. That is, secondary industry is the main area in which private-enterprise production is concentrated.

Within secondary industry, Zhejiang private enterprises have often developed along with the regional economy. Many economic regions with agglomerate effects have been formed, which is characterized by "one village, one product". For instance, Yiwu's "small goods city", Shaoxing's "light industries and textiles", Liushi's "low-voltage electrical appliances", Haining's "leather", Yongkang's "hardwares", and Tongxiang's "woolen sweater", are famous in China. At present, there are more than 300 economic regions with an output of special local products over 100 million RMB in Zhejiang province, and 13,000 firms producing special local products, with 6 million employees (Blue Book of Private Enterprises, 2002). Another result of the regional economy is that professional (products) markets emerge to form productive and sales networks, which connect tens of thousands of individual businesses and family firms.

3.2.2.3 Emergence of large enterprises and diffuse ownership structure

Many large private enterprises have emerged and developed recently, meaning that Zhejiang had 183 firms in the largest 500 private enterprises in China in 2003, which was the highest of any of the Chinese provinces

(Report of China's Citizen-run Enterprises, No.1, 2004, p.584).[31]

Meanwhile, private enterprises have developed a more diffuse ownership structure. There were 140,000 limited liability companies, which accounted for 59% and 84% in terms of firm number and registered capital respectively in total private enterprises in Zhejiang province in 2004 (Report of China's Citizen-run Enterprises, No.1, 2004, p.587). The reasons are twofold. The first reason is that when private enterprises grow, they themselves have the incentive to merge, acquire, and cooperate with others. Taking industrial private-run enterprises with annual sales revenue over 5 million RMB for example, in 1998, there were 952 solely-run companies and 937 limited liability companies in Zhejiang province, accounting for 42.3% and 41.6% of total private enterprises, respectively. In 2004, limited liability companies increased to 7467, accounting for 72.5% of total private enterprises, while the ratio of solely-run companies declined to 21.9%. The second reason is the ownership reform of state-owned enterprises (SOEs) and collective-owned enterprises (mainly TVEs). By the end of 2002, 92% of SOEs and 96.5% of TVEs had transferred to registered private enterprises in Zhejiang province (Report of Zhejiang Provincial Bureau of Statistics, 2003), many of which were often formed as limited liability companies.

However, individual business constitutes a large part of private enterprises in terms of absolute number of heads in Zhejiang (see Table 3.3), while many private-run enterprises are developed from individual business, especially at the early stage of development. In general, the expansion of Zhejiang private enterprises relies heavily on quantity, so that most of them are characterized by sparse, small, and low technology. Within the secondary industrial private enterprises, there were 18,000 firms with annual sales revenue over 5 million RMB in 2004, accounting for only 5% of total private enterprises (Zhejiang Statistical Yearbook, 2005). Consequently, most private enterprises are still small firms owned and managed along family lines. This will be further examined in the next section, as part of the discussion of ownership structure in private enterprises.

3.2.3 Some stylized facts of Zhejiang private enterprises

3.2.3.1 From the Wenzhou model to the Zhejiang model

The development of Zhejiang private enterprises constitutes the so-called "Zhejiang model," which is derived from the well-known Wenzhou model. Wenzhou is a prefecture-level municipality located in the south-east corner

---

[31] The second was Jiangsu with 105 firms, and the third was Shandong with 45 firms.

of Zhejiang. The Wenzhou model is a pattern characterized by the development of private enterprises, which differs not only from the Sunan pattern that characterized the development of collective TVEs, but also from the Pearl-river Delta pattern where private enterprises are often promoted by foreign capital. The notion of the Wenzhou model first appeared in 1985 because of the impressive economic achievement of Wenzhou.[32] Since then, the Wenzhou model has expanded to typify the ownership characteristics of private enterprise province-wide and is frequently citied in the literature (Yuan, 1987; Sun, 2000; Blue Book of Private Enterprises, 2001, 2002).

Wenzhou was once a small city with poor resources, density population and few lands, and occlusive transportation. Since the reform period, Wenzhou has achieved great economic growth and social development that mainly contributed by its highly-developed private enterprises, resulting in the following facts. Calculated in real terms, between 1978 to 2003 Wenzhou's real GDP increased from 1.32 billion to 43.45 billion RMB, increasing more than 5-folds, with an average annual growth rate of 15%; real fiscal revenue increased from 0.14 billion to 5.43 billion RMB with an average annual growth rate of 16%; real retail sales of social commodities increased from 0.51 billion to 52.3 billion RMB with an average annual growth rate of 21%; and average net real incomes of rural residents increased from 114 RMB to 1,981 RMB with an average annual growth rate of 12%. From 1981 to 2003, average disposable real incomes of urban residents also increased from 423 RMB to 5,939 RMB, with an average annual growth rate of 13%, which ranked No.3 among 33 Direct Jurisdiction Cities, Economic Special Zones, and Opening Coastal Cities in China (Report of China's Citizen-run Enterprises, No.1, 2004, pp.183-184).

The rapid economic and social development in Wenzhou is closely associated with the highly-developed private enterprises. At present, there are about 350 thousand private enterprises (including privately-run enterprises and individual businesses) in Wenzhou, accounting for 98.8% of total industrial firms. Industrial output produced by private enterprises in Wenzhou accounts for 96% of total industrial output, tax revenue from private enterprises accounts for about 70% of total fiscal revenue, exports of private enterprises account for more than 95% of total exports, and employees within private enterprises account for about 80% of total employees.

---

[32] See "Three-hundred Thousand People Engage in Family Industry in Wenzhou" in *Shanghai Revolutionary Daily, May 12, 1985.*

In general, the Wenzhou model is a result of reform periods implemented since 1978. Due to Wenzhou's mountainous terrain, high population density, and natural resource shortage, life based on only agriculture was difficult in the pre-reform period (Yuan 1987). At the same time, there is a history of traditional family handicrafts such as umbrella making, shoe making and cotton shinning, weaving, and fluffing (Sun, 2000). Since 1978, the development of the private sector in Wenzhou has undergone transformations and has formed a system of "small commodities, and big markets".[33]

In terms of institutional arrangements, the Wenzhou model is famous for three innovations. The first was the practice of scattering individual household firms to business affiliation (*Guahu*), i.e. "wearing a red hat" as a collective, during the period from the late 1970s to the mid-1980s. The second innovation was the practice of business affiliation to joint-stock cooperatives from the mid-1980s to the mid-1990s (Sun, 2000). The third innovation was the transformation of joint-stock cooperatives to limited liability companies or joint-stock companies that occurred from the late 1990s. To a certain degree, the first two innovations are called "the old Wenzhou model" while the last one is called "the new Wenzhou model."[34] The New Wenzhou model is not a denial of the old one. Rather, it gives new connotations and prospects for the future of private enterprises. More precisely, ownership arrangement of the new model shifts from single capital source to multiplex capital sources. In the organization, the new model provides a solid foundation for a conglomeration of private enterprises; in the operation, it moves towards a comprehensive development that comprises both brand-name and capital operation, instead of the previous pattern of small commodities based on traditional products; in management ability, it forms a contingent of entrepreneurs. That is, private enterprises in present Wenzhou are more closely related to the modern firms in Western countries. In general, the Wenzhou model is acknowledged as a typical case of "reforming from below," that is, the radical nature of these innovations and their subsequent evolution was a result of individuals, households, and government officials at the local level pursuing their pragmatic interests, rather than following "top-down" directives (Sun, 2000). In fact, because of continuous vigor, the Wenzhou model has been again received great attention regarding the development of non-state enterprises, and it is now applied in the whole Zhejiang province, even the whole country.

---

[33] The output of small commodities accounts for about 70% of industrial output at present in Wenzhou (Report of Zhejiang Administration for Industry and Commerce, by Jiang Xue, 13 July, 2004).

[34] Report of Zhejiang Administration for Industry and Commerce, by Jiang Xue, 13 July, 2004.

The Zhejinag model is an update and extension of the Wenzhou model. In other words, the Zhejiang model is deduced from the Wenzhou model and it applies the Wenzhou model to the whole province. According to a report by the All China Federation of Industry and Commerce (ACFIC) in 2003, the "Zhejinag experience" can be summarized as following. First, popular enthusiasm for business start-up is aroused, and then a system of spontaneously starting-up a business by individuals occurs. Second, the professional (products) markets that meet the needs of socialist market emerge to form the productive and sales networks, connecting tens of thousands of individual businesses and family firms. Third, the folk (non-government) investment is active and distributed over various investment areas. Fourth, there are many "economic plates" with agglomerate and radiating effects, corresponding to the regional economy and special local products. Finally, a lot of large corporations are emerging and are encouraged to participate in national and international competitions.

However, the Zhejiang model is more or less related to the extensive administrative and fiscal decentralization at the provincial level in China due to federalism (Qian and Weingast, 1997),[35] which embodies in the fiscal contract responsibility system of the national budget as one kind of dual-track approach (see Section 3.1). That is, the provincial government has more autonomous power than the community or prefecture governments and can formulate certain policies, while the community or prefecture governments are strongly influenced by the provincial government. In this respect, the "Zhejiang experience" gives rise to the rapid development of private enterprises as a whole in Zhejinag province, and it provides an illustration of accelerating the development of private enterprises nationwide. In general, there is a common aspect of the basic Zhejiang experiences, which is an actual portrait of the development of Chinese private enterprises. That is, the development of private enterprises is not a result of the careful design by the government, which can also be seen in "reforming from below" of the Wenzhou model as discussed above, but rather, it is a result of a desire to make a living and pursue riches by individuals. This explains two important lessons of the Zhejinag experience, that is, creative initiatives of people and the proper role of the government, of which the latter will be discussed in the next Section.

---

[35] Federalism as a commitment to preserving market incentives has been studied by Qian and Weingast (1997). In their study, local governments refer mainly to community governments. In practice, however, the administrative and fiscal decentralization is more effective at the provincial level in China, such as Guangdong province which has been acknowledged as the first beneficiary of the fiscal contracting system during the early reform periods (Blue Book of Private Enterprises, 2001, and 2002).

Generally speaking, the core of "Zhejiang experience" perhaps is that the creative initiatives (pioneering spirit) of the people are treated with respect by the government, which directly gives rise to popular enthusiasm for the establishment of business by individuals. In many aspects, Zhejiang is a small province with poor natural resources,[36] and it is often subjected to natural disasters such as typhoons. The development of Zhejiang private enterprises has a close link with its history and traditional culture. Historically, many Zhejiang residents are descendants of immigrants from outside areas. Culturally, Zhejiang is a combination of traditional (mainland) and ocean (outside) culture,[37] in which the former emphasizes hard-work and thrift, harmony, and order, while the latter emphasizes openness, management consciousness, and creative consciousness. The reform and open door policy since 1978 releases the rules and regulations that fetter people's awareness and behavior, freeing people's creative initiatives. Many ground-breaking experiences are created by Zhejiang people, which provide a sound foundation for the rapid development of private enterprises. This can be seen in the institutional innovations of the Wenzhou model as discussed above.

Enthusiasm for business start-up by individuals, then gives rise to active folk (non-governmental) investment in Zhejiang province. Most private enterprises are naturally evolved from the primitive accumulation of folk capital while few are from Hongkong, Macao, and Taiwan or have foreign capital. From 1980-2001, folk investment increased from 1.7 billion to 151.8 billion RMB, with the average annual growth rate at 25.2%, which is 0.6 and 2.5 percentage points higher than the average rates of overall social fixed assets' investment and state investment, respectively (Zhejiang Statistical Yearbook, 2002). In 2001, folk capital accounted for 54.7% of overall social fixed assets' investment, becoming the main source of overall social fixed assets' investment. This differs not only from the Sunan pattern in Jiangsu province, where private enterprises are mainly spin-offs from state and collective enterprises, but also from the Pearl-river Delta pattern in Guangdong province, where private enterprises are often promoted by Hongkong, Macao and foreign capital.

---

[36] The notable feature of general situations in Zhejiang province is the large populations with small land. At present, there are more than 46 million people in Zhejiang province, with only 0.1 million squared kilometers of land. Moreover, the land is characterized by "seven-tenths are mountains, one-tenth is water, and two-tenths are farmlands".

[37] This can be seen in the geographical position of Zhejiang province in mainland China.

3.2.3.2 The role of the government

The role of central planning in the Zhejiang economy has been weak relative to many other provinces, which leads Zhejiang enterprises to rely on the market for survival. Driven by the profit motive, private enterprises, most of which operated with little investment but produced good economic results, have developed in Zhejiang. Due to the relatively weak planned economy, the correspondingly lenient government administration has provided a sound environment for economic institutional changes. However, prior to Deng Xiaoping's 1992 speech and subsequent ownership reform in the mid-1990s, the development of private enterprises was restricted and strongly influenced by central government policy. In this sort of situation, every level of the Zhejiang government offered tacit consent and even encouragement of institutional innovation. This was manifest in the practice of "wearing a red hat" to retain an affiliation to an established collectively-owned or state-owned enterprise (Sun, 2000). In this respect the role of government was to mainly serve as protection for burgeoning private enterprises.[38] In the second innovation of the Wenzhou model, the government mainly served as a market promoter and withdrew its ownership shares in private enterprises, meaning that there was almost no community shares in joint-stock cooperatives (Sun, 2000). In the third innovation of the Wenzhou model, the government generally served as a regulator to facilitate the emergence of limited liability companies and joint-stock companies in private enterprises.

In summary, the government has played a pivotal role in the Zhejiang model, as well as in recent ownership reform, because ownership reform in SOEs and TVEs in Zhejiang was implemented at every level of government. In general, the role the Zhejiang government played in the development of private enterprises is represented by the fact that local governments not only colluded with private entrepreneurs to pursue local interests, but also functioned as an active market regulator to promote the access of private enterprises to capital, and to champion the reputation of Zhejiang private enterprises' products in national and international markets (Sun, 2000; Report of China's Citizen-run Enterprises, No.2, 2004). However, the role of Zhejiang government is modest, and is characterized by the so-called "doing little". In other words, in the early development period of private enterprises, the government lacked the supportive capability (especially in physical capital) and the experience of market economy; later, the government then acted spontaneously to avoid interference in the economic activities of

---

[38] Of course, a "red-hat" firm could also enjoy some preferential policies such as taxation and bank loans under the title of a "collective" firm in the 1980s and early 1990s, as discussed in Chapter 2.

private enterprises. In short, the government acts more like a market promoter instead of a rent grabber. This has been proven by the practice of tacit consent as discussed above, and by the fact that there is almost no community share or collective share in joint-stock ownership in the Wenzhou model (Sun, 2000), thus avoiding the potential problem of "grabbing hand" by the government (Sun, 2002). In recent years, the Zhejiang government has issued several policies and regulations such as "Some Opinions of Promoting a New Leap of the Citizen-run Economy" (*13 July, 2004*),[39] in which it emphasizes that the role of government is to guide the development of the private economy. Thus, the role of the Zhejiang government has shifted from active participant in the firm's economic activities to regulator and service provider that facilitates the market environment. This provides a conducive external environment for the development of private enterprises.

3.2.3.3 The prevalence of family businesses

While a more diffuse ownership structure in Zhejiang private enterprises has emerged and developed in recent years, it is estimated that about 90% of total private enterprises are family businesses (Blue Book of Private Enterprises, 2001, 2002; Gan, 2002).[40] This includes solely-owned, family-owned, and family-holding firms. Family businesses in fact can take any legal forms as registered solely-run companies, partnerships, or limited liability companies. According to a 1999 study of 1,900 medium and large enterprises by the China Academy of Social Sciences (CASS) and the National Association Industry and Commerce (NAIC), 48 percent of the relatives of the entrepreneur were employed in management of the enterprise, including 51 percent of the spouses and 20 percent of the adult children. Another study by the All China Federation of Industry and Commerce (ACFIC) found that 98 percent of private enterprises were family-managed. In short, family businesses constitute the majority of private enterprises. Therefore, most private enterprises are in a stage of family management, where ownership and control in these businesses are not separated in terms of corporate governance (Fama and Jensen, 1983; Chandler, 1990; Gan, 2002). Many

---

[39] The phase of "citizen-run economy" is a pseudonym of the private economy.

[40] There is no commonly accepted definition of family business (Gan, 2002). The narrowly defined family business refers to a firm in which there are at least two generations of family members working in the same firm and they have effective control (say, with 50% of total property rights) of the firm, while the broadly defined family business refers to a firm in which family members, including those with blood and marriage links, have effective control of the firm. The estimation of family business here takes an extremely broad definition, including single-person type of firms because these firms represent non-separation of ownership and control in terms of corporate governance, the same as in family businesses (Fama and Jensen, 1983).

researchers have been done on Chinese family businesses (Blue Book of Private Enterprises, 2001, 2002; Gan, 2002). The prevalence of family business in China seems to be an appropriate form taken by private enterprises, subject to two constraints, one is that the current market system is in existence and, the other is that the traditional cultural context is preserved.

Markets in China are generally accepted as underdeveloped relative to Western countries (Singh, 2003) although the market-oriented reforms have been implemented. In China, the product market seems increasingly mature, mainly because after recognition of private enterprises and entering the World Trade Organizations (WTO), competition between private enterprises has become increasingly fierce. For instance, the entry of a large number of new enterprises producing poor-quality products was followed by the upgrading of product quality in the Wenzhou model. Regarding the development of private enterprises, the lack of capital and labor markets seems more serious.

Firstly, the capital market is immature in China and the banking system is less efficient. Although recently some foreign banks and some trust associations have entered China, many restrictions are imposed on them. For instance, only a few foreign banks in the big cities such as Beijing and Shanghai are allowed to run businesses dealing in saving and loans of RMB (Chinese currency) by individuals. Most banks in China are state owned, particularly the central bank and the four commercial banks that play the principal role in the Chinese financial system. The central government controls state banks, the central bank, and SOEs. Clearly the central government can order a state bank to provide funds to a state enterprise and to order the central bank to print money whenever it appears necessary. Moreover, failure to recover loans from SOEs is often not considered as a loss of state assets, but a failure to recover loans from private enterprises is considered a serious problem. On the other hand, because most private enterprises have a short history as well as being a small size generally, they lack credit to attract external financing, particularly bank loans. This consequently illustrates a serious "lending bias" against private enterprises (Perotti, 1993; Chow and Fung, 1998), meaning that the banks do not want to make loans to private enterprises. It was difficult for private enterprises to obtain bank loans, especially in their early days, when they were seriously short of capital. Only after they have developed and grown to that of considerable size and strength were banks willing to grant loans to them. In many cases, bank credit has always been unnecessary rather than being urgent for private enterprises. Moreover, in order to obtain the loan, private enterprises even needed to pay rebates demanded by some senior bank management. Due to an immature financial system in China, self-accumulation or retained profit is the basic source for private enterprises to raise capital.[41] However, this method of raising capital seems a difficult way to reach the requirement by scale economies (Blue Book of Private Enterprises, 2001, 2002).

Secondary, the lack of both qualified managers and skilled workers is a common problem facing private enterprises (Blue Book of Private Enterprises, 2001, 2002). Due to the relatively long history of the planned economy in China, a group of entrepreneurs has not yet emerged (Zhang, 1999). While more people with high educational qualifications are engaging in private enterprises, many private entrepreneurs have low levels of education.[42] There are two main reasons why many college graduates do not want to work in a private enterprise, even if it pays a higher wage than a state firm. The first is that state firms are generally able to offer greater job security and social benefits, including residence rights, housing, and health and educational benefits. The second reason is that most private enterprises are of small scale, and they cannot give full play to professional knowledge that can occur in large corporations. This is also a reflection of family management in most private enterprises, in which the owner of a firm gives more opportunities to family members. Therefore, in many cities and towns, the first choices for university graduates are foreign companies, joint ventures, and government institutions (Gregory et al., 2000).

Therefore, private enterprises face both underdeveloped capital and labour markets, in which the lack of a regulated manager market is perhaps the most serious. According to the study by ADB and CGCC in 2001 mentioned above, it was most difficult to acquire senior management personnel for private enterprises; this was followed by senior qualified technicians and general management and technical personnel. As far as settling the relations between

---

[41] According to a study of 724 medium and large private enterprises in China (including those in Zhejiang) by the Asian Development Bank (ADB) and the China General Chamber of Commerce (CGCC) in 2001, the principal capital source of private enterprises was individual and household saving (accounting for 49.4%), followed by retained earnings (41.9%), while bank loans accounted for 37.2%. (In this study by ADB and CGCC, the data had relative value and each data set indicated the proportion of enterprises that selected the relevant item as one of their principal capital sources. The data were obtained by totalling the first three fund sources, and thus the proportions do not add up to 100%.)

[42] Gregory et al. (2000, p.23) claim that, according to a 1999 study of 1,900 medium and large private enterprises in China (including those in Zhejiang) administrated by the Chinese Academy of Social Science (CASS) and the National Association of Industry and Commerce (BAIC), only 40% of entrepreneurs could read a balance sheet.

ability and morals are concerned,[43] most entrepreneurs hold that moral character is more important than ability, that is, moral character can remedy defects in ability, but defects of moral character cannot be remedied by ability. For a person without basic morals, his ability can result in disaster, and the more ability he has, the bigger the losses he could bring to the enterprise. In short, in the absence of a perfect labor market, owners have to trade off trust for competence.

In addition to this, as discussed in Chapter 2, while traditional Chinese culture, which emphasizes family-base value, strongly influences the management of private enterprises, family members are no doubt the best "bearer" of family-base value. Trust, which stems from traditional culture, is therefore culturally determined (Granovetter, 1985; Fukuyama, 1995). And trust between family members underpins the development of private enterprises (see Chapter 2).

In summary, subject to the current immature capital and labour markets in China, family members provide cheap and flexible resources to fill the void created by these markets (Roberts and Zhou, 2000; Sun and Wong, 2002), thus giving rise to the prevalence of family businesses. This pattern of corporate governance is also a reflection of a strong influence by the family-base value in traditional Chinese culture, as discussed in Chapter 2. There are two main advantages of family businesses, both of which are represented in transaction cost theory and agency theory. The first is that family relationships can reduce market transaction costs, due to self-enforced implicit contracts, and the second is that family members whose interests are expected to be closely aligned with those of the owner can significantly reduce agency costs. However, there are also disadvantages associated with family businesses. The first is the lack of access to outside resources such as bank loans that are critical for their development. Besides, the lack of managerial talents of the owners may not fit well with the changing situations, especially when the firm grows. That is, many owners are not able to provide all the management skills themselves except in the smallest enterprises (Gregory et al. 2000). The second disadvantage for family businesses is succession planning (James, 1999; Gan, 2002), and disputes relating to succession are a problem for many family businesses (Blue Book of Private Enterprises, 2001, 2002). At present, however, the advantages of family businesses seem to outweigh their disadvantages due to the imperfect

---

[43] Here morals refer to providing products of high quality and services of high grade in accordance with the principle of honesty and fairness. Thus, morals serve as an important aspect of personal trust in Chapter 2.

market in China, as discussed above. More importantly, due to the influence of the traditional cultural context, trust between family members is obviously stronger than that of members outside the family. Even though there is a potential problem with succession planning, this has not yet emerged as a major constraint because many private enterprises are still young. Considering these facts, the prevalence of family business is a successful institutional arrangement broadly adapted to the transitional economic environment in China (Blue Book of Private Enterprises, 2002).

3.3 Conclusion

Chinese private enterprises have re-emerged and flourished since the late 1970s, along with the reform and open door policy. Initially allowed only on the fringes of the economy, private enterprises now account for nearly one-quarter of gross domestic product (GDP) in China, strongly contributing to its impressive economic growth. The important role of private enterprises was formally recognized by the Chinese constitution in 1999, which gave impetus to the rapid growth of private enterprises in recent years.

The rise of private enterprises generally confirms the commonly accepted wisdom in the property rights literature that well-defined property rights are a prerequisite of economic prosperity. In comparison with SOEs, the reason for the success of private enterprises is the difference in ownership. This is evident in Zhejiang province. However, the development of Chinese private enterprises also confirms one view in the literature that there is no universally accepted approach to achieving private ownership, particularly in different cultural contexts, as some scholars suggest (see Chapter 2). This can be seen in the fact that not only is the development of Chinese private enterprises an unintentional result of market-oriented reforms, but also that there is significant government involvement in private firms, as in the Zhejiang model.

It has been argued that standard property rights theory needs to incorporate the social and cultural context in which firms operate (see Chapter 2). Regarding the development of private enterprises in Zhejiang, there are two main players defined by traditional Chinese culture, i.e., government and family, thus giving rise to two different development patterns for private enterprises. One is the phenomenon of "red-hat" enterprises in which there is a significant government involvement, and the other is the phenomenon of family businesses in which family involvement is significant.[44] In fact, there

---

[44] Of course, one can deduce that there are three cooperative patterns for a private entrepreneur; that is, cooperation with either the government only, or family only, or both the

has been almost no "red-hat" enterprises registered recently, while family businesses are still prevalent and constitute the majority of Chinese private enterprises.

Family businesses, which represent the non-separation of ownership and control, thus seem to be an appropriate governance form taken by private enterprises, subject to the constraints of currently underdeveloped markets and the preserved traditional culture in China. This chapter has discussed the different roles played by the government and family, and given stylized facts about the characteristics of family businesses in private enterprises. Chapter 4 will analyse mathematically these facts by introducing the roles of government and family into the firm's production activities. With respect to the development of private enterprises, the roles played by the government and family are also further explored in the empirical studies in Chapters 5 and 6, and in the policy implications in Chapter 7.

---

government and family. These are the basic facts of cooperative arrangements in Chapter 4.

CHAPTER 4

Models of Trust-Sharing (*Guanxi*-Sharing) in Chinese (Zhejiang) Private Enterprises[45]

4.1 Introduction

This chapter presents two related models of development patterns of Chinese private enterprises. They illustrate incentive-based reasons for ownership arrangements of private enterprises, and highlight how institutional foundations of trust (*Guanxi*),[46] particularly government and family-based cultural values, play an important role in influencing the development of private enterprises. These models attempt to explain why government and family-based culture are crucial for the ownership structure and management of private enterprises. The main argument in the models is that the structure of family businesses can be viewed, in essence, as a form of trust-sharing (*Guanxi*-sharing) arrangement within the firm. Furthermore, the increase in the prevalence of family businesses can be seen as a result of family trust (*Guanxi*) replacing government trust (*Guanxi*) in the firm's economic activities.

The conventional wisdom in the property rights literature is that clearly defined property rights are a prerequisite for economic prosperity. Indeed, as discussed in Chapter 3, private enterprises in China are the most dynamic component of the regional economy, and play an increasingly important role in the national economy. This is evident in the experience of the development of private enterprises in Zhejiang province. However, the Chinese experience presents a unique approach to developing a market economy. The development of Chinese private enterprises differs from what standard property rights theory describes, especially in the early stages of development. It is commonly acknowledged that the traditional Chinese cultural system is strongly influential in all aspects of Chinese social life, including business management (Xing, 1995). Therefore to understand the development of Chinese private enterprises we need to incorporate the social and cultural context into standard property rights theory (Weitzman and Xu, 1994). Following the approach adopted by Davis and North (1971), we distinguish two categories of institutions, the institutional environment and

---

[45] This chapter is originated from the following paper: Qin, Zhong. 2011. "Models of Trust-Sharing in Chinese Private Enterprises." Economic Modelling, Vol. 28, Issue 3, pp.1017-1029.

[46] As discussed in Chapter 2, the concepts of trust and *Guanxi* are treated as interchangeable throughout the book.

the institutional arrangement.[47] Furthermore, we consider two institutional (ownership) arrangements for a private enterprise: one is the non-cooperative arrangement which corresponds to what standard property rights theory describes, and the other is the cooperative arrangement incorporating traditional Chinese culture.

We use a general notion of trust (*Guanxi*), which has been frequently cited in recent literature, to replace the notion of cooperative culture (Weitzman and Xu, 1994) to explain the development of Chinese private enterprises. In this chapter, we mainly discuss trust (*Guanxi*) within a firm, particularly in the process of production. In relation to the development of private enterprises, as discussed in the previous chapters, trust (*Guanxi*) in China comprises two important components, i.e., the role of the government, and the role of family. As a consequence, the private entrepreneur typically pursues one of three cooperative arrangements: cooperation with the government as a "red-hat" firm, cooperation with the family as a family business, or cooperation with both the government and family. The third type of cooperation can be seen in private enterprises in the Zhejiang model, where many "red-hat" firms are also household enterprises, as discussed in Chapter 3. These three types of cooperation are in essence trust-sharing (*Guanxi*-sharing) arrangements (see Chapter 2). As discussed in the previous chapters, although "red-hat" enterprises were prevalent from the beginning of the reform period to the late 1990s, there are almost no private enterprises registered as "red-hat" firms at present, while family businesses are still prevalent in China. This chapter attempts to theoretically explain this phenomenon.

Previous research regarding the Chinese experience focuses on the role played by the government and discusses the nature of township-village enterprises (TVEs) (Weitzman and Xu, 1994; Chang and Wang, 1994; Smyth, 1997, 1998, and 2002; Tian, 2000), while few studies provide a theoretical framework to analyze directly the role played by the family and to explain the above phenomenon of Chinese private enterprises. Therefore, two related models are developed in this chapter to fill this gap in the literature. While the basic model is based on Tian's (2000) framework, we discuss how the institutional foundation (trust/*Guanxi*), which comprises the trust (*Guanxi*) of both the government and family, influences the development of Chinese private enterprises.

There is no generally accepted definition of family business in the

---

[47] The definitions of institutional environment and institutional arrangement are consistent with the approach and reasoning in Davis and North (1971). See Chapter 2.

literature.[48] A broad definition of family business includes solely-run, family run, and family holding businesses, while the narrow definition of family business excludes solely-run enterprises (namely single proprietor firms) (see Chapter 3). Although the estimation that family business accounts for about 90% of all private enterprises in China is based on the broad definition (Blue Book of Private Enterprises, 2001 and 2002; Gan, 2002), we take both definitions of family business into consideration in this chapter. In the first basic model, we consider only the narrow definition of family business, that is, a family business excludes the single proprietor form. In the second model, we take the broad definition of family business.

The remainder of this chapter is organised as follows. Section 4.2 discusses the model developed by Tian (2000). Section 4.3 presents our basic model and considers the determination of the optimal choice of ownership arrangements. Section 4.4 extends the model to explain the interplay between government and family trust (*Guanxi*) in Chinese private enterprises, discussing why family business may not need government trust (*Guanxi*). Conclusions follow in Section 4.5.

4.2 Tian's (2000) Model

Tian (2000) developed a model based on Eswaran and Kotwal (1985) to discuss the nature of TVEs, in which there is a significant involvement of the government. Our basic model adopts the framework of Tian as a starting point. Tian considers both the institutional environment and the institutional arrangements, but focuses on the determination of the optimal choice of ownership arrangements by taking the institutional environment as exogenous. He concludes that private ownership is the optimal property rights arrangement "based on a set of presumptions that may not be satisfied by transitional and other irregular economic environments, in which economic freedom is constrained and markets are absent, immature, or imperfect." (Tian, 2000, pp.248-249)

4.2.1 Structure of Tian's model

In the first step, Tian considers a private entrepreneur, denoted by e, which may be an investor or a group of investors, and a bureaucrat, denoted by b, which may be the local government or an administrator. The private entrepreneur can establish a firm by choosing one of two organizational

---

[48] In fact, a family business always refers to familistic management in terms of corporate governance (Chandler, 1990; Gan, 2002), that is, non-separation of ownership and control. See also Chapter 2.

forms: the private ownership arrangement in which e runs the firm privately, or the cooperative arrangement in which e runs the firm jointly with b. After choosing the organizational form, the firm makes a capital investment $\overline{k}$, which can be made solely or jointly by the two parties. Without loss of generality, Tian assumes that $\overline{k} = 1$.

Tian's model focuses on two specific non-marketed resources: management ability of e and procurement ability of b. He uses ρ, with $0 \le \rho \le 1$, to denote the degree of market perfection. Increasing ρ implies that the market environment is becoming more transparent. The importance of procurement ability is considered to decrease as the degree of market perfection increases. If $\rho = 0$, the economic environment is extremely irregular and procurement ability is very important. If $\rho = 1$, the market operates normally, so that procurement ability is not a necessary input for the production process since factors of production can be easily obtained in the market.

Tian assumes that effective production in imperfect markets uses three types of resources: capital investment, management ability M, and procurement ability R. The profit from the investment for given M and R can be denoted by a function, $\Pi (M, R; \rho)$, which is assumed to be increasing, continuous, and concave in its first two arguments. Both management and procurement are time-consuming processes. He assumes that both the private entrepreneur and bureaucrat each have one unit of time that can be allocated between production and alternative activities, and uses λ to denote the procurement ability of the private entrepreneur. Due to different endowment advantages, he also assumes that one hour of the private entrepreneur's time devoted to procurement is equivalent to only a fraction λ of one hour devoted to procurement by the bureaucrat. Thus, $0 < \lambda < 1$. The income from alternative activities of the private entrepreneur (opportunity income) is given by u_e

and that of the bureaucrat is given by u_b.

All opportunity incomes are assumed to be exogenous.

In the second step, Tian sets up the problem of maximizing expected welfare of a society that consists of both a private entrepreneur and a bureaucrat under two alternative arrangements, i.e., private ownership and collective ownership. Under the private ownership arrangement, the expected income of the private entrepreneur is given by

(1)
$$\Pi_p^e = \max_{M,R}\left[\Pi(M,\lambda R;\rho) + (1-M-R)u_e\right],$$
$$\text{where } 0 \le M \le 1, 0 \le R \le 1, 0 \le M+R \le 1.$$

The term $\Pi(M,\lambda R;\rho)$ is the entrepreneur's expected income from production, and the term $(1-M-R)u_e$ is the income from his alternative activity. The expected income of the bureaucrat is $\Pi_p^b = u_b$.

Therefore, expected social welfare under the private ownership arrangement is

(2) $W_p = \Pi_p^e + \Pi_p^b = \Pi_p^e + u_b$.

Under the collective ownership arrangement, the private entrepreneur and the bureaucrat run the firm jointly, and each of them receives a share of the residual income. Tian assumes that they share the profit according to some given ratio, which depends on the bargaining power of each party. He uses $0 \le \theta \le 1$ to denote the share of the private entrepreneur, such that the net income of the entrepreneur is

(3) $\Pi^e(M,R;\rho) = \theta\Pi(M,R;\rho)$.

And the net income of the bureaucrat is

(4) $\Pi^b(M,R;\rho) = (1-\theta)\Pi(M,R;\rho)$.

Given the bureaucrat's procurement ability R, the private entrepreneur will allocate his time between management and his next best alternative, such as being employed by another employer or leisure to maximize

69

(5) $\Pi_c^e = \max_M \left[\theta \Pi(M, R; \rho) + (1 - M) u_e \right]$, where $0 \le M \le 1$.

Similarly, given the entrepreneur's management ability M, the bureaucrat will allocate his time between procurement and the alternative activity to maximize

(6) $\Pi_c^b = \max_R \left[(1 - \theta) \Pi(M, R; \rho) + (1 - R) u_b \right]$, where $0 \le R \le 1$.

The above maximization problems form a two-person non-cooperative game with a Nash equilibrium. At the Nash equilibrium pair $\left(M^*, R^* \right)$, (5) and (6) are satisfied simultaneously. Expected social welfare under the collective ownership arrangement is

(7) $W_c = \Pi_c^e + \Pi_c^b$.

Once expected social welfare under the two ownership arrangements is determined, the optimal ownership arrangement will be given by the ownership arrangement that provides the highest social welfare.

In the third step, Tian assumes a profit function and solves for the optimal ownership arrangement. He assumes a Cobb-Douglas profit function as

(8) $\Pi(M, R; \rho) = A M^{\alpha_1} R^{(1-\rho)\alpha_2}$, where $\alpha_1, \alpha_2 > 0$, and $\alpha_1 + \alpha_2 < 1$.

He denotes $\alpha_3 = 1 - \alpha_1 - \alpha_2$, which can be regarded as the relative importance of capital input. Under the private ownership arrangement, solving this problem for interior solutions, i.e., $0 < M + R < 1$, the expected social welfare in (2) is given by

70

(9)

$$W_P = \left[1-\alpha_1-(1-\rho)\alpha_2\right]\left\{A\lambda^{(1-\rho)\alpha_2}\alpha_1^{\alpha_1}\left[(1-\rho)\alpha_2\right]^{(1-\rho)\alpha_2}\right\}^{1/\left[1-\alpha_1-(1-\rho)\alpha_2\right]}$$
$$\times u_e^{-\left\{\alpha_1+(1-\rho)\alpha_2\right\}/\left[1-\alpha_1-(1-\rho)\alpha_2\right]} + u_e + u_b.$$

Under the collective ownership arrangement, solving the reaction functions of the entrepreneur and bureaucrat for an interior Nash equilibrium, expected social welfare in (7) is given by

(10)

$$W_c = \left[1-\theta\alpha_1-(1-\theta)(1-\rho)\alpha_2\right]\times\left\{A\theta^{\alpha_1}(1-\theta)^{(1-\rho)\alpha_2}\alpha_1^{\alpha_1}\left[(1-\rho)\alpha_2\right]^{(1-\rho)\alpha_2}\right\}^{\frac{1}{1-\alpha_1-(1-\rho)\alpha_2}}$$
$$\times u_e^{\frac{\alpha_1}{1-\alpha_1-(1-\rho)\alpha_2}} u_b^{\frac{(1-\rho)\alpha_2}{1-\alpha_1-(1-\rho)\alpha_2}} + u_e + u_b.$$

By comparing (9) and (10), Tian derives the following three theorems:

Theorem 1. *For the Cobb-Douglas technology specified in (8), the private ownership arrangement dominates the collective ownership arrangement when the economic environment is close to regular. That is, $W_p > W_c$ when ρ is sufficiently close to 1.* (Tian, 2000, p.259)

Theorem 2. *For the Cobb-Douglas technology specified in (8), suppose* $\lambda < (u_e/u_b)(1-\theta)^2$. *Then, when*

$$0 < \rho < \frac{\ln(1-\theta)-\ln(\lambda u_b/u_e)}{\ln(1-\theta)/\theta-\ln(\lambda u_b/u_e)} < 1, \text{ the collective ownership}$$

71

arrangement will dominate the private ownership arrangement.
(Tian, 2000, p.260)

Theorem 3. *For the Cobb-Douglas technology specified in (8),*

suppose $\overline{\lambda} \leq 1$. *Then the collective ownership arrangement would*

dominate the private ownership arrangement if and only if $\lambda \leq \overline{\lambda}$.

(Tian, 2000, p.262)

The critical value of λ in his model is

$$(11) \quad \overline{\lambda} = \left(\frac{u_e}{u_b}\right)(1-\theta)\theta^{\frac{\alpha_1}{(1-\rho)\alpha_2}}\left[\frac{1-\theta\alpha_1-(1-\theta)(1-\rho)\alpha_2}{1-\alpha_1-(1-\rho)\alpha_2}\right]^{\frac{1-\alpha_1-(1-\rho)\alpha_2}{(1-\rho)\alpha_2}}.$$

4.2.2 Tian's main conclusions

In the above model, Tian determines the relative superiority of private ownership and collective ownership for varying degrees of imperfection of the economic environment, and specifies mathematical conditions of the parameters to determine the optimal arrangement. He also examines the effects on the critical value of λ of changes in the degree of irregularity in the economic environment (ρ), changes in the sharing rule (θ), changes in the relative opportunity incomes of the private entrepreneur and bureaucrat (u_b / u_e), changes in the relative importance of procurement ability to capital input (α_3 / α_2), and changes in the relative importance of management ability to capital input (α_3 / α_1). As $\overline{\lambda}$ falls, the collective ownership arrangement is more likely to be dominant.

In summary, Tian shows that collective ownership dominates private ownership in a transitional (and/or developing) economic environment, while private ownership dominates collective ownership in a developed economic environment. In Tian's opinion, however, private ownership is the appropriate mechanism to achieve an efficient allocation of resources. Therefore, he concludes that privatization requires that the economic environment is improved first.

4.2.3 Comments on Tian's model

Tian's model fits well with the development of Chinese TVEs, especially given the gradual nature of privatization in China, particularly when TVEs are viewed as an intermediate form of "pure" private enterprise, as discussed in Chapter 2. Tian's model can also be used to explain the phenomenon of "red-hat" firms within the context of the development of Chinese private enterprises. However, his model does not clearly explain the phenomenon of family businesses. As noted earlier, there are almost no private enterprises registered as "red-hat" firms in present-day China. This can be partially explained by improvements in the economic environment, but more importantly, by the increasing importance of family trust (*Guanxi*) relative to government trust (*Guanxi*) in the economic activities of firms. The reason behind this argument is that the economic environment in present-day China is still generally accepted as immature, as discussed in Chapter 3. That is, the fading out of government ownership has been widely accepted as a means to promote, rather than a result of, marketization and rule of law (Sun, 2002). Therefore, we extend Tian's model to provide an explanation for this feature of the development of Chinese private enterprises in the following sections.

4.3 Our Basic Model

4.3.1 Differences from Tian's (2000) model

4.3.1.1 General differences

Based on Tian's (2000) framework, we develop a general model for private enterprises, and introduce both government and family trust (*Guanxi*) into the firm's economic activities to examine the interplay of the two types of trust (*Guanxi*) and its effects on the equilibrium ownership structure. Our model differs from Tian's model in the following aspects.

First, we discuss the optimal arrangement for Chinese private enterprises from the perspective of the agent who has superior management ability. In contrast, Tian discusses the optimal ownership in terms of social welfare that consists of the expected incomes of both the private entrepreneur and the government. Of course, the profit maximization of individuals (or firms) does not necessarily lead to welfare maximization of the society as a whole, particularly in a developing country where the government institution is imperfect. As explained in Chapter 3, the development of Chinese private enterprises is a result of the profit motive of firms rather than careful design of the government. Therefore, our model seems more suitable for explaining the reality of private enterprises in China. In particular, profit maximization by individuals (firms) is very important when we discuss the interplay of government and family trust (*Guanxi*) in Section 4.4.

Second, we use a more general notion of trust (*Guanxi*) and attempt to distinguish the role of government from that of the family, while Tian considers only the role played by the government. In our model, there is a distinction between the manner in which family and government trust (*Guanxi*) enter the firm's economic activities. In particular, the use of government trust (*Guanxi*) gives rise to separation of ownership and control, but the use of family trust (*Guanxi*) does not, as discussed in Chapter 2. The distinction between family and government trust (*Guanxi*) is the underpinning idea of our theoretical model. On the other hand, both family and government trust (*Guanxi*) present necessary inputs for successful production. In particular, family trust (*Guanxi*) (in addition to government trust) can have an important role in obtaining information and resources through extending networks (Sun and Wong, 2002).[49] In this manner, family and government trust (*Guanxi*) are viewed as being of equal importance and are inputs to the firm's production in our model.

Thus, the institutional foundations of trust (*Guanxi*) in our model comprise both the roles of government and the family, which are treated as symmetric. Consequently, we assume a more complicated profit function which consists of both government and family trust (*Guanxi*), instead of only government ability as in Tian's model. In this sense, the situation that Tian describes is a special case of our model.

Third, we go further than Tian's model and get more enriched conclusions than Tian's theorems. Since our model is more general, we can derive Tian's

---

[49] The government has the procurement ability to obtain necessary inputs for a firm's production in Tian's (2000) model. However, according to a national survey conducted by the Chinese Academy of Social Sciences and the State Administration of Industry and Commerce in 1995, the occupation containing most close relatives in urban private enterprises was "Cadre[s] at [government] institution[s]" (Sun and Wong, 2002, Table 2 in p.76). Therefore, private owners may get help from these relatives who can play a procurement role similar to that of the government.

theorems and conclusions, which are presented in our first proposition. More importantly, our models give new results, in particular, those that explain the interplay of government and family trust (*Guanxi*), thus providing an explanation for the prevalence of family businesses in China.

4.3.1.2 Different assumptions of our basic model

The basic idea of the model is that non-marketed resources are considered to be inputs in the production process. We focus on two specific non-marketed resources: management ability and *Guanxi* ability. These two abilities constitute the core of private enterprise management, and they are crucial for successful production in a developing market such as China.[50]

Consider two agents: Agent 1 is a private entrepreneur (or investor) with superior management ability, *M*, while Agent 2 processes superior *Guanxi* ability, *G*. Agent 1 can establish a firm by choosing one of two organizational forms. In one organizational form, he runs the firm solely by himself, i.e., there is a non-cooperative arrangement, and in the other, he runs the firmly jointly with Agent 2, i.e., there is a cooperative arrangement.

The other assumptions are the same as those in Tian's (2000) model except that procurement ability *R* is replaced by *Guanxi* ability *G*, and *G* is assumed to take a CES (constant elasticity of substitution) form as $G = (G_g^\beta + G_f^\beta)^{1/\beta}$, where G_g is government *Guanxi* and G_f is family *Guanxi*, with $0 \leq G_g, G_f \leq 1$, $G_g + G_f \leq 1$, and $0 < \beta < 1$. The introduction of G_f is a key feature that distinguishes our model from that of Tian.

Under this assumption, government and family *Guanxi* can take the value of zero separately, but they cannot be zero simultaneously. When $G_g = 0$ or $G_f = 0$, it indicates that Agent 1 or 2 has only family or government *Guanxi*, respectively. When $0 < G_g, G_f < 1$, Agent 1 or 2 has both family and

---

[50] We do not attempt to measure the degree of market imperfection in China in this chapter.

government *Guanxi*. These correspond to cooperation with family only, or government only, or both, respectively. In this model, the latter case is a general one while the others are the special cases described in Tian's (2000) model.

Given technology and price for simplicity, the profit function in (8) becomes

(12) $\Pi(M, G; \rho) = M^{\alpha_1} (G_g^\beta + G_f^\beta)^{(1-\rho)\alpha_2/\beta}$, where $\alpha_1, \alpha_2 > 0$, and $\alpha_1 + \alpha_2 < 1$.

4.3.2 Arrangement choices and solutions

We first consider the general case, i.e., cooperation with both government and family *Guanxi*. In this case, both agents may, of course, focus on only one kind of *Guanxi* ability for production while gain from the opportunity income from the other kind of *Guanxi* ability. In other words, the idleness of other *Guanxi* ability is not a problem for the general case.

4.3.2.1 Non-cooperative arrangement

Under this type of arrangement, Agent 1 runs the firm exclusively, makes one unit of capital investment, hires unskilled labour and allocates his time between management, *Guanxi*, and his alternative activity such as being employed by another employer or just enjoying leisure time in order to maximize his expected income. That is, with the profit function given by (12), Agent 1's income maximization problem in (1) becomes

(13)

$$\Pi_1^s = \max_{M_1, G_{1g}, G_{1f}} \left[M_1^{\alpha_1} \lambda_1^{(1-\rho)\alpha_2} (G_{1g}^\beta + G_{1f}^\beta)^{(1-\rho)\alpha_2/\beta} + \left(1 - M_1 - G_{1g} - G_{1f}\right) u_1 \right],$$

where $M_1, G_{1g}, G_{1f} \geq 0$, and $M_1 + G_{1g} + G_{1f} \leq 1$.[51]

When $M_1 + G_{1g} + G_{1f} = 1$, the solution is given by

---

[51] Note that here and elsewhere in this chapter, quantities subscripted by 1 refer to Agent 1, and quantities subscripted by 2 refer to Agent 2.

(14) $M_1^{s*} = \dfrac{\alpha_1}{\alpha_1 + (1-\rho)\alpha_2}$, and $G_{1g}^{s*} = G_{1f}^{s*} = \dfrac{(1-\rho)\alpha_2}{2[\alpha_1 + (1-\rho)\alpha_2]}$.

When $M_1 + G_{1g} + G_{1f} < 1$, the interior solution is given by

$$(15) \quad G_{1g}^{s*} = G_{1f}^{s*} = \left\{ u_1^{-1} \lambda_1^{(1-\rho)\alpha_2} \alpha_1^{\alpha_1} [(1-\rho)\alpha_2]^{1-\alpha_1} 2^{\frac{(1-\rho)\alpha_2 - \beta(1-\alpha_1)}{\beta}} \right\}^{\frac{1}{1-\alpha_1 - (1-\rho)\alpha_2}},$$

and $M_1^{s*} = \dfrac{2\alpha_1}{(1-\rho)\alpha_2} G_{1g}^{s*}$.

Substituting (15) into (13), the expected income of Agent 1 is
(16)

$$\Pi_1^s = \left[1 - \alpha_1 - (1-\rho)\alpha_2\right] \left\{ \lambda_1^{(1-\rho)\alpha_2} \alpha_1^{\alpha_1} \left[(1-\rho)\alpha_2\right]^{(1-\rho)\alpha_2} 2^{(1-\rho)\alpha_2(1-\beta)/\beta} \right\}^{1/[1-\alpha_1 - (1-\rho)\alpha_2]}$$

$$\times u_1^{-[\alpha_1 + (1-\rho)\alpha_2]/[1-\alpha_1 - (1-\rho)\alpha_2]} + u_1.$$

4.3.2.2 Cooperative arrangement

Under this arrangement, Agent 1 and Agent 2 run the firm jointly, and each of them receives their share of the residual income. We assume that they share the profit according to some given ratio, which depends on the bargaining power of each agent. Again let $0 \le \theta \le 1$ be the profit share of Agent 1, then the net income of Agent 1 in (5) becomes

$$(17) \quad \Pi_1^c = \max_{M_1} \left[\theta M_1^{\alpha_1} (G_{2g}^{\beta} + G_{2f}^{\beta})^{(1-\rho)\alpha_2/\beta} + (1 - M_1)u_1 \right], \quad \text{where}$$

$0 \le M_1 \le 1$, $0 \le G_{2g}, G_{2f} \le 1$, and $G_{2g} + G_{2f} \le 1$, .

Solving this problem, Agent 1's reaction function is

$$(18) \quad M_1 = \min\left\{1, \left[u_1^{-1}\theta\alpha_1(G_{2g}^{\beta}+G_{2f}^{\beta})^{(1-\rho)\alpha_2/\beta}\right]^{\frac{1}{1-\alpha_1}}\right\}.$$

Similarly, Agent 2's income maximization problem in (6) is

$$(19) \quad \Pi_2^c = \max_{G_{2g},G_{2f}}\left[(1-\theta)M_1^{\alpha_1}(G_{2g}^{\beta}+G_{2f}^{\beta})^{(1-\rho)\alpha_2/\beta}+\left(1-G_{2g}-G_{2f}\right)u_2\right],$$

where $0 \le G_{2g},G_{2f} \le 1$, and $G_{2g}+G_{2f} \le 1$.

Solving this problem for an interior solution, Agent 2's reaction function is

$$(20) \quad G_{2g} = G_{2f} = \min\left\{1, \left[u_2^{-1}(1-\theta)M_1^{\alpha_1}(1-\rho)\alpha_2 2^{\frac{(1-\rho)\alpha_2}{\beta}-1}\right]^{\frac{1}{1-(1-\rho)\alpha_2}}\right\}.$$

Following the approach of Eswaran and Kotwal (1985) and Tian (2000), we assume that there is an interior Nash equilibrium. The interior solution is given by

(21)

$$M_1^{c*} = \left\{u_1^{-1}\alpha_1\theta^{1-(1-\rho)\alpha_2}(1-\theta)^{(1-\rho)\alpha_2}2^{(1-\rho)\alpha_2(1-\beta)/\beta}\left[\frac{(1-\rho)\alpha_2 u_1}{\alpha_1 u_2}\right]^{(1-\rho)\alpha_2}\right\}^{\frac{1}{1-\alpha_1-(1-\rho)\alpha_2}}$$

and $G_{2g}^{c*} = G_{2f}^{c*} = \dfrac{(1-\theta)u_1(1-\rho)\alpha_2}{2\theta u_2\alpha_1}M_1^{c*}.$

78

Finally, also following the approach of Eswaran and Kotwal (1985), for a given share θ, Agent 1 will set a level of Agent 2's remuneration that holds Agent 2 at (or barely above) his opportunity income. In other words, Agent 1's expected income is the joint profit of both Agent 1 and Agent 2, less the opportunity income of Agent 2, becoming

(22)

$$\Pi_1^c = (M_1^{c*})^{\alpha_1}[(G_{2g}^{c*})^\beta + (G_{2f}^{c*})^\beta]^{(1-\rho)\alpha_2/\beta} + (1-M_1^{c*})u_1 + (1-G_{2g}^{c*}-G_{2f}^{c*})u_2 - u_2$$

$$= \left[1-\theta\alpha_1 - (1-\theta)(1-\rho)\alpha_2\right]\left\{\theta^{\alpha_1}(1-\theta)^{(1-\rho)\alpha_2}\alpha_1^{\alpha_1}\left[(1-\rho)\alpha_2\right]^{(1-\rho)\alpha_2}2^{(1-\rho)\alpha_2(1-\beta)/\beta}\right\}^{\frac{1}{1-\alpha_1-(1-\rho)\alpha_2}}$$

$$\times u_1^{-\alpha_1\left[1-\alpha_1-(1-\rho)\alpha_2\right]}u_2^{-(1-\rho)\alpha_2\left[1-\alpha_1-(1-\rho)\alpha_2\right]} + u_1.$$

4.3.3 Special cases

In practice, a private firm can choose to cooperate with government only or family only instead of with both government and family; that is, the private firm may use only one type of Guanxi input for production, i.e., $G_f = 0$, or $G_g = 0$. These are special cases of our general model, with Tian's (2000) model the special case where $G_f = 0$. In our general model, Agent 2 has superior ability with respect to both family and government *Guanxi*. In these special cases, Agent 2 has only one type of superior *Guanxi* ability. We consider these special cases below.

4.3.3.1 Non-cooperative arrangement

The calculation approach is the same as before but simpler. Under the non-cooperative arrangement, we first consider the case when Agent 1 has only family Guanxi, i.e., $G_{1g} = 0$. With the profit function given by (12), Agent 1's income maximization problem in (13) becomes

(23) $$\Pi_1^{s'} = \max_{M_1, G_{1f}} \left[M_1^{\alpha_1} \lambda^{(1-\rho)\alpha_2} G_{1f}^{(1-\rho)\alpha_2} + (1-M_1-G_{1f})u_1 \right],$$

79

where $M_1, G_{1f} \geq 0$, and $M_1 + G_{1f} \leq 1$.

Thus, if $M_1 + G_{1f} = 1$, the solution is given by

(24) $M_1^{s'*} = \dfrac{\alpha_1}{\alpha_1 + (1-\rho)\alpha_2}$, and $G_{1f}^{s'*} = \dfrac{(1-\rho)\alpha_2}{\alpha_1 + (1-\rho)\alpha_2}$.

If $M_1 + G_{1f} < 1$, the interior solution is given by

(25) $G_{1f}^{s'*} = \left\{ \lambda_1^{(1-\rho)\alpha_2} u_1^{-1} (1-\rho)\alpha_2 \left[\dfrac{\alpha_1}{(1-\rho)\alpha_2} \right]^{\alpha_1} \right\}^{\frac{1}{1-\alpha_1-(1-\rho)\alpha_2}}$,

and $M_1^{s'*} = \dfrac{\alpha_1}{(1-\rho)\alpha_2} G_{1f}^{s'*}$.

Substituting (25) into (23), Agent 1's expected income is

(26)

$\Pi_1^{s'} = \left[1 - \alpha_1 - (1-\rho)\alpha_2 \right] \left\{ \lambda_1^{(1-\rho)\alpha_2} \alpha_1^{\alpha_1} \left[(1-\rho)\alpha_2 \right]^{(1-\rho)\alpha_2} \right\}^{1/[1-\alpha_1-(1-\rho)\alpha_2]}$

$\times u_1^{-[\alpha_1+(1-\rho)\alpha_2]/[1-\alpha_1-(1-\rho)\alpha_2]} + u_1$.

In the alternative scenario where $G_{1f} = 0$, Agent 1 has only government Guanxi, and the result is almost the same as that when $G_{1g} = 0$, except that G_{1f} is replaced by G_{1g}. Therefore, Agent 1's expected income is the same as in (26). These two cases are extreme cases of the non-cooperative arrangement.

4.3.3.2 Cooperative arrangement

Under this arrangement, we first consider the case when Agent 2 has only family *Guanxi*, i.e., $G_{2g} = 0$. With the profit function given by (12), Agent 1's income maximization problem in (17) becomes

(27) $\Pi_1^{c'} = \max_{M_1} \left[\theta M_1^{\alpha_1} G_{2f}^{(1-\rho)\alpha_2} + (1 - M_1) u_1 \right]$, where $0 \le M_1 \le 1$.

Solving this problem, Agent 1's reaction function is

(28) $M_1 = \min \left\{ 1, \left[\theta u_1^{-1} \alpha_1 G_{2f}^{(1-\rho)\alpha_2} \right]^{1/(1-\alpha_1)} \right\}$.

Similarly, Agent 2's income maximization problem in (19) is

(29) $\Pi_2^{c'} = \max_{G_{2f}} \left[(1 - \theta) M_1^{\alpha_1} G_{2f}^{(1-\rho)\alpha_2} + \left(1 - G_{2f} \right) u_2 \right]$,

where $0 \le G_{2f} \le 1$.

Solving this problem, Agent 2's reaction function is

(30) $G_{2f} = \min \left\{ 1, \left[(1 - \theta) u_2^{-1} (1 - \rho) \alpha_2 M_1^{\alpha_1} \right]^{1/[1-(1-\rho)\alpha_2]} \right\}$.

Also assuming an interior solution and solving (28) and (30) for an interior Nash equilibrium, we have

(31)

$$M_1^{c'*} = \left\{ u_1^{-1}\alpha_1\theta^{1-(1-\rho)\alpha_2}(1-\theta)^{(1-\rho)\alpha_2}\left[\frac{(1-\rho)\alpha_2 u_1}{\alpha_1 u_2}\right]^{(1-\rho)\alpha_2}\right\}^{1/[1-\alpha_1-(1-\rho)\alpha_2]},$$

and $\; G_{2f}^{c'*} = \left[\dfrac{(1-\theta)u_1(1-\rho)\alpha_2}{\theta u_2 \alpha_1}\right]M_1^{c'*}.$

Finally, Agent 1's expected income is the joint profit of both Agent 1 and Agent 2, less the opportunity income of Agent 2, i.e.,

(32)

$$\Pi_1^{c'} = (M_1^{c'*})^{\alpha_1}\left(G_{2f}^{c'*}\right)^{(1-\rho)\alpha_2} + \left(1-M_1^{c'*}\right)u_1 + (1-G_{2f}^{c'*})u_2 - u_2$$

$$= \left[1-\theta\alpha_1-(1-\theta)(1-\rho)\alpha_2\right]\left\{\theta^{\alpha_1}(1-\theta)^{(1-\rho)\alpha_2}\alpha_1^{\alpha_1}\left[(1-\rho)\alpha_2\right]^{(1-\rho)\alpha_2}\right\}^{\frac{1}{1-\alpha_1-(1-\rho)\alpha_2}}$$

$$\times u_1^{-\alpha_1/[1-\alpha_1-(1-\rho)\alpha_2]}u_2^{-(1-\rho)\alpha_2/[1-\alpha_1-(1-\rho)\alpha_2]} + u_1.$$

In the alternative scenario where $G_{2f}=0$, Agent 2 has only government

Guanxi, and the result is almost the same as $G_{2g}=0$, except that G_{2f} is

replaced by G_{2g}. Therefore, Agent 1's expected income is the same as in

(32). These two cases are extreme cases of the cooperative arrangement.

4.3.4 Optimal arrangement

Having determined Agent 1's expected income under the non-cooperative and cooperative arrangements, the optimal arrangement will be given by the one that maximizes his expected income. We consider only the interior solution cases, although the results for the corner solution cases can be obtained in a similar manner.

4.3.4.1 General optimum

Proposition 1 (Tian's theorem). *For a profit-maximizing private firm, the non-cooperative arrangement dominates the cooperative arrangement when*

the economic (market) environment is close to perfect. On the other hand, the cooperative arrangement dominates the non-cooperative arrangement in a transitional and/or developing economic environment.

Comparing (16) with (22), i.e., Agent 1's expected income under the non-cooperative and cooperative arrangements, we have

(33)

$$
\Pi_1^s - \Pi_1^c = u_1^{-\alpha_1/[1-\alpha_1-(1-\rho)\alpha_2]} \times \left\{ \alpha_1^{\alpha_1} \left[(1-\rho)\alpha_2\right]^{(1-\rho)\alpha_2} 2^{(1-\rho)\alpha_2(1-\beta)/\beta} \right\}^{1/[1-\alpha_1-(1-\rho)\alpha_2]}
$$

$$
\times \left\{ \begin{array}{l} \lambda_1^{(1-\rho)\alpha_2/[1-\alpha_1-(1-\rho)\alpha_2]} \times \left[1-\alpha_1-(1-\rho)\alpha_2\right] \times u_1^{-(1-\rho)\alpha_2/[1-\alpha_1-(1-\rho)\alpha_2]} \\ -\left[1-\theta\alpha_1-(1-\theta)(1-\rho)\alpha_2\right] \times \left[\theta^{\alpha_1}(1-\theta)^{(1-\rho)\alpha_2}\right]^{1/[1-\alpha_1-(1-\rho)\alpha_2]} \times u_2^{-(1-\rho)\alpha_2/[1-\alpha_1-(1-\rho)\alpha_2]} \end{array} \right\}.
$$

The comparison of special cases between (26) and (32) is almost the same as (33) except it does not include the term $2^{(1-\rho)\alpha_2(1-\beta)/\beta}$ (which is positive and larger than 1) in the first brace. This implies that cooperation with both the government and family *Guanxi* is better than cooperation with only one type of *Guanxi*, as will be discussed further in Section 4.3.5. Considering the terms in the last brace of (33), we can prove that $\Pi_1^s > \Pi_1^c$ when ρ is close to 1 while $\Pi_1^s < \Pi_1^c$ when ρ is small enough (see Tian (2000), pp.260-261).

This result means that the non-cooperative arrangement dominates the cooperative arrangement when the quality of the economic environment is sufficiently high, and vice versa. In this model, the critical value of economic environment quality is

$$
(34)\quad \bar{\lambda} = \left(\frac{u_1}{u_2}\right)(1-\theta)\theta^{\frac{\alpha_1}{(1-\rho)\alpha_2}} \left[\frac{1-\theta\alpha_1-(1-\theta)(1-\rho)\alpha_2}{1-\alpha_1-(1-\rho)\alpha_2}\right]^{\frac{1-\alpha_1-(1-\rho)\alpha_2}{(1-\rho)\alpha_2}}.
$$

That is, when $\lambda_1 \leq \bar{\lambda}$, Agent 1 will choose the cooperative arrangement for profit maximization instead of the non-cooperative arrangement. The turning point in this model at which the cooperative arrangement switches to the non-cooperative arrangement is $\bar{\lambda}$.[52]

The above optimal solutions for the non-cooperative arrangement and the cooperative arrangement mean that the development pattern of private enterprises is endogenously determined, which will be further explored by Proposition 2. In other words, the optimal choice of arrangement is an efficient response to the economic environment. When the quality of the economic environment is low, the cooperative arrangement is optimal, i.e., the use of *Guanxi* ability is important and necessary for efficient production. On the other hand, when the quality of the economic environment is high, *Guanxi* ability is not a necessary input for production because production can be carried out with management and other marketed resources without *Guanxi*. This conclusion does not contradict standard theories, but rather extends them to take into account the role of the institutional environment. This first proposition is similar to Tian's (2000) proposition. Therefore, we label Proposition 1 *Tian's theorem.*

4.3.4.2 Local optimum for the cooperation

We now focus on the cooperative arrangement of Chinese private enterprises since the economic environment in China is commonly characterized as developing or transitional.

Proposition 2. *Given the Cobb-Douglas technology specified in (12), the ownership structure of private enterprises endogenously chosen in a developing economic environment is the cooperative arrangement.*

Under the cooperative arrangement, when the economic environment is imperfect to some degree and *Guanxi* ability is relatively more important than management ability, an optimal share θ^* can be chosen endogenously

---

[52] The critical value of $\bar{\lambda}$ is the same as in Tian's (2000) model since this model is an extension of his model.

in a way that maximizes Agent 1's expected income $\prod_1^c$. To find $\theta*$, we take the logarithm of both sides of (22), differentiate $\ln\prod_1^c$ with respect to θ, and set it equal to zero. The first-order condition is

(35)

$$f(\theta)=\left[\alpha_1-(1-\rho)\alpha_2\right]\theta^2-2\alpha_1\left[1-(1-\rho)\alpha_2\right]\theta+\alpha_1\left[1-(1-\rho)\alpha_2\right]=0$$

When $\theta=0$, $f(0)=\alpha_1\left[1-(1-\rho)\alpha_2\right]>0$, and when $\theta=1$, $f(1)=(1-\rho)\alpha_2(\alpha_1-1)<0$. Thus, there is some $0<\theta*<1$ such that $f(\theta*)=0$. Solving this problem, we have the optimal share $\theta*$, which is given by

(36)

$$\theta* = \frac{\alpha_1\left[1-(1-\rho)\alpha_2\right]-\left\{\alpha_1(1-\rho)\alpha_2(1-\alpha_1)\left[1-(1-\rho)\alpha_2\right]\right\}^{1/2}}{\alpha_1-(1-\rho)\alpha_2}.^{53}$$

Orthodox endogenous ownership theory suggests that ownership structure is endogenously determined in equilibrium, which means that the market responds to forces that create suitable ownership structures for firms. However, it restricts the endogenous ownership structure as the outcome of a perfect market. Therefore, some scholars argue that this theory is not applicable to the situation in China, as discussed in Chapter 2.

In our model, however, the optimal share $\theta*$ depends on the relative importance of management ability α_1 and *Guanxi* ability α_2, as well as

---

[53] The same result can be obtained by solving (32) for the special cases—cooperation with government only or with family only.

the degree of market perfection ρ. If we regard the share θ or $(1-\theta)$ as the residual right of claim, one important element of property rights, our model shows that the division of property rights allows people the option of combining "ownership" and control in any mixture that they wish, subject to their budget. Faced with such a situation, the private entrepreneur (Agent 1) can choose *Guanxi*-sharing (trust-sharing) cooperation with Agent 2, either with the government or the family, or with both. In short, Proposition 2 is complementary to and more specific than Proposition 1 (*Tian's theorem*).

Proposition 3. *Under the cooperative arrangement and given the Cobb-Douglas technology specified in (12), the optimal share of Agent 1 (management ability) increases as the economic environment becomes more regular.*

Differentiating (36) with respect to ρ, we have

(37)

$$\frac{d\theta^*}{d\rho} = \frac{\alpha_1^{\frac{1}{2}}\alpha_2^{\frac{1}{2}}(1-\alpha_1)^{\frac{1}{2}}}{\left[\alpha_1-(1-\rho)\alpha_2\right]^2(1-\rho)^{\frac{1}{2}}\left[1-(1-\rho)\alpha_2\right]^{\frac{1}{2}}}$$

$$\times\left\{\frac{\alpha_1+(1-\rho)\alpha_2}{2}-\alpha_1(1-\rho)\alpha_2-\alpha_1^2\left[(1-\rho)\alpha_2\right]^{\frac{1}{2}}(1-\alpha_1)^{\frac{1}{2}}\left[1-(1-\rho)\alpha_2\right]^{\frac{1}{2}}\right\}.$$

Considering the term in the brace, which is equal to

$$\frac{\left\{\alpha_1^{\frac{1}{2}}-\left[(1-\rho)\alpha_2\right]^{\frac{1}{2}}\right\}^2}{2}+\alpha_1^2\left[(1-\rho)\alpha_2\right]^{\frac{1}{2}}\times\left\{1-\alpha_1^2\left[(1-\rho)\alpha_2\right]^{\frac{1}{2}}-(1-\alpha_1)^{\frac{1}{2}}\left[1-(1-\rho)\alpha_2\right]^{\frac{1}{2}}\right\}$$

, since $0<\rho,\alpha_1,\alpha_2<1$ and $\alpha_1+\alpha_2<1$, so that

86

$$\left\{ 1 - \alpha_1^{\frac{1}{2}} \left[(1-\rho) \alpha_2 \right]^{\frac{1}{2}} - (1-\alpha_1)^{\frac{1}{2}} \left[1 - (1-\rho) \alpha_2 \right]^{\frac{1}{2}} \right\} > 0, \text{ the term in the}$$

second brace is positive.

Therefore, $\dfrac{d\theta^*}{d\rho} > 0$, which means that θ^* increases as ρ increases.

In other words, as the market environment improves, the optimal ownership share tends to be concentrated in the hands of management, no matter what kind of cooperative arrangement Agent 1 chooses cooperation with either the government or the family, or with both. This reflects the dynamic process of the development of private enterprises, and it is consistent with the tendency of many employee-joint-stock cooperatives in Wenzhou City, Zhejiang province, where share-concentration has continued to increase in the hands of the core shareholders, i.e., mainly core managers (Sun, 2000).

4.3.5 Ownership structure and management

4.3.5.1 Emergence of diffuse ownership structure

The above model shows that trust (*Guanxi*) is an important resource in a firm's production process, and it is better for a private entrepreneur to choose cooperation with *Guanxi* ability in an imperfect market, either government trust (*Guanxi*), or family trust (*Guanxi*), or both. Under the assumption of symmetry between government and family *Guanxi* in the CES specification, it is easy to show that the optimal allocation between government and family

Guanxi is $G_g^* = G_f^*$; that is, government and family *Guanxi* are equally

important. In addition, the profit of a private firm choosing only government *Guanxi* for cooperation is the same as that of choosing only family *Guanxi* for cooperation (see Section 4.3.3).[54]

Furthermore, the model also shows that when Agent 1 chooses both

---

[54] This may be a possible explanation for the argument made by many scholars that the efficiency of Chinese TVEs, in which the government plays an important role, is (at least) the same as that of private enterprises (Weitzman and Xu, 1994; Chang and Wang, 1994; Smyth, 1997, 1998, 2002).

government and family *Guanxi* abilities for cooperation simultaneously, his expected income is bigger than that when choosing only one type of *Guanxi* ability for cooperation. To see this, comparing (22) of the general case and (32) of the special case under the cooperative arrangement, the difference between Agent 1's expected income is

(38)

$$\Delta\Pi_1^c = \Pi_1^c - \Pi_1^{c'}$$

$$= \left[1 - \theta\alpha_1 - (1-\theta)(1-\rho)\alpha_2\right]\left\{\theta^{\alpha_1}(1-\theta)^{(1-\rho)\alpha_2}\,\alpha_1^{\alpha_1}\left[(1-\rho)\alpha_2\right]^{(1-\rho)\alpha_2}\right\}^{\frac{1}{1-\alpha_1-(1-\rho)\alpha_2}}$$

$$\times u_1^{-\alpha_1/[1-\alpha_1-(1-\rho)\alpha_2]}u_2^{-(1-\rho)\alpha_2/[1-\alpha_1-(1-\rho)\alpha_2]}\times\left\{2^{\frac{(1-\rho)\alpha_2(1-\beta)}{\beta[1-\alpha_1-(1-\rho)\alpha_2]}} - 1\right\}.$$

Considering the last brace, since $0 < \rho, \alpha_1, \alpha_2, \beta < 1$, and $\alpha_1 + \alpha_2 < 1$, the

term $\dfrac{(1-\rho)\alpha_2(1-\beta)}{\beta\left[1-\alpha_1-(1-\rho)\alpha_2\right]} > 0$, such that $2^{\frac{(1-\rho)\alpha_2(1-\beta)}{\beta[1-\alpha_1-(1-\rho)\alpha_2]}} > 1$. Therefore,

we have $\Delta\Pi_1^c > 0$.[55]

In other words, it seems better for a private entrepreneur to choose both *Guanxi* abilities for cooperation, although they are substitutes for each other. In practice a firm will seek help from the government even though it is a family business. This happens in cases when a private enterprise is not only a family business, but also has family members working in or connected to the government. It seems that such firms will be more successful than a "pure" family business, which has been the case in the Wenzhou model (Sun, 2000). Moreover, when we view *Guanxi* ability as allocated by many different agents, diffuse ownership (share θ of profit) seems to be inevitable, which is consistent with the existence of a diffuse ownership structure in many Zhejiang private enterprises in recent times. This confirms the intuition of "the more, the better" as long as *Guanxi* is useful for the production process. In short, in the above model the objective function is to maximize the whole profit of the firm, and the model predicts an increase in the number of private

---

[55] A similar result can be obtained by comparing (16) of the general case and (26) of the special case under the non-cooperative arrangement.

enterprises with a diffuse ownership arrangement.

4.3.5.2 Combination of endogenous ownership theory and agency theory

The property rights theory developed in the above model is an endogenous ownership theory which attempts to include the role of the institutional environment. In particular, the optimal ownership structure is related to the degree of imperfection of the economic environment (Propositions 1 and 2) as well as management ability (Proposition 3). It can be argued that there is a conflict between endogenous ownership theory and agency theory; because orthodox endogenous ownership theory implies that it does not matter whether ownership is in the hands of management, while agency theory argues that ownership is better in the hands of management. In this researcher's opinion, this does not represent a contradiction because what endogenous ownership theory emphasizes is the role of "market discipline," i.e., the role of the economic environment (see Chapter 2). This is also the reason why Tian (2000) argues that improving the economic environment first is the appropriate procedure for privatization in transitional economies (see Section 4.2).

To sum up, the above model represents a combination of endogenous ownership theory and agency theory.[56] That is, the optimal ownership of a firm depends on not only the economic environment, but also the role of management. From the perspective of the whole economy, the optimal ownership structure is determined by the market, while from the view of individual firms, ownership is better assigned to the agent with management ability when the economic environment improves. Therefore, the model developed here not only extends endogenous ownership theory to include an immature market, but also combines it with agency theory.

Although the above model shows that the importance of management increases when economic environment improves, it does not explain the importance of management in an imperfect market. Moreover, the model does not clearly show the interplay of government and family trust (*Guanxi*), which is the main purpose of this chapter. Therefore, an additional but related model provides formal analysis in the following section, showing the importance of management in determining the ownership structure in an imperfect market. More importantly, the following model also shows that the interplay of government and family trust (*Guanxi*) by the way of adopting

---

[56] Of course, endogenous ownership theory and agency theory are, in essence, not contradictory (see Chapter 2). However, we emphasize their differences here.

the definition of broadly-defined family business, which is a commonsense to solve the principle-agent problem for a private entrepreneur by cooperation with family (members) in an imperfect market.

4.4 Why a Family Business Does Not Need Government Trust (*Guanxi*)

The above model does not clearly explain the interplay between government and family trust (*Guanxi*). Therefore, in this section we present an additional but related model, showing that the interplay between government and family trust (*Guanxi*) leads private enterprises to cooperate with family members in a developing or transitional market. In the following model we further consider the important role played by management in private enterprises, in which the manager maximizes the profit of family members instead of that of the whole firm. We show that a family business may not need to cooperate with the government.

4.4.1 A cooperative model of family business with the government

As explained in the previous chapters, the development pattern of Chinese private enterprises is primarily characterized by family businesses. This is true no matter whether they take the form of "pure" private firms or "red-hat" firms, and the estimation that family businesses account for 90% of all private enterprises is based on the broad definition of family business. In this section we define *family business* in a broad way, including solely-run, family-run, and family-holding private enterprises. This differs from the narrowly defined family business of the previous model in Section 4.3, but it corresponds to the definition adopted in most research in the literature (see, for example, Chandler, 1990; James, 1999; Gan, 2002). Therefore, the problem of cooperation with both government and family *Guanxi* by a private entrepreneur in the previous model becomes only a problem of cooperation with the government by a family business in this model. That is, the firm here has already cooperated with family *Guanxi*. However, the conclusions discussed in the previous model are used in this section, particularly the necessary input of *Guanxi* ability for the production process and specific firm profits.

4.4.1.1 The assumptions and a three-date model

We assume a family business, i.e., its manager, has information that the outside investor, i.e., the government, does not have, and that both manager and government realize this. We take this information asymmetry as a given, which is similar to the situation described by Akerlof (1970).

Note again that family business is broadly defined; that is, the firm has been using available family *Guanxi* ability G_f. Now suppose that there exists a profitable project, which requires further cooperation with government *Guanxi* ability G_g. The opportunity evaporates if the firm does not cooperate with government *Guanxi* at time t=1 (when the project is introduced).

We further assume that government *Guanxi* G_g is available and can be voluntarily obtained by a firm, so that the obtained government *Guanxi* $K_g > 0$, can be viewed as the monetary value of government *Guanxi*. This makes sense when we treat *Guanxi* as an intangible asset, which is similar to "reputation capital" described by Smyth (1997).[57] Thus, the value of the firm increases when government *Guanxi* is incorporated. However, this intangible asset is totally brought by the government.

We also assume that the value of the firm's share equals their expected future profits conditional on whatever information the market has, and that there is a discount for the time value of future profits without changing anything essential. Discounting for risk is not considered because the only uncertainty important in this problem stems from the manager's special information. The government (outside investor) at time t=1 does not know whether the firm's profit will go up or down when that special information is revealed at time t=2 (when the project is completed); that is, the government is viewed as passive.[58] In addition, the risk is assumed to be diversifiable.[59]

Now a three-date model is presented as follows:

There are three dates, t=0, 1, and 2. At t=0, the market has the same information as does the management. At t=1, the management receives additional information about the profit of the family business and the project

---

[57] Smyth (1997) argues that reputation capital is a core asset of Chinese TVEs.

[58] This assumption may be controversial. However, it emphasizes the importance of management ability in firms.

[59] That is, managers may have inside information about the firm, but not about the market.

opportunity, and updates their profit accordingly. The market does not receive this information until t=2.

The profit of the family business at t=0 is the expected future profit $\overline{\Pi_0} = E(\tilde{\Pi}_0)$; the distribution of $\tilde{\Pi}_0$ represents the possible updated profit at t=1. Management's updated estimate at t=1 is π_0, the realization of $\tilde{\Pi}_0$.

The net present value (NPV) of the project profit at t=0 is $\overline{\Pi_p} = E(\tilde{\Pi}_p)$; the distribution of $\tilde{\Pi}_p$ represents the profit's possible updated NPV at t=1. Management's updated estimate at t=1 is π_p, the realization of $\tilde{\Pi}_p$.

We assume that both π_0 and π_p are positive. This makes sense for the original profit because it is better to use *Guanxi* ability in an imperfect market, as seen in Proposition 1 of the previous model, and the firm here has used available family *Guanxi* as a broadly defined family business. It makes sense for the project opportunity because the project is discarded if it turns out to have a negative NPV at t=1.

We further assume that management acts in the interests of family members, i.e., the "old" owners before the start of project at t=1.[60] This is reasonable because a family business is viewed as an owner-cum-manager firm, as discussed in Chapters 2 and 3. Thus, the manager maximises $V_f = V(\pi_0, \pi_p, K_g)$, the "intrinsic" profit of family owners, conditional on the decision to pursue the project and knowledge of realizations π_0 and π_p. However, the true profit will not generally equal V_f, since the

---

[60] This is also a key assumption in the Pecking Order Theory (Myers and Majluf, 1984; Myers, 2001), in which the managers act in the interests of existing shareholders and maximize the value of existing shares.

government only knows the distribution of $\tilde{\Pi}_0$ and $\tilde{\Pi}_p$, whether the project has commenced and gets a share of the realized future profit. If the project is not undertaken at t=1, the family owners retain the total profit of the family business, π_0. If the project is undertaken, the family owners only get a share of the total profit, π', the remaining goes to the government.

4.4.1.2 The formal analysis

If the firm (family business), knowing the profit π_0 and the profit share π', does not undertake the project, it forfeits the opportunity, so $V_f = \pi_0$. If it does undertake the project, $V_f = \dfrac{\pi'}{\pi' + K_g}(K_g + \pi_0 + \pi_p)$. Family owners are better off (or will be at t=2) if the firm chooses cooperation with the government only when $\pi_0 \leq \dfrac{\pi'}{\pi' + K_g}(K_g + \pi_0 + \pi_p)$, or when

$\dfrac{K_g}{\pi' + K_g}\pi_0 \leq \dfrac{\pi'}{\pi' + K_g}(K_g + \pi_p)$, which means that the share of existing profits going to the government is no more than the share of the increment to firm profits obtained by family owners. The condition can also be written as:

(39) $\left(K_g / \pi'\right)\pi_0 \leq K_g + \pi_p$.

Thus the line $\left(K_g / \pi'\right)\pi_0 = K_g + \pi_p$ first divides the joint probability distribution of $\tilde{\Pi}_0$ and $\tilde{\Pi}_p$ into two regions, as shown in Figure 4.1.

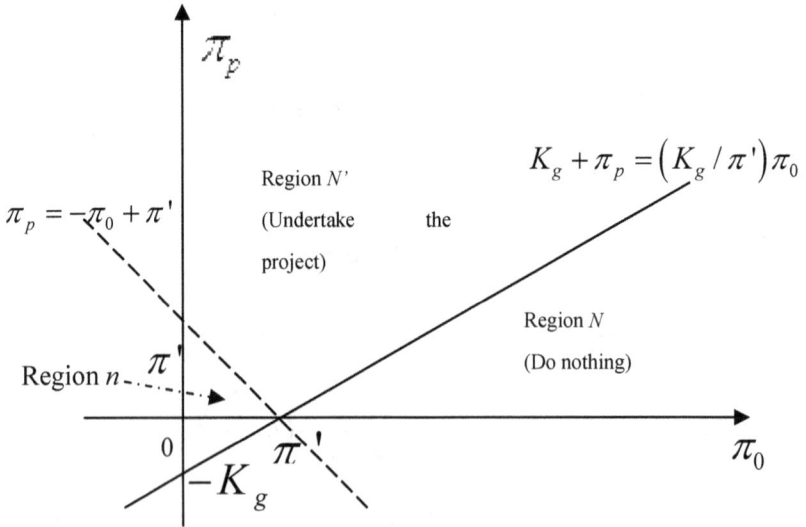

At this stage, if the actual outcome $\left(\pi_0, \pi_p\right)$ falls in region N', the firm

undertakes the project, i.e., further cooperation with the government. If the outcome falls in region N, the firm does nothing: it is willing to give up the NPV of its investment opportunity rather than undertake the project for less than the share that it is really worth. Note that the joint probability

distribution of π_0 and π_p is restricted to the northeast quadrant of Figure

4.1. Region N' is at the top left of this quadrant. The firm is most likely to

undertake the project when π_p, the realization of project NPV, is high and

π_0, the original profit of the family business, is low. The lower π_0 is, the

more attractive the project share of profit π'.

However, this is not the end of the story. Although further cooperation with the government increases the whole profit of a family firm, the family's share of profit cannot increase simultaneously with the whole profit of the firm, especially the profit created by government *Guanxi*.[61] Instead, it can only be obtained through the realization of project profit, and part of this profit has to go to the government. Therefore, the profit of family owners V_f cannot be larger than the total profit $\pi_0 + \pi_p$ if the project is undertaken; that is,

$$V_f = \frac{\pi'}{\pi' + K_g}(K_g + \pi_0 + \pi_p) \le \pi_0 + \pi_p, \quad \text{or rearranging,} \quad \pi' \le \pi_0 + \pi_p.$$

This condition can also be written as:

(40) $\pi_p \ge -\pi_0 + \pi'$.

This indicates that the project profit should be bigger than or equal to the net gains obtained by a family business after further cooperation with the government, since some parts of the project profit have to go to the government. Thus the line $\pi_p = -\pi_0 + \pi'$ further divides region N' into two regions, and converts the joint probability distribution of $\tilde{\Pi}_0$ and $\tilde{\Pi}_p$ into three regions, as shown in Figure 4.1.

4.4.1.3 When not undertaking the project

The direct result implied by the model is that the family firm may pass up good opportunities rather than cooperating with the government to undertake the project. Assuming that region N is not empty, i.e., there is some probability of not undertaking the project, then Figure 4.1 shows that all realizations of π_0 which fall in region N exceed π', i.e., $\pi_0 > \pi'$.

Put another way, the reason a family firm decides not to undertake the

---

[61] Needless to say, in many cases a family firm has to pay the costs before cooperating with the government.

project is that $\pi_0 > \pi'\left(1 + \pi_p / K_g\right)$, which follows from reversing and

rearranging (39). Since $\pi_p / K_g \geq 0$, the decision not to undertake the project

signals $\pi_0 > \pi'$. In other words, it signals that the true profit of family

owners exceeds π', the profit of family share if the project is undertaken.

Since π_0 must exceed π', then the true profit must fall if the firm decides

to undertake the project.

Furthermore, the line $\pi_p = -\pi_0 + \pi'$ makes the previous region N' smaller

by region n due to the constraint of (40). Thus region n can be interpreted as

an additional region N, which is also a region where the project is not

undertaken. In summary, region N' over the line $\pi_p = -\pi_0 + \pi'$ is the

region of undertaking the project, while region N and region n are the regions

where the project is not undertaken.

Note that both π_0 and π_p incorporate all information available to

investors. They are rationally-formed, unbiased estimates of the intrinsic

profit of the family firm. They reflect knowledge of the firm's decision rule

as well as its decision. π_0 exceeds π' because investors rationally

interpret the decision not to undertake the project as good news about the

true profit of the firm. The result is intuitive in the sense that the manager of

a family business acts in the interests of family members, and that the

manager maximizes the true profit of family owners.

4.4.2 Turning back to the previous model

Now we return to the previous model in Section 4.3, using the analysis of the

cooperative model of family business with the government. The profits in the

previous model are explicit, but specific; that is, the original profit of the family business is $\pi_0 = \prod_1^{c'}$, as in (32), while the project profit of further

cooperation with government *Guanxi* is $\pi_p = \prod_1^c - \prod_1^{c'} = \Delta\prod_1^c$, as in (38),

which is positive, as discussed before. However, we need further analysis of

π_0 and π_p to examine why a family business may not need to cooperate

with government *Guanxi*, as proposed in the cooperative model in the previous section.

4.4.2.1 The dynamic movements of (π_0, π_p) from undertaking the project

First, taking logarithms of both sides of (32) and differentiating $\ln \pi_0$ with

respect to ρ, we have
(41)

$$\frac{d \ln \pi_0}{d\rho} = \ln u_1 \times \left\{ \frac{\alpha_2 \left[2\theta\alpha_1 - (\alpha_1 + \theta) \right]}{\left[1 - \alpha_1 - (1-\rho)\alpha_2 \right]\left[1 - \theta\alpha_1 - (1-\theta)(1-\rho)\alpha_2 \right]} \right\}.$$

Since $\ln u_1 > 0$, $0 < \rho, \alpha_1, \alpha_2, \theta < 1$ and $\alpha_1 + \alpha_2 < 1$, $2\theta\alpha_1 - (\alpha_1 + \theta) < 0$,

the numerator of the term in the brace of (41) is negative while the

denominator is positive. Thus, $\dfrac{d \ln \pi_0}{d\rho} < 0$, which means that the profit of

the family business decreases as the degree of market perfection ρ

increases. In fact, $\pi_0 \to 0$ when $\rho \to 1$.

Similarly, taking the logarithms of both sides of (38) and differentiating

$\ln \pi_p$ with respect to ρ, we have

$$(42) \quad \frac{d \ln \pi_p}{d\rho} = \frac{\alpha_2 \left[2\theta\alpha_1 - (\alpha_1 + \theta) \right]}{\left[1 - \alpha_1 - (1-\rho)\alpha_2 \right] \left[1 - \theta\alpha_1 - (1-\theta)(1-\rho)\alpha_2 \right]}$$

$$+ \frac{2^D \ln 2}{2^D - 1} \times \frac{\alpha_2 (1-\beta)(\alpha_1 - 1)}{\beta \left[1 - \alpha_1 - (1-\rho)\alpha_2 \right]^2},$$

where $D = \dfrac{(1-\rho)\alpha_2 (1-\beta)}{\beta \left[1 - \alpha_1 - (1-\rho)\alpha_2 \right]}$.

Since $0 < \rho, \alpha_1, \alpha_2, \theta, \beta < 1$ and $\alpha_1 + \alpha_2 < 1$, the first term of the right-hand side is negative, the same as (41); and since $(\alpha_1 - 1) < 0$, the second term is also negative. Therefore, $\dfrac{d \ln \pi_p}{d\rho} < 0$, i.e. the project profit also decreases as ρ increases. Also $\pi_p \to 0$ when $\rho \to 1$.

Figure 4.2 The Dynamic Movements of Outcome $\left(\pi_0, \pi_p\right)$ as ρ Increases

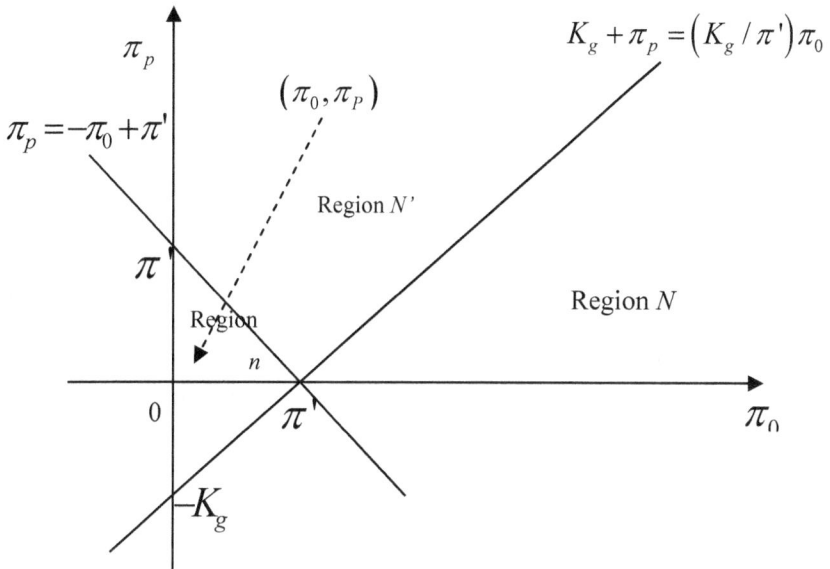

$$\pi_p$$
$$K_g + \pi_p = \left(K_g / \pi'\right)\pi_0$$
$$\left(\pi_0, \pi_p\right)$$
$$\pi_p = -\pi_0 + \pi'$$
Region N'
$$\pi$$
Region N
Region n
$$0$$
$$\pi'$$
$$\pi_0$$
$$-K_g$$

Therefore, the dynamic movements of outcome $\left(\pi_0, \pi_p\right)$ from undertaking the project, i.e., cooperation between the family business and government *Guanxi*, are shown in Figure 4.2. The original outcome $\left(\pi_0, \pi_p\right)$ falls in region N', it moves left and downwards towards the origin as ρ increases, and finally falls in region n. This result implies that when the market environment improves, the family business will not choose further cooperation with the government. This explains why no private firms are registered as "red-hat" firms in present-day China. However, the private entrepreneur still chooses cooperation with family at this stage in the model.

Summarizing the above analysis, we then have the following proposition:

Proposition 4. *When the manager acts in the interests of family, the family business may forgo good projects rather than cooperating with the government to implement them. Moreover, previous cooperation with the government will also be given up by "pure" family business when the economic environment improves.*

As argued by Lorenz's (1999, p.313), the purpose of implicit contracts is "not so much to enforce commitments as to provide a framework agreement within which on-going discussions and negotiations can facilitate their sequential adaptation", and then an inevitable consequence is that there is no guarantee that cooperation will succeed, even when the circumstances appear to promise mutual gain. Proposition 4 not only confirms this argument, but further shows that the previous cooperation with government trust (*Guanxi*) will be faded out as the market improves from imperfect to perfect. In the case of Chinese private enterprises, the forgoing of the cooperation with government by family business is given impetus by the policy of ownership reform of SOEs and the transfer of TVEs.

4.4.2.2 The decrease in cooperative profits

Furthermore, taking logarithms of both sides of (22), i.e., the profit of cooperation with both government and family *Guanxi,* and differentiating $\ln \prod_1^c$ with respect to ρ, we have

(43)

$$\frac{d \ln \prod_1^c}{d\rho} = \ln u_1 \times \left\{ \begin{array}{c} \dfrac{\alpha_2 \left[2\theta\alpha_1 - (\alpha_1 + \theta) \right]}{\left[1 - \alpha_1 - (1-\rho)\alpha_2 \right]\left[1 - \theta\alpha_1 - (1-\theta)(1-\rho)\alpha_2 \right]} \\ + \ln 2 \times \dfrac{\alpha_2 (1-\beta)(\alpha_1 - 1)}{\beta \left[1 - \alpha_1 - (1-\rho)\alpha_2 \right]^2} \end{array} \right\}.$$

Then comparing (43) and (41), which have similar structures, the second term in the brace of (43) is negative because $\alpha_1 - 1 < 0$. Therefore, we have

$$\left| \frac{d \ln \prod_1^c}{d\rho} \right| > \left| \frac{d \ln \pi_0}{d\rho} \right| = \left| \frac{d \ln \prod_1^{c'}}{d\rho} \right|, \text{ then } \left| \frac{d \ln \prod_1^c}{d \ln \prod_1^{c'}} \right| > 1.$$

100

In other words, the percentage change in $\prod_1^c$ is bigger than the percentage

change in $\prod_1^{c'}$, which means $\prod_1^c$ decreases faster than $\prod_1^{c'}$. That is, the

profit from cooperation with both government and family decreases faster than that from cooperation with only family when the economic environment improves. The rapid decrease in the profit from cooperation with the government seems to be the direct result of "mechanism degeneration" as described by Sun (2002),[62] so that a family business will forgo cooperation with government *Guanxi*.

4.4.3 Corollary of the theoretical models

Some may argue that (32) also represents the profit of cooperation with the government only by the private entrepreneur, therefore, the above analysis is also valid for "red-hat" firms (or TVEs). That is, a "red-hat" firm (or a TVE) would continue to exist in China and would perhaps drive out family firms under a similar proposition. This argument may be true if the manager acts in the interests of existing owners (both the government and manager him or herself). However, it has been acknowledged that cooperation with the government typically entails a separation of ownership and control, where there is a conflict between the firm and the government, as discussed in Chapter 2. Given the agency problem, it is hard for the manager to act in the interests of both the government and him or herself. Thus, the analysis of the above cooperative model cannot be applied to a "red-hat" firm since the assumption that the manager acts in the interests of existing owners does not hold.

In contrast, there is good reason to believe that the manager will act in the interests of family members (see Chapter 2). That is, the second model also provides a justification for the distinction between family and government *Guanxi* within a firm, which is the key underpinning idea of this chapter. Combining the above analysis in this section with the discussion in Section 4.3, particularly Proposition 1, we reach the following corollary regarding the interaction of government and family *Guanxi*:

---

[62] "Mechanism degeneration" in Sun's (2002) study refers mainly to the increasing rent-seeking and bureaucratization of local governments with successful firms. That is, these local governments are moving from the "helping hand" to the "grabbing hand" and show the tendency to abuse their ownership rights over fake collectives. In Sun's opinion, mechanism degeneration results in the fading out of local government ownership in TVEs.

Corollary: A private firm may prefer family trust (Guanxi) to government trust (Guanxi) for cooperation; that is, the prominence of family business can be explained by not only the improvement in the economic environment, but also the tendency for family trust (Guanxi) to replace government trust (Guanxi).

4.5 Conclusion

The theory of ownership structure developed in the above models takes into account the effects of an imperfect institutional environment. The first model illustrates endogenous ownership theory in which the optimal arrangement, i.e., non-cooperative or cooperative arrangement with trust (*Guanxi*) for private enterprises, is related to the degree of imperfection of the market environment, as well as the ability of management in those firms. It explains how institutional foundations of trust (*Guanxi*), particularly the roles played by government and family, are crucial for the development of private enterprises. The first three propositions discuss the optimal arrangements for the development of private enterprise in an imperfect market such as China. These propositions hold for any ownership share, including the optimal share θ^*, which maximizes Agent 1's expected income under the cooperative arrangement. The second model further confirms the importance of management in determining optimal ownership, but more importantly, it discusses the interplay of government and family *Guanxi* within the same configuration of general *Guanxi* ability in the production process. The last proposition and its corollary explain why family business is the most common ownership structure chosen by private enterprises and why direct involvement of the government in private business is fading out.

In this chapter we have focused on two types of trust (*Guanxi*); that is, government and family trust (*Guanxi*). In practice, there may be other types of trust (*Guanxi*), which may be labelled "friendship trust (*Guanxi*)," in influencing the development of Chinese private enterprises.[63] It has been argued that in China the family is the most important social institution and family life is the most important aspect of social life, while the relationships of kinship, neighbours and friends are secondary (Lu, 1987). This view has been supported by the fact that private entrepreneurs normally seek help

---

[63] Williamson (1993, p.484) suggests that personal trust is "reserved for very special relations between family, friends, and lovers," indicating that friendship trust is one type of trust. Weitzman and Xu (1994, p. 138) point out that there is a popular "*Gemen*" spirit (buddy commitment and loyalty) which plays an important role in substituting for formal rules in Chinese TVEs. The term "*Gemen*" in their study is the same as the concept of friendship trust.

from their friends and old colleagues when there is a limit in terms of the number and capacity of family members (Sun and Wong, 2002). This is also consistent with the "pecking order" theory as described by Myers and Majluf (1984) and Myers (2001).[64] In other words, a private entrepreneur prefers family members over friends for cooperation (see, for example, Schlevogt, 2001; Li, 2002).[65] Our model provides an explanation for this argument. Although friendship trust (*Guanxi*) is not examined in this chapter, the analysis here could be extended to examine friendship trust (*Guanxi*) simply because cooperation between a private entrepreneur and friends also represents the separation of ownership and control. In short, the pecking order theory of choosing different types of trust (*Guanxi*) for cooperation, i.e., family trust (*Guanxi*) first and then others, works well in Chinese private enterprises as the above research suggests.

In summary, the theoretical models developed in this chapter represent a combination of orthodox endogenous ownership theory and agency theory. These models provide plausible explanations for the development pattern of Chinese private enterprises. Although the theoretical models consider only a single dominant ownership arrangement, it may be used to explain the co-existence of different ownership arrangements in private firms, even in the same industry or the same area. Since management ability, *Guanxi* ability, the sharing rule, and market environment affect the optimal ownership arrangements, differences in these parameters could lead to the co-existence of different ownership arrangements in the same area or sectors. However, there are certain caveats that are worth noting. For the first model, the assumption of only two classes and a single profit function inevitably leads to a single dominant arrangement. In addition, the model describes a one-period non-cooperative game, but typically cooperative patterns are of a long-run nature. The exercise under the assumption of a repeated cooperative game needs further analysis. For the second model, the analysis is also based on certain restricted assumptions such as the manager acting in the interests of existing owner(s) and passive outside investor(s). Further research that relaxes these assumptions is also warranted.

---

[64] The pecking order theory states that when facing a hierarchy of financial sources, firms normally rely heavily on internal cash flow to finance their investment needs. When they require further resources, they restore first to bank borrowing and long-term debt, and only as a last resource do they go to the stock market to raise funds (Myers and Majluf, 1984; Myers, 2001).

[65] For example, Li (2002) argues that the Asian wisdom is first do business with one's siblings, then with one's cousins, then with people from one's hometown or classmates, and finally—and reluctantly—with strangers.

CHAPTER 5

Formal Ownership Structure as a Corporate Governance Mechanism: Evidence from Private Enterprises in Ningbo City, Zhejiang Province[66]

5.1 Introduction

As discussed in Chapter 2, the relationship between ownership structure and firm performance is far from conclusive. While agency theory stresses the importance of ownership in the hands of management to improve firm performance, endogenous ownership theory, which emphasizes the importance of the market environment, yields conflicting results.[67] The theoretical models developed in Chapter 4, which are a combination of orthodox endogenous ownership theory and agency theory, show that for a profit-maximizing private firm, the optimal ownership arrangement relates to the market environment as well as the role of management. This finding suggests that firm performance is closely linked to its ownership arrangement in a given market environment.

This chapter contains two empirical studies of the relationship between firm performance and ownership structure, paying particular attention to the specific characteristics of the developing market environment in China. The first test examines the relationship between firm performance and formal ownership structure in private enterprises. The second test analyses the effect of firm performance on managerial shareholding. The empirical study in this chapter is based on an analysis of a survey of 296 private enterprises in Ningbo City, Zhejiang province.

The rest of this chapter is organized as follows. Section 5.2 briefly describes the general development of private enterprises in Ningbo and gives an overview of the survey. Section 5.3 describes the data and definitions of the variables, and discusses the methodology for examining the relationship between ownership structure and firm performance. Section 5.4 presents the empirical results for the relationship between ownership structure and firm performance. Foreshadowing the main results, both the single largest shareholder and the proportion of shares held by management have strong

---

[66] This chapter is originated from the following paper: Qin, Zhong and Deng, Xin. 2009. "Ownership Structure and Performance in Family Businesses at Early Development Stage: Evidence from China." Corporate Ownership & Control, Vol. 7, Issue 1, pp.135-147.

[67] Demsetz and Villalonga (2001) provide a comprehensive review of the existing literature on the relationship between ownership and firm performance.

effects on firm performance, measured as the average profit rate. However, the relationship between family shareholding (including the shares jointly owned by the largest shareholder and his/her family members) and firm performance is insignificant. Given the importance of management shareholding for improving firm performance, Section 5.5 presents the empirical results for the determinants of the ownership decision to give firm shares to management. From the perspective of the firm (owners), willingness to give ownership shares to management personnel outside the owner's family is negatively related to firm performance. Conclusions are then presented in Section 5.6.

5.2 Overview of Data Collection

5.2.1 The general development of private enterprises in Ningbo

Ningbo, the second largest city in Zhejiang province,[68] had a population of 5.53 million in 2004 (Zhejiang Statistical Yearbook, 2005). The development of private enterprises in Ningbo corresponds generally with that of private enterprises in the whole of Zhejiang province, as discussed in Chapter 3. In 2004, there were 68,500 privately-run enterprises (employing more than eight people) and 233,388 individual businesses (employing no more than eight people), with 1.23 and 0.41 million employees respectively, while registered capital of privately-run enterprises and individual businesses were 66.21 and 7.22 billion RMB respectively (about USD$8.0 billion and USD$0.87 billion respectively) (Report of Development of Ningbo's Private Enterprises, 2005).[69] Private enterprises are an important factor propelling economic growth in Ningbo. In 2004, the industrial output of private enterprises in Ningbo was 186.95 billion RMB, accounting for 86% of Ningbo's total industrial output; the retail sales of private enterprises were 57.81 billion RMB, accounting for 97% of Ningbo's total retail sales; taxation revenue from private enterprises was 5.58 billion RMB, accounting for 35.05% of Ningbo's total taxation revenue and exports of private enterprises were US$5.58 billion, accounting for 33% of Ningbo's exports (Report of Development of Ningbo's Private Enterprises, 2005).

Within privately-run enterprises in Ningbo, in terms of legal form, there were 25,000 solely-owned companies, 4,700 partnerships, 38,600 limited liability companies, and 45 companies limited by shares (joint-stock companies) in 2004, accounting for 36.7%, 6.8%, 56.4%, and 0.1% respectively (Report of Development of Ningbo's Private Enterprises, 2005). Thus, limited liability

---

[68] The largest city in Zhejiang province is the provincial capital, Huangzhou City.

[69] USD$1=RMB8.28yuan in 2004, and henceforward.

companies have been the main organizational form for privately-run enterprises. In terms of industrial distribution primary, secondary, and tertiary industries accounted respectively for 1.2%, 58.2%, and 40.6% of total privately-run enterprises in 2004 (Report of Development of Ningbo's Private Enterprises, 2005). In other words, secondary industry is the main area in which private-enterprise production is concentrated, followed by tertiary industry, then primary industry. In short, the development of Ningbo's private enterprises is similar to that of the Zhejiang model, as discussed in Chapter 3.

5.2.2 Description of the survey

The survey was administrated by this researcher to private enterprises in Ningbo between December 2005 and February 2006. The questionnaire was first translated into Chinese and translated back into English to ensure the accuracy of the original translation (see Appendices). Altogether 400 copies of questionnaires were distributed to privately-run enterprises (excluding individual businesses), with assistance from the Ningbo's Bureau of Industrial and Commercial Administration and the Association of Ningbo's Private Enterprises. By the end of the survey, 327 copies of the questionnaires had been collected, accounting for 82% of total distributed questionnaires. After removing incomplete questionnaires, there were 296 valid questionnaires, accounting for 91% of total collected copies or 74% of total distributed copies. All valid questionnaires were checked for accuracy twice prior to being entered into a database.

In the sample of 296 firms from which valid results were obtained, five firms were privatized state-owned enterprises, accounting for 1.7% of the sample and 63 firms had been transformed from collective-owned enterprises, whereby they took off their "red-hats," accounting for 21.3% of the sample. The remaining 228 firms were green-field private firms accounting for 77.03% of the sample, of which 12 firms had started out as individual businesses previously employing no more than eight people, while 216 firms were registered as privately-run enterprises from the beginning employing more than eight people. Within these 296 private firms, although there were 20 firms with government shares when they started as private businesses, there was no government shareholding in the private enterprises in the sample at the time of the survey. Overall, there were 283 firms where families controlled at least 50% of the shares, accounting for 95.6% of the 296 firms. That is, most private enterprises in the sample were characterized as broadly-defined family businesses, as discussed in the previous chapters. In terms of legal form there were 97 solely-owned companies, 14 partnerships, and 185 limited liability companies in the surveyed firms, accounting for 32.8%, 4.7%, and 62.5%, respectively. There were no firms in the survey limited by shares. The sector distribution of these 296 firms corresponds with the sector distribution of privately-run enterprises in Ningbo as a whole, as shown in Table 5.1. Overall, the 296 firms in the survey are generally representative of the basic characteristics of privately-run enterprises in Ningbo.

Table 5.1 Industrial Distributions of Ningbo's Private Enterprises and Survey Firms at the End of 2004

	Ningbo City		Survey Firms	
	firms	propor-tion	firms	propor-tion
Total firms	68,500		296	
Primary Industry	840	1.20%	8	2.70%
Secondary Industry	39,860	58.20%	163	55.07%
Of the total: Manufacturing	37,395	54.59%	152	51.35%
Construction	2,090	3.05%	10	3.38%
Tertiary Industry	27,800	40.60%	125	42.23%
Of the total: Wholesale and retail trade and catering service	17,590	25.68%	66	22.30%

(Source: Report of Development of Ningbo's Private Enterprises (2005) and Researchers' Survey)

5.3 Data Specification and Methodology

The main purpose of this chapter is to discuss the formal ownership structure as a corporate governance mechanism within private enterprises. Following the studies of Demsetz (1983), Demsetz and Lehn (1985), and Demsetz and Villalonga (2001), among others, we examine the relationship between firm performance and formal ownership structure by also taking into account factors such as firm age, firm size and the instability of the business environment. In the first empirical study which examines the role of ownership arrangements on firm performance we consider ownership in terms of the single largest shareholder, family shareholding, and management shareholding.

5.3.1 Data description and specification of variables

5.3.1.1 Measurement of firm performance

Firm performance is measured by the average profit rate (AvPR) of the firm, which is defined as the annual average rate of net profits to gross assets over the three years prior to the survey.[70] This variable is the dependent variable in our econometric model.

Table 5.2 Descriptive Statistics for the 296 Survey Firms

Variables	Definition	Mean	Standard Deviation	Min	Max
AvPR (%)	Average profit rate in three years prior to the survey	4.1975	25.9170	-306.424	114.9124
T1 (%)	The largest shareholder	78.3586	21.7889	10	100
Family (%)	Family shares (including the largest shareholder and family members)	92.8711	17.9405	10	100
Manage-ment (%)	Shares of top management	58.6309	36.7944	0	100
Age (Year)	Years registered as a private firm	6.4466	3.3253	2.08	20.17
LnAsset	Natural log of average gross assets in three years prior to the survey (million RMB)	0.7971	1.5692	-4.1626	6.1257
Instability (%)	Standard deviation of sales in three years prior to the survey	630.6928	2,956.836	0.1637	25,166.12

5.3.1.2 Ownership structure variables

To examine the role of ownership structure on firm performance, we break ownership structure into three types, as follows:

1) *The single largest shareholder (T1).* This stands for the percentage of shares held by the single largest owner. This variable serves as a proxy for

---

[70] The profit rate is a better measure of firm performance than the market value measured by Tobin's Q because market value cannot be easily obtained for most Chinese private enterprises.

ownership concentration and was used in Chen's (2001) study of Chinese publicly listed companies and a number of other studies for similar countries.[71] As shown in Table 5.2, the average shareholding of the largest owner is 78.36%, reflecting a high ownership concentration. This percentage primarily reflects the fact that most Chinese private enterprises are of relatively small size (Schlevogt, 2001; Sun and Wong, 2002) and the sample of 296 firms comprises 97 solely-owned companies, as discussed above.[72] In general, previous studies have found a positive relationship between ownership concentration and firm performance in developing countries, which is attributed to the impact of better monitoring (see, for example, Barberis et al., 1996; Xu and Wang, 1997; Claessens and Djankov, 1999; Chen, 2001). On this basis, a positive relationship between firm performance and the single largest shareholder (T1) is expected.

2) *Percentage of shares jointly owned by the largest owner and each of his/her family members (Family)*. This variable corresponds to a broadly-defined family business and can be used to explain the non-separation of ownership and control. As shown in Table 5.2, the average shareholding jointly owned by the largest owner and his/her family members (Family) is 92.87%, reflecting a high concentration of family ownership.

There is a sizeable literature that examines the effect of family ownership on firm performance. Fama and Jensen (1983) note that combining ownership and control allows concentrated shareholders to exchange profits for private rents, while Demsetz (1983) argues that such owners may choose non-pecuniary consumption and thereby draw scarce resources away from profitable projects. However, Demsetz and Lehn (1985) note that combining ownership and control can be advantageous, as large shareholders can act to mitigate managerial expropriation. James (1999) posits that families have longer investment horizons, leading to greater investment efficiency.

Using data for the United States, Morck et al. (2000) find that continued founding-family ownership is an organizational form that leads to poor firm performance. In contrast, McConaughy et al. (1998), and Anderson and Reeb (2003) find that family-controlled firms perform better than non-family firms. Their explanation for this finding is that family relationships improve monitoring while also providing incentives that are associated with better

---

[71] For example, see studies by Faccio et al. (2001) for East Asian countries, including Hong Kong, Indonesia, Japan, Malaysia, Philippines, Singapore, South Korea, Taiwan and Thailand, and Dogan and Smyth (2002) for Malaysia.

[72] According to the legal definitions of Chinese private enterprises (see Section 2.1.2), the total ownership shares in a solely-owned company are held by the single shareholder.

firm performance. Using data for developing countries, Faccio et al. (2001) studied family firms in East Asian companies and reported that family control leads to wealth expropriation in the presence of less than transparent financial markets, thus harming firm performance. However, the Faccio et al. study (2001) uses a sample of large corporations with a relatively low proportion of family shares compared with our sample. Khaemasunun (2004) argues that family firms in Thailand perform better because they are relatively small in size, and family members working in the firm tend to attach importance to firm performance since they have a high proportion of the total shares. This argument might be true for Chinese private firms because families (including the largest shareholder and his/her family members) have a very high proportion of the total shareholding in our sample. Therefore, a positive relationship between family ownership (Family) and firm performance is expected.

3) *Percentage of shares owned by top management (Management) refers to the percentage of shares owned by CEOs, deputy CEOs, general managers, and deputy general managers.* As shown in Table 5.2, the average shareholding of top management in the sample is 58.63%, which is also high. Jensen and Meckling (1976) stress that managers act in their own self-interest and argue that managers perform better the higher their ownership stake within the firm. The higher the percentage of shares owned by management, the harder managers will work to improve firm performance, which leads to an increase in firm value and hence an increase in the managers' private wealth. The agency problems in emerging markets are relatively more severe than in developed economies due to the absence of strong legal protection and other governance mechanisms (La Porta et al., 1998). Dyck and Zingales (2004) study private benefits of control around the world and find that higher private benefits of control are associated with less developed capital markets and more concentrated ownership. In the case of China, Chen (2001) finds that an increase in management shareholding improves firm performance for publicly listed companies. All these findings suggest that increasing management shareholding is an obvious remedy to mitigate the problem of agency. On this basis, we expect a positive relationship between firm performance and management shareholding.

5.3.1.3 Control variables

Firm age, beginning from the date the firm registered as a private enterprise (Age). Ang et al. (1998) argue that due to the effects of a learning curve and survival bias older firms are likely to be more efficient than younger ones. Thus firm performance should improve with age. However, Chen (2001) finds that the performance of Chinese publicly listed companies decline with their listed age, mainly due to problems of adverse selection and moral hazard subsequent to listing. After classifying a sample of United States family firms as "young" and "old" based on whether the firm is under or over 50 years of age, Anderson and Reeb (2003) find both young and old family firms exhibit a significant and positive association between age and firm performance. They also point out that better firm performance is attributed primarily to the youngest firms in their sample because the new founders bring unique, value-adding skills to the firms that result in superior accounting performance and market valuations; that is, younger firms seem more efficient. As shown in Table 5.2, the average age of our sample firms was six years at the end of 2004, indicating that most private firms were established after the commencement of ownership reform of state-owned enterprises (SOEs) and township-village enterprises (TVEs) at the Fifteenth Congress in 1997 and after the recognition of private enterprises in the Chinese Constitution in 1999. We include the firm's age to test whether firms with shorter histories have better performance. On the basis of the extant literature a negative relationship between firm age and firm performance is expected.

Firm size (LnAsset). This is measured by the natural logarithm of annual average total assets over the past three years. One argument is that firm size negatively affects not only firm performance, but also ownership concentration (Demsetz, 1983; Demsetz and Lehn, 1985; Demsetz and Villalonga, 2001). Chen (2001) finds a negative correlation between firm size and firm performance in a sample of Chinese publicly listed companies and Anderson and Reeb (2003) reach the same result for a sample of family firms in the United States. An alternative argument is that firm size improves firm performance due to the importance of capital stock. Barth et al. (2005) recently found a positive relationship between firm size and firm performance in Norwegian family firms. Most Chinese private enterprises are relatively small (Schlevogt, 2001), as shown in Table 5.2. Larger private firms may exhibit better performance because capital resources are critical for the development of private firms (Sun and Wong, 2002). As discussed in Chapter 3, larger firms are better placed to access capital and banks are more ready to lend to large firms. This would suggest a positive relationship between firm performance and firm size for Chinese private firms.

Instability of the business environment (Instability). Demsetz and Lehn (1985) identify the instability of a firm's performance as a factor determining ownership concentration. They argue that firms with more stable prices, technology and market share need less managerial discretion and therefore managers can be monitored at a relatively low cost. In contrast, frequent changes in relative prices, technology, and market shares require timely managerial decisions concerning redeployment of corporate assets and personnel. The more unstable a firm's environment, the greater the cost to the owner of maintaining tighter control. Hence, a more unstable business environment should give rise to a more concentrated ownership structure. For instance, under the Japanese Main Bank system, Japanese banks had equity holdings in firms to which they made loans, which could be considered additional insurance for loan repayment in a volatile environment (Chen, 2001). We use the standard deviations of changes in firm's sales revenue over the past three years to proxy the instability of the business environment. As shown in Table 5.2, the instability indicator is quite large with a mean of 631 in a range of 0.16 to 25,166. This strongly implies that the business environment in China is volatile. Under these circumstances there is a need for the firm's owners (as well as managers) to concentrate their shareholdings, because the owners and managers of Chinese private firms are generally not separated, as discussed in Chapters 2 and 3. Therefore, we expect that a more stable business environment will be reflected in improved firm performance. That is, we expect a negative relationship between firm performance and the instability of the business environment.

5.3.2 Econometric methodology

To examine the relationship between firm performance and ownership arrangements in Chinese private enterprises, an Ordinary Least Squares (OLS) model is employed:

$$AvPR = \alpha + \beta_1 DTO + \beta_2 Age + \beta_3 LnAsset + \beta_4 Instability + \mu_i ,$$

where α is the intercept; $\beta_1 ... \beta_4$ are the regression coefficients to be estimated; μ_i is the random error term; and DTO is a vector of three different types of ownership shares; that is, the shares owned by the single largest owner (T1), the shares jointly owned by the largest owner and family members (Family), and the shares owned by top management (Management). The OLS estimation will take into account multicollinearity and heteroskedasticity, as discussed below.

5.3.2.1 Correlations of variables

To assess potential bias due to multicollinearity, we examine the pair-wise correlation coefficients between each pair of variables. The problem of multicollinearity is not well defined (Wooldridge, 2006). Gujarati (1995, pp.335-336) suggests that multicollinearity is of concern if the simple correlation is higher than 0.6 and a serious problem if the simple correlation is higher than 0.8. In their seminal study of firm performance and ownership structure in the United States, Demsetz and Lehn (1985) run separate models when the simple correlation between ownership variables is 0.71. More recently, Demsetz and Villalonga (2001) consider multicollinearity to be a problem requiring remedy when the simple correlation is greater than 0.6.[73]

Table 5.3 shows the correlation matrix for the sample used here. The only simple correlation in excess of 0.6 is between the single largest shareholder (T1) and family shareholding (Family). To address the issue of multicollinearity in our study, the effect of these two ownership variables will be estimated separately. Therefore, we perform two hypothesis tests with the ownership structure variables. In the first OLS regression, the ownership variables include the single largest shareholder (T1) and top management shareholding (Management); in the second OLS regression, the ownership variables include family shareholding (Family) and top management shareholding (Management). Among these three ownership variables, top management shareholding (Management) will be examined in both tests.

Table 5.3 Correlation Matrix

	AvPR	T1	Family	Management	Age	LnAsset	Instability
AvPR	1						
T1	0.0878	1					
Family	0.0828	0.6811	1				
Management	0.1888	0.2460	0.3525	1			
Age	0.0211	0.3150	0.1176	0.1442	1		
LnAsset	0.2613	-0.2585	-0.1183	0.2134	-0.0789	1	
Instability	0.2680	-0.0667	-0.0755	0.0650	-0.0569	0.5008	1

5.3.2.2 Heteroskedasticity

Models employing cross-sectional data may be affected by heteroskedasticity.

---

[73] In terms of the measurement of firm performance, Demsetz and Villalonga (2001) present no regression models using the accounting profit rate because the simple correlation between Tobin's Q and the accounting profit rate was 0.61 in their study.

This problem is especially serious when we use a sample including firms with large differences in size and in variance of sales, as shown in Table 5.2. After checking for heteroskedasticity using the Breusch-Pagan / Cook-Weisberg test in the two OLS regression models described above, we find these OLS models are affected by heteroskedasticity, as shown in Table 5.4. Our diagnostic testing shows that each test rejects the null hypothesis of constant variance for fitted values of the average profit rate. To address the problem of heteroskedasticity in the OLS regression, we employ a robust regression model with White's heteroskedastic consistent t-statistics.

Table 5.4 Breusch-Pagan / Cook-Weisberg Test for Heteroskedasticity of OLS

Ho: Constant variance		
Variables: fitted values of AvPR		
	First OLS with T1 and Management	Second OLS with Family and Management
Chi2(1)	266.64	201.88
Prob>Chi2	0.000	0.000
Results	Reject Ho	Reject Ho

5.4 Empirical Results of the Relationship between Firm Performance and Formal Ownership Structure

5.4.1 The relationship between firm performance and the single largest shareholder together with top management shareholding

In the first model, the dependent variable is the profit rate (AvPR), and the explanatory variables are the single largest shareholder (T1), top management shareholding (Management), firm age (Age), firm size (LnAsset), and the instability of the business environment (Instability). The results are reported in Table 5.5.

The coefficient on the single largest shareholder (T1) is positive and significant in the OLS model with robust estimation, suggesting that large shareholders may help reduce agency costs caused by the principal-agent problem in private enterprises, and hence are better for firm performance. The finding here is consistent with many studies for developing countries, as discussed above. In the survey of the 296 firms, the average shareholding of the single largest owner increased from 74.63% when starting a private business to 78.36% by the end of 2004.

Top management shareholding (Management) also has a statistically significant positive coefficient in the firm performance regression, which is consistent with expectations. That is, increasing the proportion of shares owned by top management might significantly strengthen managers' incentive to improve firm performance. In the sample, the top management shares also increased from 54.93% at the beginning of private business start-up to 58.73% by 2004. Considering the importance of shares held by management, together with the importance of the largest shareholder, our findings suggest that it is better for a firm to combine its ownership and control.

Table 5.5 The Relationship between Firm Performance Measured as Average Profit Rate (AvPR) and the Single Largest Shareholder (T1) together with Management Shareholding (Management)

OLS with robust standard errors	AvPR
T1	0.1446011[c]
	(1.95)
Management	0.0777436[b]
	(2.36)
Age	-0.0687814
	(-0.15)
LnAsset	2.955494[c]
	(1.86)
Instability	0.0015675[a]
	(2.80)
Constant	-14.59993[c]
	(-2.49)
R^2	0.1260
F-statistic	8.36
P-value	0.000

Notes: a, b, c stand for significant at 1%, 5%, and 10% level respectively. t-statistics are in parentheses.

The results suggest that larger firms perform better, indicating that agency costs do not increase when the firm grows larger. This is true particularly because most private firms are small, while at the same time capital resources are vital for their development, indicating that increasing firm size with more capital improves firm performance. This result underscores the importance for private firms to seek more physical capital.

Interestingly, there is a statistically significant positive relationship between firm performance and the instability of the business environment, contradicting our prediction. Demsetz (1983), Demsetz and Lehn (1985), and Demsetz and Villalonga (2001) argue that changes in business circumstances, which are defined as the standard deviations of monthly stock market rates of return or annual accounting profit rates, are not beneficial for the performance of firms. However, those studies use sample firms from mature markets such as the United States, which have a relatively stable business environment. Hence their argument may not be appropriate for developing markets.

There are two reasons for our different results here. The first reason is that the business environment in a developing market such as China is more volatile relative to many developed markets. As noted by Singh (2003, p.459), in broad terms developing markets are essentially characterized by "pervasive and inefficient government control [of] economic activity, lack of competition, [and] immature and imperfect capital markets" and hence it is expected that there will be a relatively volatile business environment. Su and Fleisher (1998) and Rogers (2004) find that returns in Chinese stock markets are relatively volatile. Moreover, Su and Fleisher (1998) argue that higher average returns are associated with larger exposure to risks in Chinese publicly listed companies, and Khaemasunun (2004) argues that higher returns are associated with higher risks in Thai family firms. These studies use the changes in market returns as an indicator of instability, which is the same as in the Demsetz studies except that different results are obtained. The instability indicator in our model refers to the changes in sales, and the positive relationship between firm performance and changes in sales suggests that increases in sales, rather than stable sales, contributes more to better firm performance. That is, firms experiencing a greater increase in sales revenue exhibit better performance.

The second reason, more importantly, comes from the essence of endogenous ownership theory, which is that the market environment affects the ownership structure. When the business environment is relatively volatile, decisions need to be made more quickly and flexibly in response to market fluctuations (Yeung, 2000). Our findings show that a higher ownership concentration is associated with a more unstable business environment, which is consistent with endogenous ownership theory and indicates that private firms have to adopt an appropriate corporate governance mechanism to changing business circumstances. That is, ownership shares should be concentrated in the hands of decision-makers of the firm, i.e., the owner and the manager, since the owner and the manager are usually not separated in most private firms. Therefore, our results do not contradict orthodox ownership theory, but rather extend it to reflect conditions in developing markets. The positive effect of ownership concentration (T1 and Management) on firm performance generally suggests that an overly dispersed ownership structure may not be the best way to improve the economic efficiency of Chinese private enterprises. In contrast, the findings show that it is better for a private firm (including family business) to combine ownership and control to improve firm performance. However, it is still worthwhile to test the role of family ownership on firm performance, which is what we do in the following section.

5.4.2 The relationship between firm performance and family shareholding together with management shareholding

In the second model, the dependent variable is the profit rate (AvPR), and the explanatory variables are family shareholding (Family), management shareholding (Management), and other control variables (Age, LnAsset, Instability). The results are reported in Table 5.6.

Table 5.6 The Relationship between Firm Performance Measured as Average Profit Rate (AvPR) and Family Shareholding (Family) together with Top Management Shareholding (Management)

OLS with robust standard errors	AvPR
Family	0.1073285
	(1.23)
Management	0.0811907[b]
	(2.34)
Age	0.1445348
	(0.33)
LnAsset	2.494881[b]
	(2.27)
Instability	0.0016789[a]
	(3.00)
Constant	-14.51778[c]
	(-1.81)
R^2	0.1193
F-statistic	7.85
P-value	0.000

Notes: a, b, c stand for significant at 1%, 5%, and 10% level respectively. t-statistics are in parentheses.

Contrary to our expectation, family shareholding jointly owned by the largest owner and all family members (Family) has an insignificant effect on firm performance in the OLS robust regression. This indicates that an increase in family ownership might not be beneficial to firm performance.

The fact that family controlled businesses represent the majority of Chinese private firms seems inconsistent with this result. In our sample of 296 firms, the family shares jointly owned by the largest owner and his/her family members increased to 92.87% by 2004 compared with 89.28% when starting as private businesses. However, this evidence should be viewed with caution. Firstly, the 3.59 percentage-point increases in family shares were a reflection of the increase in the single largest shareholder rather than an increase in the shares owned by his/her family members. In the sample of 296 firms, there was an increase of 3.73 percentage points in the single largest shareholder from 74.63% to 78.36%, as discussed in the previous section, while the shares owned by family members except the largest shareholder experienced a downward trend with a decrease of 0.14 percentage points from 14.65% to 14.51%. The second reason was that private businesses were established at different times. As discussed in Chapter 3, Zhejiang private enterprises have developed a more diffuse ownership structure in recent years. When establishing a limited liability company, family members are considered first because they provide cheap and flexible capital resources. Thirdly and more importantly, as discussed in the theoretical models in Chapter 4, owners and managers in family firms will act in the interests of the family and hence may give up good opportunities to increase the profits of the whole firm, thus weakening firm performance. The empirical result here is consistent with the argument in our theoretical models and with the wealth-expropriation argument by Faccio et al. (2001), as discussed in Section 5.3.1. This seems an accurate depiction of Chinese private enterprises when firms grow larger, particularly for private firms that are relatively large in the Zhejiang model (including Ningbo), as discussed in Chapter 3. However, the insignificant relationship between firm performance and family shareholding does indicate that some other factors such as the use of family trust (*Guanxi*) may not be well explained by the formal ownership structure. This is an issue that will be discussed further in Chapter 6.

The significant and positive relationship between top management shareholding (Management) and firm performance confirms the importance of management shareholding in improving firm performance. Firm size (LnAsset) and the changes in business environment (Instability) also have a significantly positive effect on firm performance, confirming the findings in the previous model.

However, firm age (Age) does not have a significant effect on firm performance in the second model, confirming the findings in the first model and running contrary to our expectation. On the face of it, this result implies that both old and young firms exhibit the same level of efficiency (or inefficiency) in Chinese private firms. A possible explanation for this result is that most private firms in the sample are young and they have relatively short histories, while other factors such as firm size and business instability might be more influential in determining firm performance.

5.4.3 Reverse Causality and Control for Growth Opportunities

The results presented in Tables 5.5 and 5.6 may suffer from the problem of reverse causality. Because performance improvements are anticipated by insiders, i.e., the largest shareholder (T_1), family members and management, reflecting their information advantage, insiders are able to increase their share-holding. Therefore, there is a need to address this possible problem.

5.4.3.1 The problem of reverse causality between firm performance and ownership variables

As shown in Table 5.7, the effects of firm performance (AvPR) on the single largest shareholder (T1), family shareholding (Family), and top management shareholding (Management) are statistically positive in the sample. The coefficients on these variables are significant at the 5%, 1%, and 1% level respectively. Thus, a problem of reverse causality exists between firm performance and the ownership variables in Tables 5.5 and 5.6.

5.4.3.2 Control for growth opportunities

To overcome the problem of reverse causality, a proxy for growth opportunities is introduced in Tables 5.5 and 5.6 in this subsection. For the example used here, growth opportunities (Growth) are defined as the average growth of sales revenue over the past three years prior to the survey, which is the same definition as in previous studies (see, for example, Chen, 2001).

Table 5.7 The Relationships between Ownership Variables (T1, Family, Management) and firm performance (AvPR)

OLS with robust standard errors	T1	Family	Management
Age	1.910242[a]	0.5552705[b]	1.709018[b]
	(6.00)	(2.07)	(2.52)
LnAsset	-4.24035[a]	-1.393015	5.316277[a]
	(-4.43)	(-1.40)	(3.27)
Instability	0.0004741	-0.0002566	-0.0009864[c]
	(1.08)	(-0.63)	(-1.82)
AvPR	0.1213123[b]	0.0871072[a]	0.20957[a]
	(2.14)	(3.11)	(3.00)
Constant	68.61531[a]	90.1982[a]	43.21927[a]
	(25.43)	(36.84)	(9.06)
Number of firms		296	
R^2	0.1791	0.0404	0.0934
F-statistic	18.99	4.21	9.55
P-value	0.0000	0.0025	0.0000

Notes: a, b, c stand for significant at 1%, 5%, and 10% level respectively. t-statistics are in parentheses.

In the empirical specifications reported in Table 5.8, the independent variables is the profit rate (AvPR), while the explanatory variables are the single largest shareholder (T1), family shareholding (Family), management shareholding (Management), growth opportunities (Growth), and other control variables (Age, LnAsset, Instability). The empirical specifications in Table 5.8 correspond to the models reported in Tables 5.5 and 5.6, respectively.

As shown, both the single largest shareholder (TI) and top management shareholding (Management) have a statistically significant positive coefficient in the first regression, which are significant at the 10% level, respectively. In the second model, while family shareholding (Family) has an insignificant effect on firm performance, the relationship between top management shareholding (Management) and firm performance is significantly positive (which is significant at the 10% level). Additionally, both firm size (LnAsset) and the instability of the business environment (Instability) have a significant effect on firm performance in these two regressions. In other words, even after introducing a proxy of growth

121

opportunities (Growth) in the regressions in Tables 5.5 and 5.6, the results in Table 5.8 are consistent with the findings reported in Tables 5.5 and 5.6 in the sample.

Table 5.8 The Relationships between Firm Performance and Ownership Variables by Control for Growth Opportunities (Growth)

OLS with robust standard errors	AvPR	
T1	0.1385819^c	
	(1.86)	
Family		0.1070568
		(1.23)
Management	0.0711119^c	0.0727299^c
	(1.68)	(1.65)
Growth	0.011298	0.0126145
	(1.13)	(1.25)
Age	0.0457702	0.2616412
	(0.10)	(0.59)
LnAsset	2.959583^a	2.531531^b
	(2.61)	(2.31)
Instability	0.0015496^a	0.0016538^a
	(2.77)	(2.96)
Constants	-15.00304^b	-15.35994^c
	(-2.55)	(-1.91)
Number of firms	296	296
R^2	0.1299	0.1241
F-statistic	7.19	6.82
P-value	0.0000	0.0000

Notes: a, b, c stand for significant at 1%, 5%, and 10% level respectively. t-statistics are in parentheses.

5.4.4 Robustness of the Results

An assumption of the analysis above in Tables 5.5 and 5.6 is that the specifications and proxies adequately capture the appropriate attributes. The results are also robust to an alternative measurement of firm performance, the return over sales (ROS) ratio, which is defined as the annual average rate of net profits to sales revenue over the three years prior to the survey. The results are reported in Table 5.9. In Table 5.9 each of the variables has the

122

same signs and similar statistical significance as those reported with AvPR as the measure of firm performance in Tables 5.5 and 5.6. In other words, the robust check confirms the findings as discussed in Sections 5.4.1 and 5.4.2.

Table 5.9 The Relationships between Firm performance Measured as Return over Sales (ROS) Ratio and Ownership Variables (T1, Family, and Management)

OLS with robust standard errors	ROS	
T1	0.1989445[b]	
	(2.35)	
Family		0.0062702
		(0.06)
Management	0.1959317[c]	0.2548592[a]
	(1.69)	(2.69)
Age	-0.1676201	-0.2168694
	(-0.31)	(-0.81)
LnAsset	2.130348[c]	1.997617[c]
	(1.66)	(1.65)
Instability	0.0018295[a]	0.0020031[a]
	(2.78)	(3.06)
Constants	-15.24921[b]	-24.67344[a]
	(-2.21)	(-2.65)
Number of firms	296	296
R^2	0.0805	0.0859
F-statistic	5.28	5.45
P-value	0.0002	0.0001

Notes: a, b, c stand for significant at 1%, 5%, and 10% level respectively. t-statistics are in parentheses.

5.5 The Determinants of Giving Ownership Shares to Management outside the Family

The empirical study in the previous section shows that ownership concentration of the single largest shareholder and top managers has an important role in firm performance, suggesting that family business, which characterized by high concentrated ownership and combination of ownership and control, is an optimal corporate governance to avoid the principal-agent problem. However, family business cannot completely rule out the principal-agent problem although it has certain advantages of reducing agency costs. The reasons are as follows. Firstly, even the managers and shareholders come from the same family, the interests of managers are not perfectly aligned with the interests of other family members and that of the whole family, and managers' interests are partly or completely driven by their self-interests (Morck et. al., 1998). In other words, perfect alignment is implausible in theory and impossible in practice. Secondary, the existence of economy of scale requires the use of agents (Demsetz, 1997),[74] and a private firm has to expand its scale in order to take advantages in competition when the firm grows at a certain stage. Thirdly, even in a firm with absolutely-dominate family shareholdings, the firm still need to recruit some managers outside the owner's family due to the advantages of specialization.

In practice, family managers might lack sufficient management skills, thus reducing the profitability of family firms. Barth et al. (2005) find that Norwegian family-owned firms are less productive than non-family-owned firms and attribute this finding to the skill-gap between family managers and outside professionals, which is consistent with Demsetz's (1997) argument about the specialization of agents. That is, firms owned and managed by a single person cannot be the optimal organization for most firms because specialization and scale can be productive, which usually requires the use of agents. By choosing a more diffuse ownership structure, owners are choosing to increase the agency cost they bear. However, this reduces the risk-weighted cost of capital to the firm, so that the total cost of operating the firm is not necessarily raised by greater agency cost (Demsetz, 1997). Therefore, family firms may recruit outside professionals to management. In many cases, the larger the firm size, the higher level of dependency on professionals outside the owner's family.

There are many studies discussing firm performance by classifying the managers of family firms into two groups, i.e., from the owner's family or outside the owner's family (see, for example, Anderson and Reeb, 2003; Barth et al., 2005). Given the fact that most Chinese private enterprises are characterized by family businesses and that there is a high degree of centralization of power in the hands of the owner (Schlevogt, 2001), this raises a question: under what conditions would the owner of the firm give ownership shares to its managers from outside the owner's family? To answer this question, we perform a probit model to examine the determinants of willingness to give ownership shares to management personnel outside the owner's family.

---

[74] Demsetz (1997) argues that the two main reasons to use agents are to take advantage of economies of scale and specialization.

5.5.1 The determinants of willingness to give ownership shares to professional managers outside the owner's family

In answering the question "Do you plan to give shares in the firm to management personnel other than family members?" (see Appendix 1), 141 owners answered "yes" while 155 owners answered "no," accounting respectively for 47.6% and 52.4% of the total 296 firms. In the probit model here, the dependent variable, i.e., the willingness to give ownership shares to managers outside the owner's family (GM), is a binary variable set equal to 1 if the answer is "yes" and set equal to zero otherwise. The control variables are family shareholding (Family), firm age (Age), firm size (LnAsset), the instability of the business environment (Instability), and the average profit rate (AvPR), which are defined as in Section 5.3. The results are reported in Table 5.10.

Conceptually, the proportion of family shareholding may be an important factor determining the willingness to give ownership shares to managers outside the owner's family. If the family holds a solid control position, it would grant ownership shares to hired managers without being concerned about losing control and would treat such share-granting as an incentive plan. In contrast, if the family's share proportion is at, or lower than, a certain critical point, it would not grant any shares to the hired managers simply because of the cost of losing control. This also indicates that the impact of the family's equity position is not linear and has a switch point. However, as shown in Table 5.10, the relationship between family shareholding and GM is statistically insignificant, indicating that the family's share position does not affect the willingness to give ownership shares to managers outside the owner's family. One possible explanation is that in the sample of 296 firms, there are 241 firms (including 97 solely-run enterprises) with a total family shareholding of 100%. This meant that there is a very high concentration of family ownership with the mean at 93%, as shown in Table 5.2. In other words, there is very little variation in the data to find a switch point for the impact of the family's equity position. This result reflects the lack of variation in the data collected.

Table 5.10 The Probit Regression for the Determinants of
Giving Ownership Shares to Management outside the Family (GM)

Probit regression	GM
Family	0.000609
	(0.14)
Age	0.0232396
	(1.03)
LnAsset	0.0691885
	(1.18)
Instability	0.0001283 [b]
	(2.20)
AvPR	-0.0192099 [b]
	(-2.46)
Constant	-0.29085
	(-0.68)
Number of firms	296
Log likelihood	-194.77082
Pseudo R^2	0.0492
LR chi2(5)	20.14
Prob>chi2	0.0012

Notes: a, b, c stand for significant at 1%, 5%, and 10% level respectively.
z-statistics are in parentheses.

The positive relationship between GM and the changes in business environment (Instability), which is significant at the 5% level, shows that the owners of the firm will be more likely to give shares to managers outside the family under conditions of increasing instability in the business environment, confirming the findings in the previous section. This result is consistent with the Demsetz (1983), Demsetz and Lehn (1985), and Demsetz and Villalonga (2001) studies.

Although they argue that there is no systematic relationship between management shareholding and firm performance, Demsetz and Villalonga (2001) point out that firm performance is at least as likely to affect ownership structure as ownership structure is to affect performance. This is also supported by the results in the probit model where there is a negative relationship between GM and firm performance (AvPR), which is significant at the 5% level, indicating that management shareholding is perceived by firm owners as a critical factor for better firm performance. In other words, when the firm performs worse, the owners will be more likely to give ownership shares to managers outside the family, thus strengthening managers' incentives to improve firm performance. This finding is consistent with the argument by Claessens and Djankov (1999) that profitability affects ownership structure in the Czech Republic, and with findings for Norwegian family firms by Barth et al. (2005) that professional managers are called for in difficult times while family owners enjoy maintaining control in good times or in good firms. Therefore, our second test of the willingness to give ownership shares to management outside the owner's family is also consistent with endogenous ownership theory.

5.5.2 The reasons for giving, or not giving, ownership shares to professional managers outside the owner's family

As discussed in Chapters 2 and 3, however, every ownership structure, including management shareholding, has both benefits and costs associated with different incentive effects. As shown in Table 5.11, of the 141 firms answering "yes" to giving professional managers ownership shares, most firms regarded "convergence of interests" as the main reason (42 firms, accounting for 29.8%). The second most popular response was that "manager(s) will be more responsible" (38 firms, accounting for 27%). These factors represent benefits of giving ownership shares to management, and hence increasing management shares as a corporate governance mechanism. On the other hand, of the 155 firms not giving management shares, the main reason was that "it would create disputes within the firm" (50 firms, accounting for 32.3%). The second most common reason was that it will be "hard to dismiss the manager(s) if they under-perform" (49 firms, accounting for 31.6%). These responses indicate the costs of giving management shares as a corporate governance mechanism.

Table 5.11 The Reasons for Giving, or Not Giving, Ownership Shares to Professional Management outside the Owner Family in the Survey Firms

Reasons	Giving Ownership Shares		Not Giving Ownership Shares	
	firms	proportion	firms	proportion
Total	141		155	
It facilitates a convergence of interests	42	29.80%		
Manager(s) will be more responsible	38	27.00%		
It shares the risk between owner(s) and manager(s)	17	12.00%		
It reduces managerial turnover	24	17.00%		
It improves decision making	20	14.20%		
The profits should be restricted to the owner(s)			16	10.30%
Concerned about the loyalty and capability of the manager(s)			16	10.30%
Paying a high salary is enough to motivate management			24	15.50%
Hard to dismiss the manager(s) if they under-perform			49	31.60%
It would create disputes within the firm			50	32.30%

5.6 Conclusion

The study of formal ownership structure as a corporate governance mechanism in Chinese private enterprises suggests that the importance of ownership structure is more complicated than previously understood. Ownership arrangements such as placing ownership concentration in the hands of the largest shareholder and management shareholding exhibit important effects on firm performance, which is consistent with agency theory. On the other hand, the economic environment is an important determinant of ownership arrangements, which is consistent with endogenous ownership theory. More precisely, the study in this chapter presents a combination of agency theory and endogenous ownership theory, as discussed in Chapter 4. In this sense, our study extends endogenous ownership theory to take into account the impact of the economic environment on ownership decisions. This extension has enabled us to study ownership structure and performance in a developing market such as China. In other words, it is better for the owners and managers of the firm to concentrate ownership given the volatile business environment in current China. This practice is very easy for most private enterprises whose size is relatively small. Therefore, the combination of ownership and control seems to be an inevitable tendency of corporate governance in private enterprises, which provides an explanation for family businesses constituting the majority of private firms.

There are two related empirical tests in this chapter, with the main purpose of examining the relationship between firm performance and formal ownership structure in Chinese private enterprises. The first test shows that not only does the distribution of ownership rights have an impact on firm performance, but also the type of large shareholders is an important determinant of firm performance. The increase in ownership concentration in the single largest shareholder and the increase in top management shareholding contributes to better firm performance. Thus, the combination of ownership and control is good for corporate governance in Chinese private firms, which provides an explanation for why the majority of Chinese private enterprises choose family business as a formal ownership structure. However, family shareholding does not have a significant effect on firm performance, requiring further research with respect to trust (*Guanxi*) in Chinese private firms. The second test in this chapter supplements the first by examining what determines whether firm owners give shares to professional managers. The results show that willingness to give ownership shares to outside professionals is negatively related to firm performance, confirming the effect of management shareholding on firm performance.

On the other hand, the market environment in China is characterized as relatively immature compared with the markets in developed countries. Such a business environment is important to understand corporate governance in private firms. However, we do not claim that the unstable business circumstances are beneficial to firm performance, but rather, the firms with better performance experience the greater increase in sales revenue. More importantly, the changes in business circumstances are a key factor to determine the ownership arrangements. That is, ownership shares should be concentrated in the hands of owners as well as managers in an unstable business environment, thus improving firm performance.

129

CHAPTER 6

The Determinants of the Importance of Government and Family Trust (*Guanxi*) in Chinese Private Enterprises

6.1 Introduction

Most Chinese private enterprises are best characterized as family businesses, as discussed in the previous chapters. The empirical results in Chapter 5 showed that the combination of ownership and control, particularly ownership concentration, in the hands of the single largest owner and top management, is beneficial for Chinese private enterprises. However, this kind of corporate governance practice has been criticized by some scholars as representing "poor corporate governance" (see, for example, Demsetz, 1983, 1997; Singh, 2003). If these ownership arrangements are in fact poor corporate governance, this seems to represent a contradiction, especially given China's impressive economic growth in recent decades. This argument, together with the empirical results in Chapter 5 which revealed the insignificant effect of family shareholding on firm performance, indicates that there may be other factors at play in Chinese private enterprises such as trust (*Guanxi*) which may not be well explained by orthodox ownership theory.

As discussed in Chapter 2, there are two important components of trust (*Guanxi*) in the literature on Chinese private enterprises. One subset of the literature emphasizes government trust (*Guanxi*) and the other emphasizes family trust (*Guanxi*). In the theoretical models developed in Chapter 4, the core argument was that the structure of Chinese private enterprises can be viewed as a form of trust-sharing (*Guanxi*-sharing), and that a Chinese private firm may prefer family trust (*Guanxi*) to government trust (*Guanxi*) as the primary vehicle for facilitating cooperation. To put the argument differently, the findings in Chapter 4 suggest that the dominance of family businesses in Chinese private enterprises is a result of not only the improvement in the economic environment, but also the tendency for family trust (*Guanxi*) to replace government trust (*Guanxi*) as the means of cooperation within the firm.

This chapter tests the core argument in the theoretical models in Chapter 4. In contrast to Sun and Wong's (2002) treatment of government and family trust (*Guanxi*) in Chinese private enterprises,[75] government trust (*Guanxi*) in

---

[75] See discussion in Section 2.3.3.3.

this study comprises both institutional and personal trust (*Guanxi*), as discussed in Chapter 2. Moreover, government and family trust (*Guanxi*) are examined separately in terms of firm characteristics such as firm age, firm size, and the instability of the business environment in the context of the gift economy in China.[76] Based on an analysis of a survey of 296 private firms administrated in the period from December 2005 to February 2006 in Ningbo, Zhejiang province, this chapter examines the determinants of the perceived importance of government and family trust (*Guanxi*) as well as the firm's preference for government or family trust (*Guanxi*). The econometric results in this chapter are supplemented with findings from a limited number of interviews with firm owners and managers that were conducted at the same time as the survey was administrated. With assistance from the Association of Ningbo's Private Enterprises, this researcher conducted in-depth interviews with four owners of private firms on the importance of government and family trust (*Guanxi*) in Chinese private enterprises.

The remainder of this chapter is organized as follows. Section 6.2 describes the data and gives the definitions of the variables used in the study, as well as discussing the econometric methodology. Section 6.3 presents the empirical results pertaining to the determinants of the perceived importance of government and family trust (*Guanxi*). The analysis indicates that the instability of the business environment has a significant and positive effect on the perceived importance of both government and family trust (*Guanxi*). In addition, firm size and gift-giving have positive effects on the perceived importance of government trust (*Guanxi*), while the age of the firm has a positive influence on the perceived importance of family trust (*Guanxi*). Section 6.4 discusses the factors which explain firm preference for government or family trust (*Guanxi*) in Chinese private enterprises. The results show that a private firm will choose family members for cooperation as the age of the firm and instability of the business environment increase. Conclusions are presented in Section 6.5.

6.2 Data Specification and Methodology

The main purpose of this chapter is to examine the determinants of the importance of government and family *Guanxi*, and to provide an explanation for the prevalence of family businesses among Chinese private enterprises. The analysis utilizes the same survey as used in the previous chapter and the data collection was the same as discussed in Section 5.2. The total sample of 296 firms included in the survey were generally representative of the basic

---

[76] Chinese *Guanxi*-based business practice has been called the "gift economy" (Yang, 1994). For further discussion see Section 6.2.1.

characteristics of privately-run enterprises in Ningbo as well as Zhejiang province, as discussed in Chapter 5. It is worth noting that although there were 20 firms with government shares within these 296 private firms when they started as private businesses, there was no government shareholding in the private enterprises in the sample at the time of the survey. That is, all firms in the sample have been completely privatized. However, this does not mean that government *Guanxi* is not important at all in contemporary China.

6.2.1 Empirical specification

In order to examine the determinants of the perceived importance of government and family *Guanxi* in Chinese private enterprises, we employed two ordered logit models as follows:

$$Gg \quad = \quad \alpha_g + \beta_{1g} Age + \beta_{2g} LnAsset + \beta_{3g} Instability + \beta_4 Gift + \mu_g$$

$$(1)$$

$$Gf = \alpha_f + \beta_{1f} Age + \beta_{2f} LnAsset + \beta_{3f} Instability + \mu_f$$

$$(2)$$

Gg and G_f in the above equations denote the importance of government *Guanxi* and family *Guanxi*, respectively, as perceived by private entrepreneurs.

Following previous studies of the determinants of *Guanxi* by Xin and Pearce (1996) and Lovett et al. (1999), the explanatory variables in our empirical models include firm age, firm size, and the instability of the business environment.[77] In addition, we also include a variable denoting "gift-giving" in the first model examining the determinants of government *Guanxi*. We do so because given Chinese *Guanxi*-based business practice has been called "the gift economy" (Yang, 1994), and gift-giving is critical to building and maintaining relationships with government officials. In gift-giving (*Songli*) an entrepreneur offers a material reward, which may take the form of money given in a red envelope (*Hongbao*) to government officials (Wank, 1996). However, the gift is not a fee-for-service bribe as they often are in other countries where import licenses or construction contracts have a well-known

---

[77] Xin and Pearce (1996) examine the determinants of *Guanxi* by controlling for firm age and firm size. Lovett et al. (1999) argue that changes in the business environment represent a determinant of *Guanxi*.

"price" (Xin and Pearce, 1996), because the gift is usually offered without an explicit demand for a return (Wank, 1996).[78] Instead, the practice of gift-giving provides the entrepreneur with an intangible future claim for the government official's support where the entrepreneur can call on the official's goodwill. Xin and Pearce (1996) further argue that private executives' expectations of cultivating connections with the government will be reflected in their gift-giving patterns, and find that private executives make more extensive use of gift-giving to build connections with the government than executives in state-owned enterprises (SOEs) and collective-owned companies (COEs). Indeed, gift-giving refers to building relationships with the government in much of the literature (Yang, 1994, 2002; Xin and Pearce, 1996; Wank, 1996; Guthrie, 1998). In these studies gift-giving is viewed as an effective vehicle for investing in *Guanxi* that can enhance bureaucratic support to protect private enterprises from the risks inherent in China's uncertain legal environment. For this reason we include the gift-giving variable as a determinant in the model of the perceived importance of government *Guanxi*. In contrast, family *Guanxi*, which is unusually strong and prevalent in Chinese private enterprises (Whyte, 1995; Xing, 1995; Schlevogt, 2001), is not affected by gift-giving patterns. On this basis, the gift-giving variable is measured by a question asking respondents whether they give gifts to government officials to build connections,[79] which is related directly to government *Guanxi*. In short, the gift-giving variable is included in the government *Guanxi* model, but not in the family *Guanxi* model.

6.2.2 Descriptive statistics

The descriptive statistics for each variable are reported in Table 6.1. The perceived importance of Government *Guanxi* to the firm and family *Guanxi* to the firm is respectively the dependent variable in the above two ordered logit models. In the first model, government *Guanxi* (Gg) is a variable measuring the perceived importance of government *Guanxi*; 1= "not helpful at all," 2= "relatively not helpful," 3= "neutral," 4= "relatively helpful," 5= "very helpful." In the second model, family *Guanxi* (Gf) is a variable measuring the perceived importance of family *Guanxi*; 1= "not helpful at all," 2= "relatively not helpful," 3= "neutral," 4= "relatively helpful," 5= "very helpful."

---

[78] This is not to say that straightforward bribery does not occur in China. In fact, the practice of gift-giving is remarkably reminiscent of bribery and corruption, which explains why *Guanxi* is easily mistaken for bribery or corruption, as discussed in Section 2.3.2.2.

[79] This question employed in the survey is the same as in Xin and Pearce's study (1996) (see Appendices for details).

The mean of government and family *Guanxi* were 3.79 and 3.80 respectively, indicating that government and family *Guanxi* were viewed by private firms in the sample as almost of equal importance. As a rough indicator, this result confirms the theoretical argument in Chapter 4 that proposed government and family *Guanxi* should be treated as being of equal importance in our mathematical models.

Table 6.1 Descriptive Statistics of the 296 Private Enterprises

Variable name	Description of variable	Means/Frequencies
Government	The importance of Gg on a 5-point scale	Mean=3.79 (SD=1.02)
Guanxi (Gg)	1=not helpful at all	Freq.=6 (2.03%)
	2=relatively not helpful	Freq.=31 (10.47%)
	3=neutral	Freq.=60 (20.27%)
	4=relatively helpful	Freq.=120 (40.54%)
	5=very helpful	Freq.=79 (26.69%)
Family *Guanxi*	The importance of Gf on a 5-point scale	Mean=3.80 (SD=0.96)
(Gf)	1=not helpful at all	Freq.=8 (2.70%)
	2=relatively not helpful	Freq.=19 (6.42%)
	3=neutral	Freq.=65 (21.96%)
	4=relatively helpful	Freq.=136 (45.95%)
	5=very helpful	Freq.=68 (22.97%)
Age (Years)	Years registered as a private firm	Mean=6.45 (SD=3.33)
LnAsset	Natural log of average gross assets over the past three years (million RMB)	Mean=0.80 (SD=1.57)
Instability (%)	Standard deviation of sales over the past three years	Mean=630.69 (SD=2956.84)
Gift-giving (Gift)	A binary dummy variable where 1=giving gifts to government officials to build connections, 0 otherwise	21.28% (63 firms) of the total were giving gifts to government officials to build connections

The independent variables used to explain the perceived importance of government and family *Guanxi* are as follows:

1) *Firm age (Age)*. This variable denotes length of time between when the firm registered as a private enterprise and the date of the survey. As shown in Table 6.1, the average age of firms in the sample was six years at the end of 2004, indicating that most private firms were established after the commencement of ownership reform of COEs and SOEs in 1997, and after

the recognition of private enterprises in the Chinese Constitution in 1999.

Generally speaking, *Guanxi* as reputation capital requires an investment of time (Lovett et al., 1999; Standifird et al., 1999), and becomes stronger when the time passes. However, firm age can also be an indicator to denote changes in the business environment. As proposed by North (1990), when economic exchanges are simple, informal arrangements such as tradition, religious morals and ritual are sufficient to sustain stable structures for human interaction. However, as complexity increases, tradition no longer suffices. In the context of *Guanxi*-based business practices in China, Guthrie (1998) and Li (2002) further argue that the significance of *Guanxi* is declining due to the development of a rational-legal system and the evolution of increasingly competitive markets (Li, 1998; Gregory et al., 2000; Singh, 2003). The theoretical considerations in Chapter 4 follow this argument; that is, the importance of both government and family *Guanxi* is decreasing as the economic environment improves. Most private firms in the sample were established recently in a relatively improved market environment compared with that in the early reform period, seemingly suggesting that the significance of both government and family *Guanxi* has declined in contemporary China. However, our theoretical models in Chapter 4 further suggest that government *Guanxi* is being replaced by family *Guanxi* in private enterprises, implying that the importance of government and family *Guanxi* would be viewed differently by private firms. More precisely, because government connections allowed many firms that were actually private-owned enterprises in Zhejiang province (including Ningbo) to register as "red-hat" firms in the early reform period (Wank, 1996; Sun, 2000, 2002), old firms seem more likely to regard government *Guanxi* as more important than young firms. On the other hand, most firms in the sample were family businesses, as discussed in Section 5.2.2, and they were newly-established, which seems to suggest that young firms view the importance of family *Guanxi* as more important than old firms. Therefore, we expect that old firms are more likely to regard government *Guanxi* as more important while young firms are more likely to regard family *Guanxi* as more important.

2) *Firm size (LnAsset)*. This variable is measured by the natural logarithm of annual average total assets over the past three years.

Standifird and Marshall (2000) argue that the key factors in determining a *Guanxi*-based network's level include network size and scope, and that the transaction costs associated with the *Guanxi* network decrease as network size and scope increase. In other words, there are economies of scale and scope to the development of *Guanxi* networks. Following this argument, firm size, which can be an indicator of network size and scope, would have a positive relationship with the level of the *Guanxi* network. However, this view does not show the influence of firm size on the perceived importance of *Guanxi*.

Wank (1996) argues that firm size is irrelevant to government *Guanxi* because Chinese pursue business in networks rather than as part of corporate strategies, in which profits are not reinvested in existing firms, but into new firms linked to the parent firm through overlapping kinship ties of management and ownership. This creates business groups that embody sizeable investments, even though the size of any one member firm is small. Xin and Pearce (1996) also find that the size of Chinese private firms does not affect the importance of government *Guanxi*. This is because government *Guanxi* plays different roles in private enterprises, where large firms rely more on government trust to enhance their credibility within society and with banks while smaller firms often seek government protection against various kinds of tax and administrative fees (Sun and Wong, 2002). However, capital stock is critical to the development of Chinese private enterprises, as discussed in the previous chapters. Sun and Wong (2002) point out that due to the small size of most private firms, few people would have enough funds, either from their own savings or from borrowing from family members and friends, to start an enterprise. Thus enterprises have to rely heavily on government and banks in accessing capital for their development. This consideration would suggest that large firms would be more likely to regard government *Guanxi* as more important than small firms. As discussed in Chapter 3, although most Zhejiang private enterprises have evolved from the primitive accumulation of non-governmental capital, the government has played an important role in the Zhejiang model, particularly with respect to "red-hat" enterprises (Sun, 2000, 2002).[80] As many Zhejiang private enterprises have recently developed into large enterprises, they would perceive government *Guanxi* to be important in accessing capital resources because private resources are relatively limited compared with governments and banks (Sun and Wong, 2002) and the capital market in contemporary China is still immature, as discussed in Chapter 3. Therefore, we expect that large firms in the sample would be more likely to regard government *Guanxi* as more important.

---

[80] In the modelling in Chapter 4, the role of government *Guanxi* played in Chinese private enterprises includes both "protection" and "procurement ability" (Tian, 2000) such as obtaining necessary information and materials for the production process. The "red-hat" phenomenon is representative of the use of government *Guanxi* in Chinese private enterprises in the early reform period.

For family *Guanxi*, which is unusually strong in Chinese private firms (Whyte, 1995; Xing, 1995), Schlevogt (2001) finds that the decision for private firms to remain small is due to the greater emphasis on family *Guanxi*. In other words, the decision to stay small is motivated by the desire to maintain personal relationships with important shareholders (especially other respected and trusted family members) and avoid the inclusion of outsiders, who are viewed with suspicion and distrust. According to Schlevogt (2001), this is a major reason why Chinese private enterprises keep business within the family. Following this argument, small private firms are more likely to regard family *Guanxi* as more important than large firms.

3) *Instability of the business environment (Instability)*. This variable is defined as the standard deviation of changes in sales revenue over the past three years. As shown in Table 6.1, the instability indicator in the sample was quite large with a mean of 631, indicating that markets in China are volatile, as discussed in Chapter 5.

Fligstein (1996) argues that an ineffective or non-facilitative government such as in many developing countries creates an environment characterized by greater uncertainty, and more political and financial risk for independent organizations. In these circumstances, *Guanxi* can be used to reduce the transaction costs associated with environmental uncertainties and to improve efficiency (Lovett et al., 1999; Standifird and Marshall, 2000), particularly in a situation where the haphazard enforcement of laws by state agents is a major source of uncertainty (Wank, 1996). Greater business instability seems to be associated with greater need for both government *Guanxi* (Peace, 2001; Rao et al., 2005) and family *Guanxi* (Yeung, 2000; Schlevogt, 2001). Therefore, we expect a positive relationship in the sample between the instability of the business environment and the perceived importance of both government and family *Guanxi*.

The above three explanatory variables (Age, LnAsset, Instability) are the same as in the previous econometric models in Chapter 5. They are used here not only to examine whether they affect the importance of government and family *Guanxi*, but also to establish the links between the use of *Guanxi* and formal ownership structure with respect to these three firm characteristics.

4) Respondents were asked "Do you give gifts to government officials in order to build connections?" (see Appendix 1) Gift-giving (Gift) is a binary variable set equal to 1 if firms responded that they give gifts to government officials in order to build connections; set equal to zero otherwise. There were 63 firms who reported that they gave gifts to government officials to

138

build connections, accounting for 21.28% of the total 296 firms. As discussed above, in the context of the gift economy in China and given the general expectation that gift-giving will cultivate connections (Xin and Pearce, 1996; Wank, 1996), a positive relationship between gift-giving and the perceived importance of government *Guanxi* is expected. In the model examining the factors determining the importance of government *Guanxi*, we will employ a Hausman specification error test to examine whether gift-giving is endogenous. If gift-giving is found to be endogenous a structural equation will be estimated after substituting estimates of the endogenous variable.[81]

6.2.3 Econometric methodology

To examine the determinants of the perceived importance of government and family *Guanxi* in the two ordered logit models, we take into account multicollinearity, heteroskedasticity, and possible endogeneity of the gift-giving variable.

6.2.3.1 Multicollinearity and heteroskedasticity

As shown in Table 6.2, there is no simple correlation in the sample between any two variables in excess of 0.6, which means that multicollinearity is not a concern and does not require any remedy (Gujarati, 1995).

Table 6.2 Correlation Matrix

	Gg	Gf	Age	LnAsset	Instability	Gift
Gg	1.0000					
Gf	0.0414	1.0000				
Age	-0.0281	0.1285	1.0000			
LnAsset	0.2380	0.1796	-0.0789	1.0000		
Instability	0.1913	0.1924	-0.0569	0.5008	1.0000	
Gift	0.1545	-0.0384	0.0033	0.1054	0.0900	1.0000

However, heteroskedasticity may be a problem in models employing cross-sectional data, with firms with large differences in size and in variance of sales, as shown in Table 6.1. In order to avoid the potential problem of

---

[81] Lee (1979) has shown that the resulting parameter estimates from this procedure in models with limited (censored) dependent are consistent if the structural equation is identified exactly. For a recent application to the determinants of support for marketization in Russia, see Clark et al. (2003).

heteroskedasticity in the sample, we employed a robust technique with White's heteroskedastic consistent z-statistics in both ordered logit models.

6.2.3.2 Is gift-giving endogenous in the model of government *Guanxi?*

We employed Hausman's specification error test to examine whether the gift-giving variable is endogenous in the government *Guanxi* model. The test is reported in Table 6.3, where model (b) refers to the government *Guanxi* model without the gift-giving variable and model (B) refers to the government *Guanxi* model with the gift-giving variable. Our diagnostic testing shows that the difference in coefficients between models (b) and (B) fits the asymmetric assumptions, indicating that the coefficients in the government *Guanxi* model with the gift-giving variable are consistent and efficient. Therefore, gift-giving is not an endogenous variable in the government *Guanxi* model.

Table 6.3 Hausman's Specification Test for Gift-Giving

	Coefficients			
	(b) partial	(B) all	(b-B) Difference	sqrt(diag(V_b-V_B)) s.e.
Age	-0.006801	-0.0071415	0.0003406	0.0019216
LnAsset	0.2016485	0.1949353	0.0067131	0.0182806
Instability	0.0001773	0.0001732	4.09e-06	0.0000147
Test	Ho: difference in coefficients not systematic			
	chi2(3) = (b-B)'[(V_b-V_B)^(-1)](b-B)			
	=	0.21		
	Prob>chi2 =	0.9754		
Result	Do not reject Ho			

Notes: b = consistent under Ho and Ha; obtained from ologit.
B = inconsistent under Ha, efficient under Ho; obtained from ologit.

6.3 Empirical Results for the Determinants of the Perceived Importance of Government and Family *Guanxi*

6.3.1 What explains the perceived importance of government *Guanxi*?

6.3.1.1 The determinants of government *Guanxi*

In the first ordered logit model, the perceived importance of government *Guanxi* is the dependent variable and the explanatory variables are firm age (Age), firm size (LnAsset), the instability of the business environment (Instability), and gift-giving (Gift). The results are reported in Table 6.4.

Table 6.4 The Determinants of the Importance
of Government *Guanxi* (Gg)

Ordered logistic regression with robust standard errors	Gg
Age	-0.0071415
	(-0.20)
LnAsset	0.1949353[b]
	(2.28)
Instability	0.0001732[a]
	(3.58)
Gift	0.5954213[b]
	(2.50)
Number of firms	296
Log pseudolikelihood	-386.50838
Pseudo R^2	0.0380
Wald chi2(4)	43.05
Prob>chi2	0.0000

Notes: a, b, c stand for significant at 1%, 5%, 10% level respectively. z-statistics are in parentheses.

Firm age (Age) has an insignificant effect on the perceived importance of government *Guanxi*, contradicting our expectation that old firms are more likely to regard government *Guanxi* as more important than young firms. Instead, this finding suggests that the importance of government *Guanxi* does not decrease in newly-established private enterprises. An explanation for this

141

result is that the owner/manager of the firm may be a cadre entrepreneur, i.e., a former government official (Wank, 1996; Sun and Wong, 2002), who may have pre-existing *Guanxi* capital before the establishment of the firm. These firms may attach importance to government *Guanxi*. More importantly, this result can be explained by the enduring strength of government *Guanxi* due to its deep embeddedness in Chinese culture (Granovetter, 1985), which is consistent with the argument that traditional culture is difficult to change (North, 1990; Weitzman and Xu, 1994). In this manner, it can be argued that the significance of government *Guanxi* has not diminished in contemporary China, as some researchers have suggested (see, for example, Yang, 1994, 2002; Xin and Pearce, 1996; Standifird and Marshall, 2000).[82]

The positive relationship between firm size (LnAsset) and the perceived importance of government *Guanxi*, which is significant at the 5% level, suggests that large firms care more about government *Guanxi* than small firms. That is, although many small firms may seek more government protection against tax and administrative fees, firms perceive government *Guanxi* as important in obtaining financial resources. This reflects the fact that capital stock is critical to their development (Gregory et al., 2000; Sun and Wong, 2002). This result is also consistent with the argument that their larger scale and scope place these firms in a better position to initiate larger projects, and that these larger-scale projects are often much more attractive to the government and to banks (Guthrie, 1998). This result also reflects the incentive of private firms to seek more capital resources, as discussed in Chapter 5. This is because the larger the firms, the better the development of their *Guanxi* network (Standifird and Marshall, 2000), and hence it is easier for them to get support from the government.

To obtain closer connections with the government, Sun and Wong (2002) suggest that private firms need to take the initiative in getting involved in government-sponsored projects such as the "Hope Project" and the "Glorious Program." [83] This may generate, as Wank (1996) put it, "mutual understanding" or "mutual concern" between the government and private

---

[82] For example, Standifird and Marshall (2000) argue that *Guanxi*-based business practices offer certain transaction cost advantages over existing structural alternatives identified in transaction cost theory. Even with the transformation to a more market-based economy, the enduring strength of *Guanxi* lies in conducting moderately asset specific activities such as long-term supplier relationships for industrial machinery. These types of exchanges will continue to be performed via the *Guanxi* network whereas less asset-specific functions, such as equipment leasing, will be performed through market-based exchange.

[83] The objective of the "Hope Project" is to improve basic education in remote villages while the objective of the "Glorious Program" is to develop western China. They are both organized by the Chinese government.

firms. Therefore, the finding here poses a concern that how the government treats equally most private firms that are of small size, particularly for providing financial support. The difficulty that small firms face in getting assistance from the government was emphasized in some interviews in the survey. For example, an owner of one private firm stated:

> "Every enterprise has to establish all kinds of links with the government. In so doing, besides considering our business interests we are also seeking some kind of protection from the government, particularly before the recognition of private firms by the government in the early reform period. However, we have many difficulties in communicating with the government, as in the old saying 'we present the pig-head but the temple does not accept it' (*Tizhezhutoumeimiaojin*).[84] That is, the government does not really care about us." (Personal interview in Ningbo, 2005)

The instability of the business environment (Instability) has a strongly positive effect on the perceived importance of government *Guanxi*, which is significant at the 1% level, confirming our expectation. This result is consistent with the findings in many studies as discussed above (see, for example, Xin and Pearce, 1996; Wank, 1996; Rao et al., 2005), as well as the argument in Chapter 4 that it is better for private firms to use government *Guanxi* in a developing market such as China, where government *Guanxi* is a necessary input in the firm's production process.

The positive effect of gift-giving (Gift) on the perceived importance of government *Guanxi*, which is significant at the 5% level, means that those firms who give gifts to government officials to build connections are statistically more likely to regard government *Guanxi* as being more important. This confirms our expectation.

6.3.1.2 The usefulness of government *Guanxi*

Government *Guanxi* was viewed as quite useful by private firms during the interviews. For example, an owner-manager of one private firm stated:

> "Government *Guanxi* matters for getting things done in our business. In the past we relied on government *Guanxi* to obtain some kinds of advantage such as material needs. Nowadays, a good relationship with the government can enhance business in the market because the government still dominates almost every aspect of our business. At

---

[84] In this expression, the "pig-head" refers to gifts and favours while the "temple" refers to authorities such as the government.

present the importance of government *Guanxi* may decline in some social domains, but flourish in new areas ..." (Personal interview in Ningbo, 2005)

This statement illustrates that government *Guanxi* is considered important in private enterprises. With respect to the roles played by government *Guanxi* for private enterprises, another manager of a green-field private firm stated:

"Government *Guanxi* is very important everywhere in China because the government controls state contracts, banks loans, access to imports, favourable tax incentives, access to valuable market information, exemptions from troublesome laws and regulations, and so on ... We hope, however, that we can do our business relying on market rules instead of the government." (Personal interview in Ningbo, 2005)

This view is supported in the survey in response to the question: "what is the main role that the government has been playing and the role that you expect the government will play in the future within your firm?" (see Appendix 1). The results are reported in Table 6.5. As shown, 59 firms, accounting for 19.9% of the sample, reported that the most important role for government *Guanxi* was to facilitate "access to financial resources." This result supports the argument by Sun and Wong (2002) that the government is important in providing the foundations for institutional trust for private firms, particularly in accessing bank loans. Overall 57 firms, accounting for 19.3% of the sample, viewed government *Guanxi* as most important for "protection." This result confirms the argument that the government supports the institutional innovations of the Zhejiang model, as discussed in Chapter 3, where the first innovation of the Zhejiang model was the practice of "wearing a red hat" during the period from the late 1970s to the mid-1980s. The second innovation was the formation of joint-stock cooperatives from the mid-1980s to the mid-1990s, and the third was the practice of limited liability companies or joint-stock companies that occurred from the late 1990s. Particularly in the early reform period, local governments allowed private entrepreneurs to register their firms as "collectives," thus releasing them from the restrictions placed on private firms (Wank, 1996; Sun, 2000, 2002). As discussed in Chapter 5, there were 63 private firms in the sample transferred from "collectives," accounting for 92.7% of the total 68 transferred firms. Most of these collectives had been "red-hat" firms that had taken off their "red hats" since the ownership reform policy in 1997, meaning that there were no "red-hat" firms in the survey.

Table 6.5 The Usefulness of Government *Guanxi* in Private Firms

	Freq.	Percent	Cum.
Protection	57	19.26	19.26
Market access	38	12.84	32.09
Tax preference	51	17.23	49.32
Assess to financial resources	59	19.93	69.26
Technological support and services	91	30.74	100.00
Total	296	100.00	

Altogether 91 firms, accounting for 30.7% of the sample, reported that the most important role for government *Guanxi* was to provide "technological support and services." These responses relate to one of the indirect roles of government trust (*Guanxi*), i.e., improving the overall economic environment, as discussed in Chapter 2. In fact, it has been argued that along with the market-oriented reforms in China, government *Guanxi* has moved away from the acquisition of consumer goods and the provision of everyday needs. However, it has flourished in the realm of business and the urban-industrial sphere, whether in dealings among private entrepreneurs or between private entrepreneurs and local officials (Yang, 2002). Since the role played by the government in private enterprises may have changed, this result also reflects the expectations of Chinese private enterprises with respect to the role played by the government. This result is consistent with the argument by Sun (2000, 2002) that the role of the government should be to withdraw from direct involvement in a firm's economic activities.

6.3.2 What explains the perceived importance of family *Guanxi*?

6.3.2.1 The determinants of family *Guanxi*

In the second ordered logit model, the dependent variable is the perceived importance of family *Guanxi* and the explanatory variables are firm age (Age), firm size (LnAsset), and the instability of the business environment (Instability). The results are reported in Table 6.6. The instability of the business environment (Instability) has a positive effect on the perceived importance of family *Guanxi*, which is significant at the 5% level, confirming our expectation. This finding is consistent with other studies discussed above (see, for example, Lovett et al., 1999; Yeung, 2000).

145

Table 6.6 The Determinants of the Importance of Family *Guanxi* (Gf)

Ordered logistic regression with robust standard errors	Gf
Age	0.0920613[a]
	(2.72)
LnAsset	0.1304204
	(1.52)
Instability	0.0001731[b]
	(2.49)
Number of firms	296
Log pseudolikelihood	-371.49164
Pseudo R^2	0.0360
Wald chi2(3)	19.84
Prob>chi2	0.0002

Notes: a, b, c stand for significant at 1%, 5%, 10% level respectively. z-statistics are in parentheses.

There are two empirical results that contradict our expectations. First, firm age (Age) has a strongly positive effect on the perceived importance of family *Guanxi*, which is significant at the 1% level, indicating that old firms are more likely to regard family *Guanxi* as being more important than young firms. This finding seems to suggest that the significance of family *Guanxi* decreases in newly-established private firms. However, this finding should be viewed with caution. Since most firms in the sample were young and family *Guanxi* presumably predates the establishment of private firms, these firms may be less likely to view family *Guanxi* as important because it is less necessary for them to evoke *Guanxi* practices within the family due to the inherently close connections (Guthrie, 1998). Instead, the result shows that family *Guanxi* is given more importance by private firms as firm age increases. This result differs from the finding for government *Guanxi*, as discussed above, which implies that old private firms regard family *Guanxi*

146

as more important than government *Guanxi*. This result will be further analysed in Section 6.4 below where firm preferences for family versus government *Guanxi* are examined.

Second, firm size (LnAsset) has an insignificant effect on the perceived importance of family *Guanxi*, indicating that small firms do not view family *Guanxi* as more important than large firms. This result does not support the argument by Schlevogt (2001) that stronger family *Guanxi* leads Chinese private firms to stay small. Instead, it suggests that due to the prevalence of family-based values, private firms may grow larger while keeping the strength of family relationships (Yeung, 2000). This finding is consistent with the argument in Chapter 5 that agency costs do not increase when Chinese private enterprises grow larger because family relationships can be used to improve monitoring and to provide incentives to reduce agency costs.

6.3.2.2. The Usefulness of family *Guanxi*

Family *Guanxi* was viewed as very useful in private firms during the interviews. For example, an owner of one green-field private firm stated:

> "Family relationships are the core of the moral system defined by traditional Confucius thought. For my business, my family has been a reliable source of cheap and flexible capital and labour, particularly in the business start-up phase. However, this is not the end of family *Guanxi*. In fact, family *Guanxi* enables me to embrace others who may assist my business ... My firm faced a threat of serious 'punishment' several years ago for a tax infringement, but one of my father's friends [working in the government] intervened and we only received a minimal level of 'punishment' ..." (Personal interview in Ningbo, 2005)

Indeed, it has been shown in many studies that family *Guanxi* is important for the development of Chinese private firms (see, for example, Schlevogt, 2001; Gan, 2002), particularly in providing cheap and flexible resources, and in extending network resources (Sun and Wong, 2002). This view is supported in the survey in responses to the question: "what is the main role that family members have been playing or will play in your firm?" (see Appendix 1). The results are reported in Table 6.7.

Table 6.7 The Usefulness of Family *Guanxi* in Private Firms

	Freq.	Percent	Cum.
Provide cheap/flexible resources	152	51.35	51.35
Manage financial affairs	7	2.36	53.72
Assist in decision making	62	20.95	74.66
Extend network resources	74	25.00	99.66
Build up family reputation	1	0.34	100.00
Total	296	100.00	

Overall 152 firms reported that the most important role of family *Guanxi* was to "provide cheap and flexible resources such as capital and labour," accounting for 51.4% of the sample. This was a major reason why family businesses account for the majority of private firms, and also the fact that most firms are small because private resources are relatively limited compared with those of the government and banks (Sun and Wong, 2002). However, this view implies that it is easy for private entrepreneurs to get help from their family members. In addition, 74 firms, accounting for 25% of the sample, considered that the most important role of family *Guanxi* was to "extend the firm's network of connections outside the firm." This supports the argument that although family-centred, family *Guanxi* is an important avenue to extend networks of the firm (Sun and Wong, 2002). Altogether 62 firms, accounting for 21% of the sample, considered that the most important role of family *Guanxi* was to "assist in decision making within the firm," so that family relationships can be used to reduce agency costs, as discussed in the previous chapters.

6.4 Private Firms' Preference for Government or Family *Guanxi*

The empirical results in the previous section showed that there is a significant and positive effect of business instability on the perceived importance of both government and family *Guanxi*, confirming the argument in Chapter 4 that both government and family *Guanxi* are important for Chinese private firms in a relatively imperfect market environment. However, the differences are notable between government and family *Guanxi* in private firms with respect to firm age and firm size. To examine the decision whether to choose government or family *Guanxi* for cooperation in terms of firm characteristics in Chinese private enterprises, a probit model was employed to test which factors explain the firm's *Guanxi* preference. The results of this model can be used to predict preference for government or family *Guanxi* in private firms.

6.4.1 Description of the model

6.4.1.1 The dependent variable

Respondents were asked the question: "would you prefer to cooperate with government or family members in your firm?" (see Appendix 1). The dependent variable is a binary variable set equal to 1 if the firm prefers government for cooperation and set equal to zero if the firm prefers to cooperate with family members. In the sample 135 firms chose the government and 161 firms chose family members for cooperation, accounting for 45.6% and 54.4% respectively of the total 296 firms.

6.4.1.2 The independent variables

The independent variables are firm age (Age), firm size (LnAsset), the instability of the business environment (Instability), and gift-giving (Gift), which were defined in Section 6.3.2. Based on the analysis in the previous ordered logit models, these variables may have different effects on the firm's *Guanxi* preference. In concrete terms, because firm age has a significantly positive effect on the importance of family *Guanxi* without statistically affecting the importance of government *Guanxi*, this suggests that old firms would prefer family members for cooperation more than young firms. Firm size positively affects the importance of government *Guanxi* but it does not have a significant influence on the importance of family *Guanxi*, suggesting that large firms would prefer government for cooperation more than small firms. The instability of the business environment has a more significantly positive effect on the importance of government *Guanxi* than the importance of family *Guanxi*, suggesting that firms in a more volatile business environment will prefer government for cooperation. Because gift-giving has a positive effect on the importance of government *Guanxi*, a positive relationship between gift-giving and the preference for government would be expected in the sample.

149

6.4.2 Regression results

In contrast to the previous ordered logit models where government and family *Guanxi* were examined separately, in this model firms have to make a trade-off between government and family *Guanxi* for cooperation. In other words, although government and family *Guanxi* are regarded as important in private firms, a private firm may prefer one over another if the firm has a choice. This is because government and family *Guanxi* differ in terms of trustworthiness, as well as their effect on the firm's economic activities which represent respectively the separation or combination of ownership and control in terms of corporate governance, as discussed in Chapter 2. Given these two options, the empirical results of the probit model of the firm's preference for government or family *Guanxi* are directly opposite. The results are reported in Table 6.8, where the positive coefficients indicate a preference for government and the negative coefficients refer to a preference for family members.

The negative coefficient on firm age (Age), which is significant at the 5% level, is consistent with our expectation. The result indicates that young firms prefer government for cooperation while old firms prefer family members for cooperation. For newly-established private firms, however, although the significance of government *Guanxi* might not diminish in a transitional economy, as discussed above, cooperation with the government is not facilitated by improvement in the economic environment. [85] More importantly, the finding suggests that private firms will prefer family *Guanxi* over government *Guanxi* for cooperation as the firm's age increases. This is true even for those firms who experienced the early reform period containing the "red-hat" phenomenon in which the government had played an important role. In this sense, the importance of government *Guanxi* is declining relative to family *Guanxi* in private firms.

---

[85] For example, due to the development of a rational-legal system and the evolution of increasingly competitive markets in China (Li, 1998; Gregory et al., 2000; Singh, 2003), cooperation with the government is restricted by policies such as ownership reform, which require the government to withdraw from direct involvement in the firm's economic activities (Sun, 2000, 2002).

Table 6.8 Probit Regression of Firm Preference for Government or Family
Guanxi on Control Variables (Age, LnAsset, Instability, Gift)

Probit regression with robust standard errors	Firm's *Guanxi* Preference
Age	-0.0541167[b]
	(-2.40)
LnAsset	-0.0468863
	(-0.77)
Instability	-0.0006551[b]
	(-2.39)
Gift	0.2897219
	(1.53)
Constant	0.3389908[b]
	(1.96)
Number of firms	296
Log pseudolikelihood	-190.78767
Pseudo R^2	0.0649
Wald chi2(4)	16.20
Prob>chi2	0.0028

Notes: a, b, c stand for significant at 1%, 5%, 10% level respectively. z-statistics are in parentheses.

Firm size, which has a significant positive effect on the importance of government *Guanxi*, does not statistically affect the firm's preference for government or family members. In other words, firm size is not a factor determining the firm's *Guanxi* preference. While large firms care more about government *Guanxi* than small firms because government *Guanxi* is very useful in accessing financial resources, as discussed in the previous section, small and large private firms have the same preference for cooperation with either the government or family. This reflects the importance of family *Guanxi* in private firms (Whyte, 1995; Xing, 1995; Schlevogt, 2001), even for those firms which have grown larger in size (Yeung, 2000). This implies that a private firm might choose family members for cooperation after obtaining capital assets from the government, which sets the government in an embarrassing situation in private firms.

The instability of the business environment (Instability) has a negative sign in the probit model, which is significant at the 5% level, contradicting our expectation. The result indicates that government is chosen in a relatively stable business environment compared with family members who are chosen in a relatively unstable business environment. Because government and family *Guanxi* represent separation or non-separation of ownership and control in private firms, as discussed in Chapters 2 and 4, this finding is consistent with the argument that because of family *Guanxi*-based inter-organization networks, decision making in family firms is more efficient and flexible than in firms managed by professional managers in responding to environmental changes (Yeung, 2000). This result does not deny the important role played by the government in a volatile business environment, but rather suggests that in a more volatile business environment firms need to have a more rapid response to changing market conditions in order to ensure better firm performance,[86] and this may be realized more effectively if ownership and control are not separated. In other words, due to the relative difficulty of monitoring an agent's performance in a more volatile business environment, the owner of the firm will prefer to exercise control to ensure that his or her interest is protected.[87] The result is consistent with the empirical findings in Chapter 5, which indicates that a private firm should adopt an appropriated corporate governance mechanism in the volatile business environment where the combination of ownership and control is the most efficient one.

Gift-giving (Gift) does not have a statistically significant effect on the firm's *Guanxi* preference, meaning that firms who give gifts to government officials to build connections do not statistically prefer cooperation with the government. That is, gift-giving is not a determinant of preference for government *Guanxi* although it positively affects the importance of government *Guanxi* in China's gift economy. This finding is consistent with the argument that the gift is usually offered without an explicit demand for a return (Xin and Pearce, 1996; Wank, 1996), especially if the cooperation with government is viewed as the result of the exchange.

6.4.3 Firm preference for family *Guanxi* or government *Guanxi*

The above analysis in the probit model showed that young firms are more likely to choose the government for cooperation in a relatively stable

---

[86] The empirical results in Chapter 5 showed that private firms experiencing a greater increase in sales perform better.

[87] As discussed in Chapter 4, the owner-manager of family business acts in the interests of family members.

business environment while old firms prefer family members for cooperation in a relatively volatile business environment. These two significant factors, firm age and the instability of the business environment, which affect the firm's *Guanxi* preference, are consistent with the findings for the determinations of the perceived importance of family *Guanxi* in the previous ordered logit model. That is, as firm age increases in a relatively volatile business environment, a private firm is more likely to regard family *Guanxi* as more important and hence prefer family members to government for facilitating cooperation. To put this argument differently, the findings in the firm's *Guanxi* preference model indicate that in the currently immature market environment in China, as discussed in the previous chapters, although a newly-established private firm prefers government for cooperation, the firm will choose family members for cooperation as firm age increases. In this sense, government *Guanxi* is replaced by family *Guanxi* in facilitating cooperation in private firms, confirming the core argument of Chapter 4.

In addition, relating to the different effects of government and family trust (*Guanxi*) on a firm's economic activities, reliability or loyalty have been emphasized in many studies of corporate governance in private firms (see, for example, James, 1999; Lovett et al., 1999; Yeung, 2000; Schlevogt, 2001; Gan, 2002; Sun and Wong, 2002). The following statement by one owner-manager is representative of many Chinese private enterprises:

> "To be honest, the practice in my firm is to promote those who are loyal, and to use those who are capable. In other words, the loyal will supervise the capable, and not the other way around." (Personal interview in Ningbo, 2005)

Although this statement does not clearly refer to the government or to family members, the distinction between government and family trust (*Guanxi*) is reflected in its essence. As discussed in Chapter 2, family *Guanxi* generally embodies a higher level of "loyalty" while the use of government *Guanxi* is represented as a higher level of "ability." When facing these options, a private firm would choose family members ahead of those outside the family circle, confirming the "pecking order" theory of choosing different types of trust (*Guanxi*) for cooperation in Chinese private enterprises, as discussed in Chapter 4.

6.5 Conclusion

The study of the determinants of government and family trust (*Guanxi*) in this chapter suggests that both government and family trust (*Guanxi*) are perceived as important for the development of Chinese private enterprises, particularly in the relatively volatile markets in China compared with many developed countries. However, given the significance of both government and family trust (*Guanxi*), the empirical results show that private firms prefer family members to the government for cooperation as the firm ages and the instability of the business environment increases. This confirms the core argument in the theoretical models in Chapter 4 that family trust (*Guanxi*) is replacing government trust (*Guanxi*) within Chinese private enterprises.

There are two related empirical tests in this chapter. The first test examines the determinants of the perceived importance of government and family *Guanxi* respectively. The results show that the importance of both government and family *Guanxi* is positively associated with the instability of the business environment. In addition, firm size and gift-giving have a statistically significant positive effect on the perceived importance of government *Guanxi,* while firm age has a significant positive effect on the perceived importance of family *Guanxi*. These results indicate that although government and family *Guanxi* are regarded as important to private firms, they are perceived differently with respect to the firm characteristics of age and size. The second test examines the firm's preference for government or family *Guanxi*. The results show that the decision to choose family members for cooperation is associated with an increase in firm age, coupled with the instability of the business environment. This provides evidence of a preference for family members over the government in private enterprises in the volatile business environment currently being experienced in China.

In conclusion, the empirical results in this chapter show that although both government and family trust (*Guanxi*) are important for private enterprises in the Chinese transitional economy, government trust (*Guanxi*) is being replaced by family trust (*Guanxi*). Together with the empirical results in Chapter 5, which found that it is better for a private firm to combine its ownership and control, the findings in this chapter give additional support to our understanding of why family businesses constitute the majority of Chinese private firms. The results in this chapter also reflect the different effects of government and family trust (*Guanxi*) on the firm's economic activities, representing respectively the separation or combination of ownership and control in terms of corporate governance in private firms. This confirms the underpinning idea of our theoretical considerations in Chapter 4. The policy implications of the different roles played by the government and the family will be presented in Chapter 7.

CHAPTER 7

Policy Implications

7.1 Introduction

The development of Chinese private enterprises in recent decades differs from what standard property rights theory describes, particularly in the early stages of development. The main theme of this book has been to incorporate social and cultural contexts into standard property rights theory, with emphasis on the institutional foundations of trust (*Guanxi*), in order to better understand the development of Chinese private enterprises. The theoretical models developed in Chapter 4 represent a combination of orthodox endogenous ownership theory and agency theory, in which the ownership arrangement in private enterprises is related to the degree of perfection of the market environment and the ability of management in those enterprises. These models show how institutional foundations, particularly the role of government and family trust (*Guanxi*), which are culturally determined, are crucial for the development of private enterprises, and provide an explanation for why family businesses constitute the majority of Chinese private enterprises. Chapters 5 and 6 provided empirical tests of the main propositions in the theoretical models.

Based on the analysis of the previous chapters, this chapter presents policy implications not only for the future development of Chinese private enterprises but also for foreign-invested enterprises entering China. The chapter is organized as follows. Section 7.2 discusses privatization in transitional economies and management implications for foreign-invested enterprises in China. The role of government in improving the overall economic environment in order to facilitate the development of Chinese private enterprises is discussed in Section 7.3. The discussion in Section 7.4 suggests that while management capacity is important to private firms, private enterprises should emphasize managerial loyalty in order to continue to develop and grow in the future. Section 7.5 summarizes the main arguments put forward in this chapter.

7.2 Cultural Embeddedness and Enduring Strength of Trust (*Guanxi*)

This book has set out to incorporate the role of trust (*Guanxi*), as an indicator of traditional culture, into standard property rights theory. The hope is that such an approach will help to better understand the development of Chinese private enterprises since the introduction of market reforms in the late 1970s.

The Chinese experience with the development of private enterprises, which has contributed to remarkable economic growth in recent decades, also raises policy implications for other transitional economies in existing and former socialist countries as well as foreign-invested enterprises entering China.

7.2.1 Privatization in transitional economics

The study in this book has provided an explanation for the gradual nature of privatization in China along two tracks. First, the property rights theory developed in Chapter 4 is an endogenous ownership theory, showing that the optimal ownership arrangement is related to the degree of market perfection. Hence, the ownership arrangement cannot be altered independently of the economic environment. Moreover, because developing new markets and establishing a mature market system are time-consuming and costly, complete and immediate privatization may not be the best choice for an economy with imperfect institutions. This is consistent with the argument that rapid and comprehensive privatization cannot succeed in the absence of an appropriate institutional and legal framework and such a framework cannot be created overnight (Murrell, 1992; Stark, 1996). In other words, unconditional mass privatization is not appropriate for a transitional economy that lacks a perfect textbook institutional environment. Therefore, first getting the economic environment right is critical for successful privatization in transitional economies.[88]

Second, the notion of trust (*Guanxi*) employed in this book is culturally determined and hence has a deep embeddedness in particular cultures (Granovetter, 1985; Fukuyama, 1995). In the context of Chinese culture, Confucian ideology has long been established as the system governing nearly all aspects of social life (Xing, 1995). Government trust (*Guanxi*), which is one type of group cooperative ability (Weitzman and Xu, 1994) defined by traditional Confucian ideology, provides another reason for the gradual nature of privatization in China. The cultural embeddedness of government trust (*Guanxi*) ensures that the role played by the government remains important in China's market reforms, as discussed in Chapter 6. This is consistent with the coexistence of ongoing market-oriented ownership reform and a political dictatorship, a dictatorship which shows no signs of weakening (Brezis and Schnytzer, 2003). Moreover, since it is better for a private firm to cooperate with government in a developing grey market, as discussed in Chapters 4 and 6, Chinese private enterprises have incorporated

---

[88] This is the main conclusion in Tian's (2000) study. Building on Tian (2000), the propositions derived in the theoretical models in Chapter 4 include *Tian's theorem* (see Proposition 1 in Chapter 4).

the role of government trust (*Guanxi*). One example is that private enterprises masqueraded as "red-hat" enterprises in the Zhejiang model in the early reform period. Another example is the use of government trust (*Guanxi*) in township-village enterprises (TVEs),[89] in which TVEs can be viewed as an intermediate form of private enterprises, as discussed in Chapter 2. The important role of government trust (*Guanxi*) within firms provides an explanation for the success of Chinese private enterprises.

Therefore, given the importance of first creating the right environment for ownership reform, coupled with the cultural embeddedness of government trust (*Guanxi*), it makes sense that China has proceeded with gradual privatization. In contrast, a rapid and comprehensive privatization program was undertaken in other transitional economies in Central and Eastern Europe and the former Soviet Union.[90] Given the success of China's transitional economy in recent decades, it is suggested that privatization in other transitional economies should take into account not only the effects of the imperfect market environment but also the role of the cultural context in which the reforms take place, in particular the significance of government trust (*Guanxi*). For this reason it may not be a realistic option for Central and Eastern Europe and the former Soviet Union to be thinking in terms of the Chinese experience, simply because of the considerable difference in culture and hence the differing roles of government trust (*Guanxi*). However, it is possible to envisage other Asian socialist countries, such as Vietnam and North Korea, seeking to follow China's privatization path because these countries have cultures similar to Chinese culture or have been strongly influenced by it. In other words, due to similar cultural backgrounds, the Chinese experience of gradual privatization provides a useful reference for these Asian countries to improve economic efficiency and achieve long-term economic growth. In this context, it is noteworthy that Vietnam, which has followed a similar approach to China, has achieved impressive economic growth since the late 1980s (Brezis and Schnytzer, 2003).[91] Of course, further research is required to determine how China's experience has translated to these countries. The point is that gradual privatization may be

---

[89] The concept of government trust can be interpreted in several ways. For example, while Weitzman and Xu (1994) use the notion of group cooperative ability, Smyth (1997) employs the notion of reputation as a core asset and Tian (2000) uses the notion of procurement ability. These alternative formulations are all treated as government trust (*Guanxi*) in this book (see Chapter 2).

[90] We do not make a normative judgment about whether rapid or gradual privatization in transitional economies is preferable, but rather emphasize the importance of cultural heritage, particularly trust (*Guanxi*), in the process of privatization.

[91] The market-oriented privatizing reforms in China and Vietnam have been termed "Market-Leninism" by some scholars (see, for example, Brezis and Schnytzer, 2003).

more practical than rapid privatization in these countries, and policy decisions should take into account the effects of both the imperfect market environment and cultural heritage.

7.2.2 Enduring strength of trust (*Guanxi*) for foreign-invested enterprises

The enduring strength of trust (*Guanxi*) comes from the deep embeddedness of Chinese traditional culture. As noted by North (1990, p.45), cultural traits have "tenacious survival ability" and most cultural changes are "incremental." In other words, traditional culture is not easy to change and is often costly to change (Weitzman and Xu, 1994). As discussed in the theoretical models in Chapter 4, private firms perform better when they incorporate trust (*Guanxi*) ability in a developing market such as China. The empirical results in Chapter 6 further showed that the significance of both government and family trust (*Guanxi*) has not declined in contemporary China, which reflects the enduring strength of trust (*Guanxi*) in Chinese business practices. Since the introduction of market reforms in the late 1970s, many foreign enterprises have entered China and invested heavily in the Chinese market. This development has been given impetus by China's accession to the World Trade Organization (WTO) since 2001, making China the third largest recipient of foreign direct investment in the world in 2005, following the United Kingdom and the United States (World Investment Report 2006, UNCTAD).

The important role played by *Guanxi* in the development of Chinese private enterprises raises managerial implications for foreign-invested enterprises entering China. The most important managerial implication is the recognition of *Guanxi*'s continued influence on business transactions amid China's market reforms (Standifird and Marshall, 2000; Yang, 2002). The failure to appropriately assess the persistence of *Guanxi*-based business practices can be problematic for managers attempting to enter the Chinese market. In fact, it has been argued that the Chinese economy is not moving towards market capitalism, but rather towards a relationship-based "network capitalism" (Lovett et al., 1999),[92] in which *Guanxi* has significant potential to facilitate the building of inter-firm and firm-government relationships in China's increasingly market-oriented environment. Therefore, Western firms investing in China may benefit more from seeking long-term partnerships through the gradual development of *Guanxi* networks than from relying strictly on more familiar contract-based agreements.

---

[92] "Network capitalism" is also called "relationship marketing" or "virtual integration" (Lovett et al., 1999).

To make better use of *Guanxi* networks, specific managerial implications can be considered in terms of a sequence of involvement for foreign-invested enterprises entering the Chinese market. It is suggested that sound practice for a foreign firm entering China is to first establish distribution channels, if possible, then follow up with a greater level of commitment, such as establishing a subsidiary office, assembly operations, and/or local (Chinese) sources of supplies (Standifird and Marshall, 2000). This approach, which can be colloquially described as a "toe in the water" strategy, is similar to the so-called "step-by-step" procedural rule of trust prescribed by Lorenz (1999).[93] During this entry process, due to the importance of gift-giving in Chinese business relationships, which was discussed in Chapter 6, "gifts" can be provided to related Chinese partners. However, foreign firms should not consider such gift-giving as the only aspect of building the relationship. Instead, a manager should continue to nurture his or her existing *Guanxi* relationships by engaging in such activities as providing government officials and business partners with training at the company's headquarters in its home country. The timing of such visits in the entry and negotiation process would depend vitally on the aggressiveness and timing of the firm's market entry strategy.

The theoretical models in Chapter 4 suggest that in terms of corporate governance, it is better for a private firm to incorporate both management ability and *Guanxi* ability in China's emerging market. This implies that at some point control of the firm is not as critical as its use of *Guanxi* networks. In other words, a foreign manager should not seek greater equity control at the expense of the greater use of *Guanxi* networks to access markets and provide additional channels of distribution. In this manner, a second suggested practice for foreign-invested enterprises entering China is to establish joint-venture companies with Chinese partners because Chinese partners may either already have well-established *Guanxi* networks or be better placed to establish such contacts with relevant government and business organizations. The importance of *Guanxi* networks provides an explanation for the emerging importance of joint-venture companies as an organizational form in recent decades in China. Joint-venture companies have become the main organizational form for foreign-invested enterprises in China. In 2003, joint-venture companies accounted for 50.3% of total

---

[93] The "step-by-step" rule suggested by Lorenz (1999) prescribes that the firms should start by making small commitments to each other and then progressively increase their commitments depending on the quality of their exchange. In other words, trust is built up through a learning process, in which small risks are followed by larger ones, contingent on the success of cooperation.

foreign-invested companies (Yearbook of State's Industrial and Commercial Administration, 2004).

7.3 Towards a Rule-based Market Environment: The Role of the Government

While a well-developed *Guanxi* network can have a positive effect on a foreign-invested enterprise's ability to successfully operate in the Chinese market, this is not to suggest that the manager should forgo the use of contracts altogether. Because of the development of a rational-legal system and the evolution of increasingly competitive markets in China (Li, 1998; Gregory et al., 2000; Singh, 2003), formal rules are playing a more important role in the Chinese economy, particularly with respect to private enterprises, including domestic and foreign-invested enterprises.

As proposed in Chapter 4, the market environment affects the optimal ownership arrangement of private enterprises, reflecting the important role played by the overall economic environment in influencing the development of private enterprises. The theoretical models in Chapter 4 further suggested that government trust (*Guanxi*) is being replaced by family trust (*Guanxi*) in private enterprises, which indicates that the role of the government should be to withdraw from direct involvement in a firm's economic activities. This conjecture was confirmed by the empirical results in Chapter 6, and it is also given support by the fact that the largest proportion of private enterprises in this researcher's survey regarded the most important role of the government as providing "technological support and service" which is related to the overall economic environment (see Section 6.3.1.2). In other words, the argument against government interference does not imply that the government should not get involved in economic matters. On the contrary, the role of government should shift from being an active participant in the economy to being an arbitrator and service provider, as suggested by the success of the Zhejiang model discussed in Chapter 3. This is a basic policy implication of this study, which is consistent with the argument that the government should focus on indirect support, i.e., institutional environment, by establishing a policy and legal environment conducive to enterprise development (Batra and Mahmood, 2003).

There is a whole range of government activities compatible with market-oriented reforms in China, particularly with respect to the rule of law. The rule of law, as applied to the business environment, guarantees transparency, predictability, uniformity and respect for property rights (Gregory et al., 2000), all of which are necessary conditions for the efficient functioning of markets. However, building a rule-based framework is a long and complex task and there is much to be done by the Chinese government. The key elements include developing a judicial system which offers low-cost contract enforcement and a level playing field for all enterprises, and which provides easy registration and tax and investment incentives (Batra and Mahmood, 2003; Report of China's Citizen-run Enterprises, No.1, 2004). Drawing on the discussion in the previous chapters, recommendations with respect to the role of the government in facilitating the development of Chinese private enterprises are presented below.

7.3.1 Commitment to private enterprises

7.3.1.1 Protection of private property rights

One of the most important roles by government is to protect property rights. A government's commitment to the private sector is usually reflected in its willingness to support privatization and implement policies consistent with the sustainable long-term development of the private sector. As discussed in Chapter 3, the Constitutional Amendment of 1999 upgraded the status of the private sector from being a supplement to public ownership to being an important component of the market-socialist economy. The Constitutional Amendment of 2004 further stated that legitimate private property is protected by law, which means that private property is now officially recognized. This indicates that the government begins to be respectful with and to protect private property rights really and truly. At the same time, significant progress has also been made in unifying certain areas of economic law and in separating the regulators from the regulated. However, much still needs to be done. In particular, the protection of private property is not placed on the same footing as state property, which is considered "sacred and inviolable." For example, private property does not receive the same protection under criminal law. If an individual embezzles money in a private business, this would only be considered as "encroachment on the property of others." If the same crime had been committed with state property, this would be considered as corruption, which carries a much more severe punishment.

As argued by Gregory et al. (2000), the protection of private property rights is often tested in cases of conflict between public and private interests. On the one hand, the principle of "no expropriation without just compensation" is compatible with the rule of law to protect private property. On the other hand, since it is typically difficult to estimate the intangible benefits of public action, and because bureaucrats tend to overestimate these benefits, the adequate protection of private property rights may require a bias in favour of the private owner. Given this difficulty, it is recommended that the protection of private property should be placed at least on an equal footing with state property, and that this should be specified in the Chinese Constitution. Once the rational system of property rights has been established, in which all individual property rights are well-protected and widely-respected, private enterprises will readily solve the multiple obstacles in the development process, and hence will boost up their competitive power in economy corresponding to the increased globalization.

7.3.1.2 Anti-corruption

Although the status of the private sector has been improved in the Chinese Constitution, as discussed above, government interference in private economic activities is still widespread, which is reflected in the manner in which local governments encroach on firms and engage in rent-seeking activities. The ill-defined roles of government departments have resulted in the functions of many departments overlapping. Rent-seeking behaviour, which is not subject to market discipline, is evident in areas of administration as well as institutions. As discussed in Chapter 6, in the context of the gift economy in China, the practice of gift-giving (which may take the form of money in a red envelope to government officials) is easily confused with bribery and corruption. Although the government introduced the Anti-Corruption Competition Law (*Fanduibuzhengdangjinhzhengfa*) in 1994, a *Guanxi* culture has given rise to increased corruption in business-government relations amid China's market reforms (Yang, 2002).[94] The enduring strength of *Guanxi* culture in contemporary China reflects the nature of anti-corruption as being timeless, arduous, and complicated. Thus, getting corruption under control represents a long-term task for the government.

China joined the Anti-Corruption Pact of United Nations in 2005, and established the National Bureau of Anti-Corruption in 2007 as an important step to implement the Anti-Corruption Pact. However, there are no explicit legal regulation and authorizations with regard to the nature, function, and procedure of case-handling of the establishment. Therefore, it is recommended that a specific formal Anti-Corruption Law should be legislated, which may be based on the Anti-Corruption Pact of United Nations.

---

[94] The penalties for corruption are severe. Yang (2002, pp.472-473) gives the startling figure that in the anti-corruption campaign of 2001 over 3,000 people were summarily executed for corruption.

7.3.2 Reforming commercial legislation for private enterprises

As discussed in Section 2.1.3, the registration and management of private enterprises are governed by the Tentative Stipulations on Private Enterprises (TSPE, 1988) and the Company Law (1993), which has a direct impact on the market access of private enterprises. The registered capital requirement for a private limited company is an example.[95] Other constraints also arise in the application for registration. Private firms must clearly define their "business scope" (such as "food processing," "food manufacturing," "clothing manufacturing" or "furniture.") This is subject to the approval of government authorities, which makes it difficult for entrepreneurs to adapt flexibly to changing market conditions. In addition, private firms must specify a fixed site and "necessary conditions" (such as a minimum level of required equipment or professional personnel) for production, which also exposes the firm to the potential for government interference in the selection of a site and the choice of business partner.[96]

Moreover, commercial legislation for private enterprises suffers from the lack of an effective competition policy. Private enterprises may be reluctant to enter sectors dominated by state enterprises because they do not believe that conditions for fair competition exist in such markets. Thus, the legal infrastructure for private enterprise has scope for improvement. It is recommended, firstly, that minimum registered capital requirements, particularly for forming a limited liability company, should be reduced or even eliminated, as in many Western countries. Secondly, the requirement that private enterprises specify their business scope, location, and necessary conditions for production to government in advance should be relaxed in line with international practice in order to reduce the potential for bureaucratic interference.[97]

As discussed in Chapter 2, there is a distinction between an individual business (*Getigongshanghu*, employing no more than eight people) and a privately-run enterprise (*Siyingqiye*, employing more than eight people). The former is governed by the government documents: the "Several Issues on the

---

[95] The minimum registered capital requirement for a private limited liability joint stock company is RMB300,000 in retail trade and RMB500,000 in wholesale trade or manufacturing, and this must be confirmed as paid up before a business license is issued.

[96] For example, with respect to the "necessary conditions" for production, a private firm itself may not have the required equipment so that government may assign a partner with that equipment.

[97] Some progresses have been made in the Company Law amended by the National Congress in 2005. For instance, the minimum registered capital requirement for a limited liability company is RMB30,000.

Temporary Rural Economy" (1983) and the "Temporary Regulations on a Single Industrial and Commercial Proprietor in Cities and Towns" (1987) while the latter has been governed by the TSPE (1988) and the Company Law (1993). This creates two problems. First, payment of taxes in China tends to be negotiated rather than levied because of the opaque financial positions of many enterprises (Gregory et al., 2000). It is relatively more difficult for the government to access information on financial flows in an individual business (Blue Book of Private Enterprises, 2002). This means that an individual business generally pays less tax than a privately-run enterprise. Hence there is an incentive for a private owner to remain a *Getigongshanghu* for the purpose of minimizing taxes. Second, it is also difficult for an individual business to grow, because the number of salaried employees is capped at eight. Thus, the distinction between an individual business and a privately-run enterprise should be abolished.

In addition, corresponding to the further openness of foreign capital after China's accession to the World Trade Organization (WTO) and the expansion of domestic non-governmental investment, the government should break through the ownership requirements by introducing market competition mechanisms, and eliminate industrial monopolies to give private investment the same "national treatment" permission as state enterprises in various industries. Except some key industries and critical fields that count much for the national economy, all other industries should be open to private investment, particularly in allowing first domestic private capital to entry the industries that admit foreign capital. Meanwhile, the government should encourage domestic private enterprises to participate in the ownership reform and reorganization of state-owned enterprises (SOEs) and collective enterprises in various fields.

7.3.3 Improving access to financial resources for private enterprises

The empirical results in Chapters 5 and 6 showed that capital stock is critical to the development of private enterprises. However, as discussed in Chapter 3, due to the imperfect capital markets in China, private enterprises have many difficulties in accessing external financing, particularly bank loans. As discussed in Chapter 6, although building cooperative links with government is helpful for private enterprises in accessing financial resources, it remains difficult for many private enterprises, particularly the bulk of small firms, to get assistance from the government. Therefore, several recommendations are presented below with respect to the role of government in assisting private enterprises to access financial resources.

As discussed in Chapter 3, the state-owned banks play the principal role in the Chinese financial system, in which there is a strong "lending bias" against private enterprises. These banks are likely to dominate the domestic financial landscape for the foreseeable future. A preferred solution would be for the state-owned banks to treat state-owned enterprises (SOEs) and private enterprises in the same manner. To this end, an important step would be to strengthen the profit incentives of these banks through private ownership and competition. Listing the state-owned banks on the stock market or allowing strategic partnering between the state-owned banks and foreign financial institutions are alternative means to realize this objective.[98] Many private enterprises that are able to borrow from the state-owned banks have to pay effective interest rates that are significantly higher than the rates prescribed by the Central Bank (Gregory et al., 2000; Blue Book of Private Enterprises, 2002). These banks should be able to further liberalize interest rates, and to charge transaction and monitoring fees in line with international practices in banking, or lower collateral requirements, all of which would serve to improve private enterprises' access to bank loans.

At the same time, the current banking system requires private enterprises to largely seek financing from providers other than the state-owned banks. Therefore, the government should further allow the entry of new domestic private financial institutions, especially given the requirements of WTO membership which state that the Chinese government must open up entry for foreign financial institutions (Gregory et al., 2000). In addition, it is also important for the government to develop private equity markets, in particular venture capital known as "industrial investment funds" in China, and to relax requirements such as historically demonstrating profitability and the requirement for having a minimum level capital to list on the stock market (Report of China's Citizen-run Enterprises, No.1, 2004). These changes will also improve private firms' access to financial resources in the Chinese capital market.

7.4 Management Implications for Chinese Private Enterprises

As discussed in Chapters 2 and 3, the development of Chinese private enterprises has been influenced by two constraints: the market environment and traditional culture. The property rights theory developed in Chapter 4

---

[98] The state-owned banks have been given permission to list on the stock market. Following permission being granted, the China Construction Bank (CCB), the Bank of China (BC) and the Industrial and Commercial Bank of China (ICBC) have successfully debuted trading on the Shanghai and Hong Kong stock markets (see "A New Start for ICBC," *China Daily*, *October 28, 2006*).

combined orthodox endogenous ownership theory and agency theory, which demonstrated the important effects of both the market environment and management ability on the ownership arrangement of private enterprises. While the empirical results in Chapter 5 showed that ownership concentration in the hands of both the single largest owner and top managers is beneficial for firm performance, the studies in Chapter 6 demonstrated that government trust (*Guanxi*) is being replaced by family trust (*Guanxi*) in Chinese private enterprises. The study in the previous chapters provides an explanation for the prevalence of family businesses, which from a corporate governance perspective represents an appropriate combination of ownership and control. At present, family business is an appropriate governance form for private enterprises to adapt to the constraints of currently underdeveloped markets and the preserved traditional culture in China. However, family business is not the only governance option for Chinese private enterprises. And there are disadvantages with family businesses, as discussed in Chapters 3. As China moves towards a rule-based market, these disadvantages could present serious impediments in the future. Therefore, the future development of private enterprises depends heavily on the interplay of market forces, the role of the government, and the evolutionary cultural context. Private enterprises will have to take an appropriate governance form corresponding to the changing economic environment and cultural context. This is a basic conclusion of this book.

7.4.1 Connections with the government

The theoretical models in Chapter 4 suggest that the dominance of family businesses can be explained not only by the improvement of the economic environment, but also by the tendency for family trust (*Guanxi*) to replace government trust (*Guanxi*) in private enterprises. This does not mean that the importance of government trust (*Guanxi*) has declined in contemporary China, particularly in the currently immature market environment, as discussed in Chapter 6. Rather, it suggests two things. First, it points to the enduring strength of family trust (*Guanxi*) in private enterprises, which is much more powerful than government trust (*Guanxi*). Second, the relationships between private enterprises and the government have moved towards being more at arms-length, as the government shifts towards a rule-based market environment. This conclusion is illustrated by the success of the Zhejiang model in which government interference in the affairs of enterprises is rare, at least in relation to what occurs in other provinces, as discussed in Chapter 3. However, because the government plays a critical role in the reform process of Chinese socialist economy, private enterprises still need to enhance connections with the government.

As the economic environment improves, private businesses can reduce the amount of time and resources they devote to rent-seeking behaviour. Moreover, the nature of the dialogue between private enterprises and the government will change. Instead of focusing on how the government treats them as individual firms, private enterprises should shift their focus towards lobbying for policies and regulations that benefit the private sector as a whole. The best manner in which to handle relationships with the government is to lobby as a group rather than as individual firms. While there are associations of private enterprises in cities and counties,[99] there is no national association. Associations in cities and counties are organized by local governments (the Bureaus of Industrial and Commercial Administration) to serve as a means of collecting membership fees from private firms (Gregory et al., 2000; Report of China's Citizen-run Enterprises, No.1, 2004). Therefore, it is recommended that a national association should be established to represent all private enterprise, and that the role of the national association and associations at the local level should be to act on behalf of private firms as a whole in dealing with the government (Taylor, 2002).

7.4.2 Managerial loyalty and ability

As proposed in Chapter 4, the importance of management ability increases as the market environment improves, indicating that management ability is critical to the future development of private enterprises. In addition, the empirical results in Chapter 6 demonstrated that government trust (*Guanxi*) is being replaced by family trust (*Guanxi*) in private firms, reflecting the importance of loyalty and reliability amongst management. Therefore, how private enterprises improve management capacity and foster managerial loyalty is an important issue. In fact, many entrepreneurs attach considerable importance to honest and loyal behaviour by employees (Blue Book of Private Enterprise, 2001, 2002; Gan, 2002).[100] According to some studies, finding reliable managers has become the most important consideration for private enterprises (Sun and Wong, 2002). Certainly how to foster loyalty has become a critical issue for many businesses that are seeking loyal employees (James, 1999). Two recommendations are discussed below with respect to fostering managerial loyalty.

---

[99] According to the Tentative Stipulations on Private enterprises (TSPE, 1988), private enterprises are entitled to establish private enterprise associations.
[100] In terms of the relative importance of ability and loyalty, most entrepreneurs in this researcher's survey indicated that loyalty is more important than ability (see Chapter 6).

7.4.2.1 Training managers in private enterprises

Many private enterprises do not regard the training of their employees as an investment. In contrast, they treat the investment of training as production costs, which should be reduced in order to increase profits. Moreover, most of private enterprises are of small scale with limited financial resources, resulting in little investment in the training of employees and in the activities of research and development. Furthermore, many firms prefer to recruit the ready-made professionals in the labour market instead of training their employees. However, as discussed in Chapter 3, due to the immature labour market in China, it is quite difficult for private enterprises to recruit qualified managers and skilled workers.

The most common method to foster the loyalty of management is to train existing managerial personnel in private enterprises (Sun and Wong, 2002). In order to thrive in a more open and competitive market, many private enterprises will need to upgrade the capacity and skills of their managers. It is recommended that the first step is to identify what kinds of training are most needed, then to provide sufficient investment in such training programs. Since a large proportion of staff is mobile and the labour turnover rate has increased in recent years,[101] professional personnel are difficult to retain in private enterprises (Gregory et al., 2000; Blue Book of Private Enterprises, 2001, 2002). To this end, one option is to invest in firm-specific training, which promotes retention of professional personnel because firm-specific knowledge is less transferable to other firms and hence binds these people more tightly to the firm (Coff, 1997). Indeed, firm-specific training has been found to reduce labour turnover (see, for example, Munasinghe and O'Flaherty, 2005). In this manner, firm-specific training is a method to foster managerial loyalty in private enterprise.

7.4.2.2 Giving ownership shares to managers

As discussed in Chapter 5, increasing the proportion of shares in the hands of management is beneficial for firm performance. The tendency to increase the shareholding of management is also reflected in the findings of this researcher's survey (see Section 5.4.1). Therefore, a second method to foster managerial loyalty is to give ownership shares to management, making these managers the owners of the firm and hence made to feel more responsible for the success of the firm. As discussed in Chapter 3, private enterprises in the

---

[101] According to a survey published in September 2005 by Hewitt Associates, a human resources consulting firm, the average turnover rate in Chinese urban labour markets has increased from 8.3% in 2001 to 14% in 2005 (EIU, 2006).

Zhejiang model have made rapid progress in the transition to shareholding cooperatives, which is consistent with establishing corporate structures that allow firms to reward their most valuable managers with shares or share options (Coff, 1997; Gregory et al., 2000; Sun 2000, 2002).

The ultimate instance of transferring ownership shares to management is a management buyout (MBO) (Demsetz and Villalonga, 2001; Gan, 2002), which may significantly reduce agency costs.[102] As discussed in Chapter 2, the agency problem inevitably arises in corporate governance in modern corporations. At least in theory, agency costs can be ruled out only when the owner and the manager are the same, while the practice of MBO is an available way to realize the combination of ownership and control. However, the practice of MBO in China differs from that in Western countries, particularly at the beginning of reform period. At that time, MBO aimed at not only to solve the principal-agent problem, but more importantly, to solve the problem of "absence of owners." In other words, the main purpose of MBO was to solve the ownership problem or to implement ownership reform, and the reduced agency costs were by-products associated with the process of MBO. At present, since the property rights are basically and clearly defined, the task of MBO should convert to reduce agency costs, the same as in Western countries. In short, the practice of MBO is efficacious with respect to foster the loyalty of management.

7.4.3 Corporate culture and modern family firms

The basic characteristic of Chinese private enterprises is that family businesses constitute the majority of private firms. As discussed in Chapter 4, family *Guanxi* ability will become less important relative to "pure" management ability in a well-developed market, as standard property rights theory describes. Therefore, management decisions may be surrendered to professional managers as the market environment improves. This means that the family businesses will experience separation of ownership and control, as has already occurred in many modern corporations in Western countries. Separation of ownership and control is needed to foster specialization and to take advantage of scale economies (Demsetz, 1997). In this manner, specialization by professional managers outside the family circle is an avenue for the future development of family businesses (Gan, 2002), particularly for those owners who may not have sufficient management skills. In doing this, it is possible that principal-agent problems may arise in firms (Alchian and Demsetz, 1972; Jensen and Meckling, 1976). To this end,

---

[102] A related approach is to adopt employee stock ownership plans in which each staff member is given shares (Gan, 2002).

corporate culture can serve as a mechanism to cope with opportunism (Kreps, 1990; Williamson, 1993; Coff, 1997).

The enduring strength of family *Guanxi* in contemporary China reflects the continuously powerful influence of traditional Chinese culture, in which family-based values are most important (Lu, 1987; Gan, 2002). Familistic culture is the core of the moral system defined by traditional Confucius thought, which also emphasizes the importance of group-orientation and collective spirit. The studies in Chapters 5 and 6 showed that agency costs do not increase in Chinese private firms when firms grow larger in size due to the advantages of family relationships. This fact suggests the importance of the family concept as framing a corporate culture for Chinese private enterprises.[103] Indeed, the word "family" (*Jia*) is a word that can be extended to embrace anyone who one wants to include in one's own group or to express closeness with (Sun and Wong, 2002). As discussed in Chapters 2 and 4, the Chinese traditional family concept has transformed into "family-ism" in modern times and pervades almost all social organizations, and the importance of group cooperative ability is reflected in the form of family-ism's claim for solidarity in business. In this manner, the recruitment of professional managers does not contradict the governance of family businesses. Rather, professional managers can be socialized by family-based values in private firms, and, over time, become "insiders" (Yeung, 2000).

Given that family relationships can facilitate a corporate culture in private firms, family businesses can be compatible with recruiting professional managers, as suggested by other research (see, for example, Aronoff and Ward, 1995; Yeung, 2000; Blue Book of Private Enterprise, 2002). For most family businesses, while it is not optimal to introduce the modern corporation system, being blindly insistent in traditional familistic management cannot be adapted to the increasingly severe market competition. For those firms that have grown to a certain degree, the evolutionary tendency of familistic management is to incorporate traditional Chinese culture with modern corporation system in Western countries, and to establish a modern family-owned enterprise system. Therefore, it is recommended that Chinese private enterprises should become "modern family firms," which combine the advantages of family-run businesses in terms of family relationships with the advantages of modern corporations in terms of specialization of professional managers. In other words, private

---

[103] Corporate culture comprises many aspects. According to Kreps (1990) and Williamson (1993), whether added corporate culture is warranted varies with the circumstances. The argument here emphasizes the importance of family-based values that prevail in Chinese private enterprises.

enterprises can still be family-owned (with, say, at least 50% of firm shares), while professional managers are socialized into these firms. A modern family firm is the most appropriate form of corporate governance for Chinese private enterprises in the future.

7.5 Conclusion

Based on the study in the previous chapters, particularly the theoretical models in Chapter 4 and the empirical results in Chapters 5 and 6, this chapter has provided policy suggestions for the future development of Chinese private enterprises. The importance of first creating the right market environment for ownership reform, as well as the cultural embeddedness of government trust (*Guanxi*) within firms, suggests that gradual privatization is appropriate for China. However, the success of the Chinese experience raises implications for other transitional economies. The enduring strength of trust (*Guanxi*), which reflects the continued influence of trust (*Guanxi*) on business transactions amid China's market reforms, suggests that it is important for foreign-invested enterprises to establish and develop trust (*Guanxi*) networks when entering the Chinese market.

There are two basic policy implications with respect to the future development of Chinese private enterprises. The first is that instead of being an active participant in the economy, the government should focus on improving the overall economic environment in order to facilitate the development of private enterprises. Of course, building a rule-based framework for the private sector is a long and complex task for the Chinese government. It has been argued that the government needs to provide more commitment to private enterprise through improved protection of private property rights and establishment of more anti-corruption measures. Theses measures will improve the business environment in which private enterprises operate and improve their access to financial resources.

The second basic policy implication is that private enterprises must adopt an appropriate corporate governance form corresponding to the changing economic environment and evolutionary cultural context in which the firm is operating. Private enterprises need to develop connections with government while improving management capacity and fostering managerial loyalty. In this respect, investing in firm-specific skills and giving ownership shares to management are options to build managerial loyalty in private enterprises. Modern family firms, which incorporate the advantages of both family-run businesses and modern corporations, represent an appropriate form of corporate governance for private enterprises to move forward. However, research still needs to be done on the development path of private enterprises as an emerging entity in the "socialist-market" economy of China.

CHAPTER 8

Conclusions

8.1 Concluding Remarks

This book has used standard property rights theory incorporating a cultural perspective to explain the development of Chinese private enterprises since the beginning of the reform period in 1978. The specific focus has been on the changing patterns in corporate governance in private enterprises in Zhejiang province.

The success of Zhejiang private enterprises is a reflection of China's unique transition from a planned to a market-oriented economy. Within the specific Chinese context there were two important players defined by traditional culture (government and family) that have been instrumental in influencing the evolution of private enterprises. Consequently, there have been two main corporate governance patterns for private enterprises: "red-hat" enterprises and family businesses. Generally speaking, the "red-hat" phenomenon was widespread from the early reform period until the late 1990s, while family businesses are still prevalent. The changing patterns in corporate governance—the reduction in "red-hat" enterprises and the continuing dominance of family businesses in private enterprises—have been explained in this book by employing the culturally-defined notion of trust (*Guanxi*).

Following the introduction in Chapter 1, which described the structure of the book, Chapter 2 reviewed standard property rights theory in general, placing emphasis on agency theory and endogenous ownership theory. The discussion in this chapter confirmed one view in the literature that standard property rights theory might not be adequate to explain the success of Chinese private enterprises, and consequently standard property rights theory needs to incorporate a cultural perspective. The institutional foundations of trust (*Guanxi*), which stem from traditional culture, were also discussed. In particular, this chapter explored two important aspects of trust (*Guanxi*); that is, government and family trust (*Guanxi*), which provided the conceptual framework for the theoretical models developed in Chapter 4.

Chapter 3 described the general background of Chinese private enterprises and the development characteristics of private enterprises in Zhejiang province. The rise of Zhejiang private enterprises is not only consistent with the conventional wisdom in the property rights literature that clearly defined property rights are a prerequisite for economic prosperity, but also confirmed the view that there are different approaches to achieving private ownership. More importantly, the different roles played by the government and family were discussed with respect to private enterprises in the Zhejiang model.

Chapter 4 developed two related mathematical models to discuss the changing patterns in corporate governance in private enterprises in Zhejiang. The crucial assumption in the mathematical models was that some non-marketed resources, such as management ability and *Guanxi* ability, were needed for effective production in an immature economic environment. The first model showed that for a profit-maximizing private enterprise, the cooperative arrangement with *Guanxi* ability would dominate the non-cooperative ownership arrangement in a developing market environment, while the non-cooperative ownership arrangement would dominate the cooperative ownership arrangement in a developed market environment. Furthermore, within these cooperative arrangements, the second model demonstrated that the prevalence of a family business as a corporate governance pattern among Chinese private enterprises was a result of not only an improved economic environment, but also the tendency for family trust (*Guanxi*) to replace government trust (*Guanxi*) in private enterprises. This conclusion was the core argument of this book.

The two main hypotheses developed in Chapter 4, that there is a close link between ownership arrangements and firm performance in a given market environment and that private enterprises prefer family trust (*Guanxi*) to government trust (*Guanxi*) for facilitating cooperation, were empirically tested in Chapters 5 and 6. Chapter 5 examined formal ownership structure as a corporate governance mechanism in private enterprises, showing that the combination of ownership and control contributes to better firm performance, which is consistent with agency theory. In addition, the market environment had an important effect on the firm's ownership decision, which is consistent with endogenous ownership theory. The empirical results in Chapter 6 further demonstrated that although both government and family trust (*Guanxi*) were important in the immature market environment in China, private enterprises preferred family members to the government for facilitating cooperation, confirming the core argument proposed in the mathematical models developed in Chapter 4.

Based on the analysis in the previous chapters, Chapter 7 presented policy implications, which not only provided an explanation for the gradual nature of privatization in China, but also raised implications for other transitional economies; that is, gradual privatization might be more practical than rapid privatization in those countries with cultures similar to China. This chapter explored two basic policy implications for the development of Chinese private enterprises. The first was that the government should shift from being an active participant in firm's economic activities to focus on improving the overall economic environment. The second implication was that private enterprises should adopt an appropriate corporate governance pattern which corresponds to the changing economic environment and evolutionary cultural context in which firms are operating. For their future development, private enterprises should improve management capacity while fostering managerial loyalty. In addition, this chapter proposed that modern family firms, which have the advantages of being both family-run businesses and modern corporations with professional managers, are an appropriate form of corporate governance for private enterprises to move forward.

8.2 Contributions of this Book to the Literature

Based on the changing patterns in corporate governance in private enterprises in Zhejiang province, China, the objective of this book was to integrate standard property rights with cultural heritage in order to better understand the development of private enterprises. This book has sought to realize this object by modelling the roles of government and family in private enterprises in Zhejiang province.

The property rights theory developed in this book represents a combination of endogenous ownership theory, which emphasises the important role played by the market environment but restricts endogenous ownership structure to be the outcome of a perfect market, and agency theory, which emphasises the important role of management in influencing ownership decisions. The findings show that the optimal ownership arrangement of private enterprises is related to the degree of imperfection of the institutional environment as well as the ability of management in those firms. The study in this book extends orthodox ownership theory to include a developing market such as China by taking into account the impact of both the market environment and management on ownership decisions of private enterprises.

Previous research on the development of Chinese private enterprises has focused exclusively on either government trust (*Guanxi*) (see, for example, Yang, 1994, 2002; Wank, 1996; Xin and Pearce, 1996; Guthrie, 1998) or family trust (*Guanxi*) (see, for example, Xing, 1995; Yeung, 2000; Schlevogt, 2001; Gan, 2002), so that one important element of trust (*Guanxi*) has always been missing. This book represents the first attempt to model the roles of government and family together within the same framework of trust (*Guanxi*) (see Chapter 4).

While some scholars analyse both government and family trust (*Guanxi*) and attempt to make a comparison between the two (see Sun and Wong, 2002), their study is limited in that they restrict government trust (*Guanxi*) to providing institutional capital for private enterprises within society and with banks, and they do not adequately explain the role of individual firm characteristics in distinguishing between government and family trust (*Guanxi*). This book is also the first to empirically compare government *Guanxi* with family *Guanxi* in private enterprises in terms of firm characteristics and the instability of the business environment in China (see Chapter 6).

Lastly, although both government and family trust (*Guanxi*) are important in private enterprises, this book contributes to the literature by providing evidence of the "pecking order" theory with respect to non-marketed resources such as *Guanxi* ability. That is, in a developing market such as China, family trust (*Guanxi*) is normally ahead of other types of trust (*Guanxi*) for facilitating cooperation when a private enterprise faces these options.

In summary, the research of this book includes theoretical models and corresponding empirical studies. Such an approach has not only filled the gap in the literature, but also enabled us to explain the success of Chinese private enterprises, to understand the changing patterns in corporate governance in private enterprises, and to propose new insights into their future development.

8.3 Directions for Further Research

This book is a step forward in understanding the development of Chinese private enterprises and has opened up further research questions.

First, although the study has incorporated the traditional cultural context into standard property rights theory to investigate the changing corporate governance patterns within private enterprises, it is not claimed that such a cultural perspective represents the only way to explain the experience of Chinese private enterprises. Rather, there may be many other possible explanations, such as rent-seeking theory and interregional competition effects (Sun, 2000, 2002; Sun and Lu, 2004), for government's withdrawal from enterprise and the associated development of Chinese private enterprise. In fact, only an analysis that incorporates politics, sociology, and economics can describe the development path of private enterprises. This needs to be explored further.

Second, this book regarded trust (*Guanxi*), which includes both the roles of government and family, as the most important factor defined by traditional culture influencing the development of Chinese private enterprises. Although there are many types of trust (*Guanxi*), the concept itself is elusive by nature, and it is difficult to isolate and estimate. Hence, there needs to be an effort to investigate more clearly the general effect of trust (*Guanxi*) on firms, which has generally not been given enough importance in the mainstream economic literature (Williamson, 1993; Lorenz, 1999).

Third, this book treated the institutional environment as exogenous to avoid problems of measurement. However, because changes in the institutional environment certainly occur in a transitional economy, measurement of the degree of imperfection of the overall market environment needs to be more clearly specified.

Finally, because the empirical studies in this book adopted a cross-sectional design and were coupled with interviews, further case studies (particularly of well-established private enterprises) are needed to provide more support for the cultural explanation proposed in this book. In addition, an empirical study employing a nationwide sample of private enterprises is also needed.

In short, because of the uniqueness of China's transitional economy, and because private enterprises as an emerging entity are a relatively new phenomenon in the market-socialist economy, there is still much research to be done.

APPENDIX 1

Private Enterprise Questionnaire
(*English Translation*)

Dear Sir or Madam,

Thank you for your help with this study. Please answer all questions as accurately as possible. We guarantee the confidentiality of your answers. Your cooperation is highly appreciated.

In the following questionnaire, please circle your choice or complete your answers on the line as appropriate (the unit of amount is RMB 10 thousand).

1. When did your firm register as a private enterprise?

_____Year _____Month

2. What was the ownership form of your enterprise before it became a privately-run enterprise?
1) Registered as a privately-run enterprise from the beginning
2) An individual business previously employing no more than eight people
3) State-owned
4) Collective-owned (including township- or village-owned)
5) Joint venture with a foreign company

3. What is the legal form of your firm?
1) Solely-owned
2) Partnership
3) Limited liability
4) Company limited by shares (joint-stock company)

4. What is the main industry or sector in which your firm operates?
1) Farming, forestry, animal husbandry and fishery
2) Mining and quarrying
3) Manufacturing
4) Construction
5) Transport, storage, postal and telecommunication service
6) Wholesale and retail trade and catering services
7) Social services
8) Others

5. What was the structure of the shares in your firm (in percentages) when it started as a private enterprise?

1) Shares of all individuals (including jointly owned by family members): _____%

      Of which, the biggest shareholder: _____%

               Shares held by family members: _____%

2) Shares of government agencies (including the central and local governments, collectives, and government institutions such as banks): _____%

3) Among total shares, shares of top management (including CEOs, general managers, and other high level managers) in your firm: _____%

6. What is the current structure of the shares in your firm (in percentages) if there are any changes compared with when your firm commenced as a private enterprise?

1) Shares of all individuals (including jointly owned by family members): _____%

      Of which, the biggest shareholder: _____%

               Shares held by family members: _____%

2) Shares of government agencies (including central and local governments, collectives, and government institutions such as banks): _____%

3) Among total shares, shares of top management (including CEOs, general managers, and other high level managers) in your firm: _____%

7. What was the total employment in your firm in the past three years?

2002: _____ employees

2003: _____ employees

2004: _____ employees

8. What were the gross assets of your firm in the past three years?

2002: _____

2003: _____

2004: _____

9. What was your firm's sales revenue over the past three years?

2002: _____

2003: _____

2004: _____

10. What were your firm's net profits over the past three years?

2002: _____

2003: _____

2004: _____

11. When your firm selects management personnel, which one of the following factors is considered to be the most important?
1) Integrity (consistency and congruity)
2) Benevolence (caring for others and loyalty to the firm)
3) Competence (professional skills)
4) Responsibility (devotion and hard work)
5) Predictability (past experience)

12. Do you plan to give shares in the firm to management personnel other than family members?

_____Yes   _____No

A. The main reason for choosing "yes" (choose one):
1) It facilitates a convergence of interests between owner(s) and manager(s)
2) Manager(s) will be more responsible if they have shares in the firm.
3) It shares the risk between owner(s) and manager(s).
4) It reduces managerial turnover
5) It improves decision making

B. The main reason for choosing "no" (choose one):
1) The profits should be restricted to the owner(s)
2) Concerned about the loyalty and capability of the manager(s)
3) Paying a high salary is enough to motivate management
4) If you give manager(s) shares it makes it harder to dismiss them if they under-perform
5) It would create disputes within the firm

13. Is *Guanxi* (personal relationships) important for the success of your firm? *Guanxi* includes being perceived as trustworthy by others and using relationships to acquire necessary inputs and vital information to assist in firm production.
1) Not important at all
2) Relatively unimportant
3) Neutral
4) Relatively important
5) Vitally important

14. When you cultivate and maintain *Guanxi* with a person related to your business, what is the individual's primary value to the firm (choose one)?
1) Important connections in government
2) Access to suppliers
3) Access to customers
4) Control of financial resources
5) Technical or professional knowledge
6) Other purposes

15. How would you rate the role that government has been playing and the role that you expect the government will play in the future within your firm?
1) Not helpful at all
2) Relatively not helpful
3) Neutral
4) Relatively helpful
5) Very helpful

16. What is the main role that the government has been playing and the role that you expect the government will play in the future within your firm?
1) Provide protection
2) Facilitate market access
3) Provide preferential tax treatment
4) Facilitate access to financial resources
5) Provide technological support and services

17. People in business relationships often give one another gifts. Do you give gifts to government officials in order to build connections?
1) Give gifts to build connections
2) Do not give gifts to build connections

18. How do you rate the role of family members within your firm?
1) Not helpful at all
2) Relatively not helpful
3) Neutral
4) Relatively helpful
5) Very helpful

19. What is the main role that family members have been playing or will play in your firm (choose one)?
1) Provide cheap and flexible resources such as capital and labour
2) Manage internal financial affairs of the firm
3) Assist in decision making within the firm

4) Extend the firm's network of connections outside the firm
5) Build up reputation of the family

20. Would you prefer to cooperate with government or family members in your firm?
1) The government
2) Family members

[This is end of the questionnaire. Thank you for your cooperation.]

APPENDIX 2

私营企业调查问卷
(Private Enterprise Questionnaire)
(Chinese Translation)

尊敬的先生/女士：

感谢您对本次国内私营企业调查的支持和帮助。请您准确填写，我们为您所提供的资料保密。衷心感谢您的合作。

在下列问题中，有些需要您打√来选择答案，有些则需要您直接在空格线上填写相应内容。

1. 您所在的企业登记为私营企业的时间：
　　_____年　____月

2. 企业登记为私营企业前的性质为：
　　1）最早登记注册时就是私营企业
　　2）由个体户发展而来
　　3）国有
　　4）集体
　　5）与外资合资

3. 您所在的企业属于：
　　1）独资企业
　　2）合伙企业
　　3）有限责任公司
　　4）股份有限公司

4. 企业的主营业务为：
　　1）农林牧渔业
　　2）采掘业
　　3）制造业
　　4）建筑业
　　5）交通运输、仓储和邮政业
　　6）批发和零售贸易、餐饮业
　　7）社会服务业
　　8）其他行业

5. 开始登记注册为私营企业时的企业产权（股权）结构（用百分比表示）：
　　1）所有私人股东（包括私人性质的法人）所占的股份份额：_____%
　　　　其中：最大的单个股东所占的股份份额：_____%

最大股东的其他家庭成员所占的股份份额：_____%

2）国有成分（包括各级政府、城乡集体、国有单位等）所占的股份份额：_____%

3）在全部股权中，高级管理人员（即总经理和副总经理级别的人）所占的股份份额：_____%

6. 与刚成立为私营企业时比较，企业的产权（股权）结构有变化的，目前的结构为（用百分比表示）：

1）所有私人股东（包括私人性质的法人）所占的股份份额：_____%

其中：最大的单个股东所占的股份份额：_____%

最大股东的其他家庭成员所占的股份份额：_____%

2）国有成分（包括各级政府、城乡集体、国有单位等）所占的股份份额：_____%

3）在全部股权中，高级管理人员（即总经理和副总经理级别的人）所占的股份份额：_____%

7. 过去三年的企业职工人数：
2002 年：_____人
2003 年：_____人
2004 年：_____人

8. 过去三年的企业总资产：
2002 年：_____万元
2003 年：_____万元
2004 年：_____万元

9. 过去三年的企业营业收入：
2002 年：_____万元
2003 年：_____万元
2004 年：_____万元

10. 过去三年的企业净利润：
2002 年：_____万元
2003 年：_____万元
2004 年：_____万元

11. 企业在选拔和录用管理人员时，最优先考虑的是哪一项因素（请只选择一项）：

1）正直
2）忠诚和善，关心他人
3）专业技术能力
4）踏实肯干，有责任心

186

5）有经验

12. 您是否赞成对非家庭成员经理人员实施持股计划？

　　　　_____ 是　　　　　_____ 否

　　A.　　　　如果选择"是"，则您的主要理由是（请只选择一项）：
　　1）形成利益共同体
　　2）增强经理人员责任心
　　3）分担经营风险
　　4）稳定经理人员
　　5）提高企业决策水平

　　B.　　　　如果选择"否"，则您的的主要理由是（请只选择一项）：
　　1）企业的盈亏都应当由投资者（所有者）来承担
　　2）经理人员是否忠诚和有责任心是值得怀疑的
　　3）支付高薪已经足够，不需要再为经理人员提供股份
　　4）当经理人员业绩不佳时，如果他们有股份，就会难以辞退
　　5）在企业决策过程中容易引起纠纷

13. 您认为各种"关系"对企业成功经营的重要程度是：
　　1）一点也不重要
　　2）比较不重要
　　3）一般
　　4）比较重要
　　5）至关重要

14. 当您与企业生产经营活动有关的人员建立关系时，最看中的是这些人员在哪一方面的用途（请只选择一项）：
　　1）他们与相隔政府机构有重要联系或者本人就处于政府机构之中
　　2）他们能够接近供应商或者得到原材料
　　3）他们能够接近或者吸引来顾客
　　4）他们掌握着重要的资金来源
　　5）他们具备专业技术知识
　　6）其他用途

15. 您认为政府部门对企业经营是否有帮助：
　　1）一点也没有帮助
　　2）帮助不大
　　3）一般
　　4）有一定的帮助
　　5）非常有帮助

16. 政府部门对你们企业已经起到的作用，或者将会起到的作用主要体现在（请只选择一项）：
    1）提供保护
    2）允许进入市场
    3）提供税收优惠
    4）提供资金支持
    5）提供技术支持和服务

17. 人们在业务联系中经常相互赠与礼物。您在与政府官员打交道时，会怎样？
    1）会赠送礼物
    2）不赠送礼物

18. 您认为家庭成员对企业经营是否有帮助：
    1）一点也没有帮助
    2）帮助不大
    3）一般
    4）有一定的帮助
    5）非常有帮助

19. 家庭成员对你们企业已经起到的作用，或者将会起到的作用主要体现在（请只选择一项）：
    1）提供低成本的资金或者人力支持
    2）掌控财务及采购等重要部门
    3）帮助企业进行决策
    4）帮助企业进行对外沟通联络
    5）建立家族声望

20. 在企业经营中，你们更愿意与政府合作还是与家庭成员合作？
    1）政府（部门）
    2）家庭成员

[本次问卷调查结束，谢谢您的合作。]

REFERENCES

"A New Start for ICBC." *China Daily, October 28, 2006.*

Akerlof, G.A. 1970. "The Market for 'Lemons': Quality and the Market Mechanism." *Quarterly Journal of Economics, 84, pp.488-500.*

Alchian, A. and Demsetz, H. 1972. "Production, Information Costs, and Economic Organization." *American Economic Review, LXI (5), pp.777-795.*

Anderson, Ronald and Reeb, David. 2003. "Founding-Family Ownership and Firm Performance: Evidence from the S&P 500." *The Journal of Finance, LVIII (3), pp.1301-1328.*

Ang, J.S.; Colwm, R.A.; and Wuh Lin, J. 1998. "Agency Costs and Ownership Structure." *Journal of Finance, 55, pp.478-517.*

Aronoff, C.E. and Ward, J.L. 1995. "Family-owned Business: A Thing of the Past or a Model for the Future?" *Family Business Review, 8 (2), pp.121-130.*

Arrow, K.J. 1973. "Information and Economic Behaviour." *Federation of Swedish Industries, Stockholm, Sweden.*

Barberis, Nicholas; Boycko, Maxim; Shleifer, Andrei; and Tsukanova, Natalia. 1996. "How Does Privatization Work? Evidence from the Russian Shops." *Journal of Political Economy, 104 (4), pp.764-790.*

Barth, Erling; Gulbrandsen, Trygve; and Schone, Pal. 2005. "Family Ownership and Productivity: The Role of Owner-management." *Journal of Corporate Finance, 11, pp.107-127.*

Batra, Geeta and Mahmood, Syed. 2003. "Direct Support to Private Firms: Evidence on Effectiveness." *The World Bank, Policy Research Working Paper Series: 3170.*

Berle, Adolf and Means, Gardiner. 1932. "The Modern Corporation and Private Property." *New York: Macmillan.*

Blue Book of Private Enterprises (in Chinese), No.3, 2001. *Zhang, Houyi; Ming, Lizhi; and Liang, Chuanyun, Eds., Social Science Documentation Publishing House.*

Blue Book of Private Enterprises (in Chinese), No.4, 2002. *Zhang, Houyi; Ming, Lizhi; and Liang, Chuanyun, Eds., Social Science Documentation Publishing House.*

Bowles, Paul and Dong, Xiao-Yuan. 1999. "Enterprise Ownership, Enterprise Organization, and Worker Attitudes in Chinese Rural Industry: Some New Evidence." *Cambridge Journal of Economics, 23 (1), pp.1-20.*

Brezis, Elise S. and Schnytzer, Adi. 2003. "Why Are The Transitional Paths in China and Eastern Europe Different? A Political Economy Perspective." *Economics of Transition, 11 (1), pp.3-23.*

Bull, Clive. 1987. "The Existence of Self-Enforcing Implicit Contracts." *The Quarterly Journal of Economics, 102 (1), pp.147-159.*

Chandler, A.D., Jr. 1990. "Scale and Scope: The Dynamics of Industrial Capitalism." *Cambridge: Harvard University Press.*

Chang, Chun and Wang, Yijing. 1994. "The Nature of the Township-Village Enterprises." *Journal of Comparative Economics, 19 (3), pp.434-452.*

Che, Jiahua and Qian, Yingyi. 1998. "Institutional Environment, Community Government, and Corporate Governance: Understanding China's Township-Village Enterprises." *Journal of Law Economics and Organization, 14 (1), pp.1-23.*

Chen, Baizhu and Feng, Yi. 2000. "Determinants of Economic Growth in China: Private Enterprise, Education, and Openness." *China Economic Review, 11 (1), pp.1-15.*

Chen, Jian. 2001. "Ownership Structure as Corporate Governance Mechanism: Evidence from Chinese Listed Companies." *Economics of Planning, 34, pp.53-72.*

Cho, H. 1998. "Ownership Structure, Investment, and the Corporate Value: An Empirical Analysis." *Journal of Financial Economics, 47, pp.103-121.*

191

Chow, Clement Kong Wing and Fung, Michael Ka Yiu. 1998. "Ownership Structure, Lending Bias, and Liquidity Constraints: Evidence from Shanghai's Manufacturing Sector." *Journal of Comparative Economics, 26 (2), pp.301-316.*

Claessens, Stijn and Djankov, Simeon. 1999. "Ownership Concentration and Corporate Performance in the Czech Republic." *Journal of Comparative Economics, 27, pp.498-513.*

Clark, Terry D.; Goss, Ernest; and Kosova, Larisa B. 2003. "Economic Well-Being and Popular Support for Market Reform in Russia." *Economic Development and Cultural Change, 51 (3), pp.753-768.*

Coase, Ronald H. 1937. "The Nature of the Firm." *Economica, IV, pp.368-405.*

Coff, Russell W. 1997. "Human Assets and Management Dilemmas: Coping With Hazards on the Road to Resource-Based Theory." *Academy of Management Review, 22 (2), pp.374-402.*

Davis, Lance and North, Douglass. 1971. "Institutional Change and American Economic Growth." *Cambridge University Press.*

Demsetz, Harold. 1967. "Toward A Theory of Property Rights." *American Economic Review, 57 (2), pp.347-359.*

Demsetz, Harold. 1983. "The Structure of Ownership and the Theory of the Firm." *Journal of Law and Economics, 26, pp.375-390.*

Demsetz, Harold and Lehn, Kenneth. 1985. "The Structure of Corporate Ownership: Causes and Consequences." *Journal of Political Economy, 93, pp.1155-1177.*

Demsetz, Harold. 1997. "The Economics of the Business Firm: Seven Critical Commentaries." *Cambridge: Cambridge University Press.*

Demsetz, Harold and Villalonga, Belen. 2001. "Ownership Structure and Corporate Performance." *Journal of Corporate Finance, 7 (3), pp.209-233.*

Demsetz, Harold. 2003. "The Competition between Private and Collective Ownership." *Perspectives, 4 (2), pp.1-14.*

Denis, D. and Sarin, A. 1999. "Ownership and Board Structures in Public Traded Corporations." *Journal of Financial Economics, 52, pp.187-223.*

Dogan, Ergun and Smyth, Russell. 2002. "Board Remuneration, Company Performance, and Ownership Concentration: Evidence from Publicly Listed Malaysian Companies." *ASEAN Economic Bulletin, 19 (3), pp.319-347.*

Dyck, A., and Zingales, L. 2004. "Private Benefits of Control: An International Comparison." *Journal of Finance, 59, pp.537-600.*

Eswaran, Mukesh and Kotwal, Ashok. 1985. "A Theory of Contractual Structure in Agriculture." *American Economic Review, 75 (3), pp.352-367.*

Faccio, Maria; Lang, Larry P.H.; and Young, Leslie. 2001. "Dividends and Expropriations." *American Economic Review, 91, pp.54-78.*

Fama, Eugene and Jensen, Michael. 1983. "Separation of Ownership and Control." *Journal of Law and Economics, 26, pp.301-325.*

Fligstein, N. 1996. "Markets as Politics: A Political-Cultural Approach to Market Institutions." *American Sociological Review, 61 (4), pp.656-673.*

Flynn, Dave and Xu, Luodan. 2001. "Small Business Survival: Dynamics in the People's Republic of China." *Journal of East-West Business, 7 (4), pp.79-94.*

Francis, C.B. 1999. "Bargained Property Rights: The Case of China's High-technology Sector." *In Oi and Walder, (EDs.), Property rights and economic reform in China, Stanford University Press, Stanford, pp.227-247.*

Fudenberg, Drew and Tirole, Jean. 1992. "Game Theory." *Cambridge, MA: MIT Press.*

Fukuyama, F. 1995. "Trust: The Social Virtues and the Creation of Prosperity." *Free Press, New York.*

Furubotn, Eirik G. and Pejovich, Svetozar. 1974. "The Economics of

Property Rights." *Bollinger Publishing Company, Cambridge, Mass.*

Gambetta, D. 1988. "Can We Trust in Trust?" In: Gambetta, D. (Ed.), "Trust: Making and Breaking Cooperative Relations." *Blackwell, New York, pp.213-237.*

Gelb, A.; Jefferson, G.; and Singh, I. 1993. "Can Communist Economies Transform Incrementally? The Experience of China." *National Bureau of Economic Research Macroeconomics Annual, Cambridge, Mass: MIT Press, pp.87-133.*

Granovetter, M. 1985. "Economic Action and Social Structure: The Problem of Embeddedness." *American Journal of Sociology, 91 (3), pp.481-510.*

Gregory, R.G. and Meng, Xin. 1995. "Wage Determination and Occupation Attainment in the Rural Industrial Sector of China." *Journal of Comparative Economics, 21, pp.353-374.*

Gregory, Neil; Tenev, Stoyan; and Wagle, Dileep. 2000. "China's Emerging Private Enterprises—Prospects for the New Century." *International Finance Corporation, Washington, D. C.*

Grossman, Sanford and Hart, Oliver. 1986. "The Costs and Benefits of Ownership: A Theory of Vertical and Lateral Integration." *Journal of Political Economy, 94, pp.691-719.*

Gan, Dean. 2002. "The Research of Chinese Family Business." (in Chinese) *Social Science Documentation Publishing House.*

Gujarati, Damodar N. 1995. "Basic Econometrics (Second Edition)." *McGraw-Hill, Inc.*

Guthrie, Douglas. 1998. "The Declining Significance of *Guanxi* in China's Economic Transition." *The China Quarterly, 154, pp.254-282.*

Hart, Oliver and Holmstrom, Bengt. 1987. "A Theory of Contracts." *In Bewly T., (Ed.), Advances in Economic Theory, Fifth World Congress, pp.71-155, Cambridge University Press.*

Hart, Oliver and Moore, John. 1990. "Property Rights and the Nature of the Firm." *Journal of Political Economy, 98 (6), pp.1119-1148.*

194

Hermalin, B. and Weisbach, M. 1988. "The Determinants of Board Composition." *RAND Journal of Economics, 19, pp.589-606.*

Hill, C.W.L. 1995. "National Institutional Structures, Transaction Cost Economizing and Competitive Advantage: The Case of Japan." *Organization Science, 6, pp.119-131.*

Himmelberg, C.; Hubbard, R.G.; and Palia, D. 1999. "Understanding the Determinants of Managerial Ownership and the Link between Ownership and Performance." *Journal of Financial Economics, 53, pp.353-384.*

Holderness, C.; Kroszner, R.; and Sheehan, D. 1999. "Were the Good Old Days That Good? Evolution of Managerial Stock Ownership and Corporate Governance since the Great Depression." *Journal of Finance, 54, pp.453-469.*

Hsiao, Cheng; Nugent, Jeffrey; Perrigne, Isabelle; and Qiu, Jicheng. 1998. "Shares versus Residual Claimant Contracts: The Case of Chinese TVEs." *Journal of Comparative Economics, 26 (2), pp.317-337.*

James, Harvey S. 1999. "Owner as Manager, Extended Horizons and the Family Firm." *International Journal of the Economics of Business, 6 (1), pp.41-55.*

James, Harvey S. 2002. "The Trust Paradox: A Survey of Economic Inquiries into the Nature of Trust and Trustworthiness." *Journal of Economic Behaviour and Organization, 47, pp.291-307.*

Jefferson, Gary H.; Rawski, Thomas G.; Wang, Li; and Zhen, Yuxin. 2000. "Ownership, Productivity Change, and Financial Performance in Chinese Industry." *Journal of Comparative Economics, 28 (4), pp.786-813.*

Jensen, Michael and Meckling, William. 1976. "Theory of the Firm: Managerial Behaviour, Agency Costs and Ownership Structure." *Journal of Financial Economics, 3, pp.305-360.*

Khaemasunun, Kamol. 2004. "Three Essays on the Profitability, Risk, and Viability of Family Firms." *Discussion paper in microeconomic analyses of economic development conference.*

Kornai, J. 1992. "The Socialist System." *Oxford, Oxford University Press.*

Kreps, David. 1990. "Corporate Culture and Economic Theory" *In "Perspectives on Positive Political Economy," Cambridge University Press, pp.90-143.*

Krug, B. 1997. "Privatization in China: Something to Learn from?" *In Giersch, H., (Ed.), Privatization at the End of the Century, Springer, Berlin, pp.269-296.*

La Porta, R.; Lopez-de-Silanes, F.; and Shielfer, A. 1998. "Law and Finance." *Journal of Political Economy, 106, pp.1113-1135.*

Lee, Lung-Fei. 1979. "Identification and Estimation in Binary Choice Models with Limited (Censored) Dependent Variables." *Econometrica, 47 (4), pp.977-996.*

Li, David D. 1996. "A Theory of Ambiguous Property Rights in Transition Economies: The Case of the Chinese Non-state Sector." *Journal of Comparative Economics, 23 (1), pp.1–19.*

Li, David D. 1998. "Changing Incentives of the Chinese Bureaucracy." *American Economic Review, 88 (2), pp.393-397.*

Li, Shaomin. 2002. "Does East Love Guanxi More Than West? The Evolution of Relation-Based Governance: Contemporary and Historical Evidence." *Global Economic Review, 31 (1), pp.1-11.*

Li, Shaomin. 2004. "The Puzzle of Firm Performance in China: An Institutional Explanation." *Economics of Planning, 37, pp.47-68.*

Lin, Shuanglin. 2000. "Resource Allocation and Economic Growth in China." *Economic Inquiry, 38 (3), pp.515-526.*

Loderer, C. and Martin, K. 1997. "Executive Stock Ownership and Performance: Tracking Faint Traces." *Journal of Financial Economics, 45, pp.223-255.*

Lorenz, Edward. 1999. "Trust, Contract and Economic Cooperation." *Cambridge Journal of Economics, 23, pp.301-315.*

Lovett, Steve; Simmons, Lee C.; and Kali, Raja. 1999. "*Guanxi* versus the

Market: Ethics and Efficiency." *Journal of International Business Studies, 30 (2), pp.231-237.*

Lu, Zuofu. 1987. "The Issue of China's Construction and the Training of Human Beings." (in Chinese) *Study Forest Press.*

Mayer, Roger C.; Davis, James C.; and Schoorman, F. David. 1995. "An Integrative Model of Organizational Trust." *The Academy of Management Review, 20 (3), pp.709-734.*

McConaughy, Daniel L.; Walker, Michael C.; Henderson, Glenn V.; and Mishra, Chandra, S. 1998. "Founding Family Controlled Firms: Efficiency and Value." *Review of Financial Economics, 7 (1), pp.1-19.*

McConnell, John J. and Servaes, Henri. 1990. "Additional Evidence on Equity Ownership and Corporate Value." *Journal of Financial Economics, 27 (2), pp.595-612.*

Morck, Randall; Shleifer, Andrei; and Vishny, Robert. 1988. "Management Ownership and Market Valuation: An Empirical Analysis." *Journal of Financial Economics, 20, pp.293-315.*

Morck, Randall; Strangeland, David; and Yeung, Bernard. 2000. "Inherited Wealth, Corporate Control, and Economic Growth." *In Randall Morck, (eds.), Concentrated Corporate Ownership, University of Chicago Press, Chicago.*

Munasinghe, Lalith and O'Flaherty, Brendan. 2005. "Specific Training Sometimes Cuts Wages and Always Cuts Turnover." *Journal of Labour Economics, 23 (2), pp.213-233.*

Murphy, Mork K. 1985. "Corporate Performance and Managerial Remuneration." *Journal of Accounting and Economics, 7, pp.11-42.*

Murrell, P. 1992. "Evolutionary and Radical Approaches to Economic Reform." *Economics of Planning, 25, 1, pp.79-95.*

Myers, Stewart and Majluf, Nicholas. 1984. "Corporate Financing and Investment Decisions when Firms Have Information that Investors Do Not Have." *Journal of Financial Economics, 13 (2), pp.187-221.*

Myers, Stewart. 2001. "Capital Structure." *The Journal of Economic Perspectives, 15 (2), pp.81-102.*

Naughton, B. 1994. "Chinese Institutional Innovation and Privatisation from Below." *American Economic Review, Papers and Proceedings.*

North, Douglass. 1990. "Institutions, Institutional Change and Economic Performance." *Cambridge University Press.*

Oi, J.C. and Walder, A.G. 1999. "Property Rights and Economic Reform in China." *Stanford University Press, Stanford.*

Pearce, Jone L. 2001. "Organization and Management in the Embrace of Government." *Lawrence Erlbaum Associates: Mahwah, NJ.*

Perotti, Enrico C. 1993. "Bank Lending in Transition Economies." *Journal of Banking Finance, 17 (5), pp.1021-1032.*

Qian, Y. and Weingast, B. R. 1997. "Federalism as a Commitment to Preserving Market Incentives." *Journal of Economic Perspectives, 11(4), pp.83-92.*

Qin, Zhong. 2011. "Models of Trust-Sharing in Chinese Private Enterprises." *Economic Modelling, 28(3), pp.1017-1029.*

Qin, Zhong and Deng, Xin. 2009. "Ownership Structure and Performance in Family Businesses at Early Development Stage: Evidence from China." *Corporate Ownership & Control, 7 (1), pp.135-147.*

Rao, Alaka N.; Pearce, Jone l.; and Xin, Katherine. 2005. "Governments, Reciprocal Exchange and Trust among Business Associates." *Journal of International Business Studies, 36 (1), pp.104-118.*

Rawski, Thomas G. 1995. "Implications of China's Reform Experience." *The China Quarterly, 144, pp.1150-1173.*

Reid, Joseph D. 1977. "The Theory of Share Tenancy Revisited—Again." *Journal of Political Economy, 85 (2), pp.403-407.*

Report of China's Citizen-run Enterprises (in Chinese), No.1, No.2. 2004. *The China General Chamber of Commerce (CGCC).*

"Report of Development of Ningbo's Private Enterprises." (in Chinese) 2005. *Ningbo Administration for Industry and Commerce.*

"Report of Zhejiang Administration for Industry and Commerce." (in Chinese) 2004. *Zhejiang Administration for Industry and Commerce.*

"Report of Zhejiang Statistical Bureau." (in Chinese) 2003. *Zhejiang Provincial Bureau of Statistics.*

Roberts, Ken and Zhou, Changcheng. 2000. "New Private Enterprises in Three Transitional Contexts: Central Europe, the Former Soviet Union and China." *Post-Communist Economies, 12 (2), pp.187-199.*

Rogers, Mark. 2004. "Competition, Agency and Productivity." *International Journal of the Economics of Business, 11 (3), pp.349-367.*

Schlevogt, Kai-Alexander. 2001. "The Distinctive Structure of Chinese Private Enterprises: State versus Private Sector." *Asia Pacific Business Review, 7 (3), pp.1-33.*

Shleifer, Andrei and Vishny, Robert. 1986. "Large Shareholders and Corporate Control." *Journal of Politic Economy, 94 (3), pp.461-488.*

Singh, Ajit. 2003. "Competition, Corporate Governance and Selection in Emerging Markets." *The Economic Journal, 113, pp.443-464.*

Singh, I.; Ratha, D.; and Xiao, G. 1993. "Non-state Enterprises as an Engine of Growth: An Analysis of Provincial Industrial Growth in Post-Reform China." *World Bank Research Paper, CH-RPS, #20.*

Smith, Adam. 1759 [2002]. "The Theory of Moral Sentiments." *Cambridge: Cambridge University Press.*

Smith, Adam. 1776 [1937]. "The Wealth of Nations." *Cannan edition (Modern Library, New York).*

Smyth, Russell. 1997. "The Township and Village Enterprise Sector as a Specific Example of Regionalism—Some General Lessons for Socialist Transformation." *Economic System, 21 (3), pp.235-264.*

Smyth, Russell. 1998. "Township and Village Enterprises in China-Growth Mechanism and Future Prospects." *Journal of International*

Economic Studies, 12, pp.101-117.

Smyth, Russell. 2002. "Explaining the Performance of China's Collective Township and Village Enterprise Sector." *Journal of International Economic Studies, 16, pp.111-126.*

Standifird, Stephen S. and Marshall, R. Scott. 2000. "The Transaction Cost Advantage of *Guanxi*-Based Business Practices." *Journal of World Business, 25 (1), pp.21-42.*

Stark, D. 1996. "Recombinant Property in East European Capitalism." *American Journal of Sociology, 101 (4), pp.993-1027.*

Statistical Yearbook of China (in Chinese). 1990-2005. *The State Statistical Bureau of China.*

Su, Dongwei and Fleisher, Belton M. 1998. "Risk, Return and Regulation in Chinese Stock Markets." *Journal of Economics and Business, 50, pp.239-256.*

Sun, Laixiang. 2000. "Anticipatory Ownership Reform Driven by Competition: China's Township-Village and Private Enterprises in the 1990s." *Comparative Economic Studies, 42 (3), pp.49-75.*

Sun, Laixiang. 2002. "Fading out of Local Government Ownership: Recent Ownership Reform in China's Township and Village Enterprises." *Economic Systems, 26 (3), pp.249-269.*

Sun, Zao and Lu, Zhengwei. 2004. "From the Government to Enterprises—A Summarization of the Documents on the Studies of Chinese Private Enterprises." *The Chinese Economy, 37 (6), pp.53-67.*

Sun, Wen-bin and Wong, Siu-lun. 2002. "The Development of Private Enterprises in Contemporary China: Institutional Foundations and Limitations." *China Review, 2 (2), pp.65-91.*

Taxation Yearbook of China (in Chinese). 1991-2005. *The State Bureau of Taxation.*

Taylor, Bill. 2002. "Privatization, Markets and Industrial Relationships in China." *British Journal of Industrial Relations, 40 (2), pp.249-272.*

"Three-hundred Thousand People Engage in Family Industry in Wenzhou." (in Chinese) *Shanghai Revolutionary Daily, 12 May, 1985.*

Tian, Guoqiang. 2000. "Property Rights and the Nature of Chinese Collective Enterprises." *Journal of Comparative Economics, 28, pp.247-268.*

Tian, Xiaowen. 2001. "Privatisation and Economic Performance: Evidence from Chinese Provinces." *Economic Systems, 25 (1), pp.65-77.*

Wank, David L. 1996. "The Institutional Process of Market Clientelism: *Guanxi* and Private Business in a South China City." *The China Quarterly, 147, pp.820-838.*

Weitzman, Martin L. and Xu, Chenggang. 1994. "Chinese Township-Village Enterprises as Vaguely Defined Cooperatives." *Journal of Comparative Economics, 18 (2), pp.121-145.*

Whyte, M.K. 1995. "The Social Roots of China's Economic Development." *The China Quarterly, 144, pp.999-1019.*

Williamson, Oliver. 1975. "Markets and Hierarchies: Analysis and Antitrust Implication." *New York: The Free Press.*

Williamson, Oliver. 1979. "Transaction cost economics: The Governance of Contractual Relationship." *Journal of Law and Economics, 22 (2), pp.233-61.*

Williamson, O.E. 1985. "The Economic Institutions of Capitalism." *New York, Free Press.*

Williamson, O.E. 1993. "Calculativeness, Trust, and Economic Organization." *Journal of Law and Economics, 36, pp.453-486.*

Wong, C. 1996. "From Centrally Planned to Market Economies: The Asian Approach." *People Republic of China, pp.3-294 in Rana, P. and Hamid, N. (eds.), 2, Oxford University Press.*

Wooldridge, Jeffey M. 2006. "Introductory Econometrics: A Modern Approach (Third Edition)." *Thomson South-Western, Thomson Higher Education.*

"World Investment Report 2006-FDI from Developing and Transitional Economics: Implications for Development." *UNCTAD, United Nations Conference on Trade and Development.*

Xin, Katherine R. and Pearce, Jone L. 1996. "*Guanxi*: Connections as Substitutes for Formal Institutional Support." *Academy of Management Journal, 39 (6), pp.1641-1658.*

Xing, Fang. 1995. "The Chinese Cultural System: Implications for Cross-Cultural Management." *SAM Advanced Management Journal, 60 (1), pp.14-21.*

Xu, Xiaonian and Wang, Yan. 1997. "Ownership Structure, Corporate Governance, and Corporate Performance: The Case of Chinese Stock Companies." *World Bank Working Paper 1794, World Bank.*

Yang, Mayfair Mei-hui. 1994. "Gifts, Favours and Banquets: The Art of Social Relationships in China." *Ithaca, NY: Cornell University Press.*

Yang, Mayfair Mei-hui. 2002. "The Resilience of *Guanxi* and Its New Developments: A Critique of Some New *Guanxi* Scholarship." *China Quarterly, 0 (170), pp.459-476.*

Yearbook of State's Industrial and Commercial Administration (in Chinese). 1991-2005. *The State Bureau of Industrial and Commercial Administration.*

Yeung, Henry Wai-chung. 2000. "Limits to the Growth of Family-Owned Business? The Case of Chinese Transitional Corporations from Hong Kong." *Family Business Review, XIII (1), pp.55-70.*

Yuan, Enzhen. 1987. "The Wenzhou Model and the Road to Affluence." (in Chinese) *Shanghai: Shanghai Academy of Social Sciences Press.*

Zhang, Weiying. 1999. "Firm Theory and Chinese Enterprises Reform." (in Chinese) *Beijing University Press.*

Zhao, Yaohui. 2002. "Earnings Differentials between State and Non-state Enterprises in Urban China." *Pacific Economic Review, 7 (1), pp.181-197.*

Zhejiang Statistical Yearbook (in Chinese). 1990-2005. *Zhejiang Provincial*

Bureau of Statistics.

Zhu, Ying. 1995. "Major Changes under Way in China's Industrial Relations." *International Labour Review, 134 (1), pp.37-49.*

Zingales, Luigi. 1995. "What Determines the Value of Corporate Votes?" *Quarterly Journal of Economics, 110 (4), pp.1047-1073.*